Hibernia America

Recent Titles in
Contributions in Ethnic Studies
Series Editor: Leonard W. Doob

HIBERNIA AMERICA

The Irish and Regional Cultures

DENNIS CLARK

CONTRIBUTIONS IN ETHNIC STUDIES, NUMBER 14

GREENWOOD PRESS

NEW YORK · WESTPORT, CONNECTICUT · LONDON

Library of Congress Cataloging-in-Publication Data

Clark, Dennis, 1927–
  Hibernia America.

  (Contributions in ethnic studies, ISSN 0196–7088 ;
no. 14)
  Bibliography: p.
  Includes index.
  1. Irish Americans.   2. Regionalism—United States.
I. Title.   II. Series.
E184.16C68   1986   973'.049162   85–27230
ISBN 0–313–25252–1 (lib. bdg. : alk. paper)

Library of Congress Catalog Card Number: 85–27230
ISBN: 0–313–25252–1
ISSN: 0196–7088

First published in 1986

Greenwood Press, Inc.
88 Post Road West, Westport, Connecticut 06881

Printed in the United States of America

The paper used in this book complies with the
Permanent Paper Standard issued by the National
Information Standards Organization (Z39.48–1984).

10 9 8 7 6 5 4 3 2 1

Copyright Acknowledgment

"The Two-Gun Man" is taken from Joseph G. Rosa, *The Gunfighter:
Man or Myth?* copyright 1969, University of Oklahoma Press.

To Eleanor and Thomas Kinsella,
with festivity, esteem, and affection

CONTENTS

PREFACE

In a book as wide-ranging as this one, the author is tempted to thank everyone in Ireland and America with whom he has ever been in contact. I yield to that temptation and I do thank all the people who have recounted, written, sung, and manifested the Irish tradition for me. More directly, however, I owe specific debts to scores of researchers, specialists, and scholars who have charted with diligence the many paths of inquiry I have followed in compiling these chapters. Dr. John A. Murphy of University College, Cork, and Dr. Paul Bew and Dr. David Harkness of Queen's University, Belfast, were at all times patient auditors for my enthused monologues. Maurice Bric of Carysfort College, Dublin, was ever full of insights about political history, and Dr. Deirdre McGeehan of the Open University in England explored immigration with me in Philadelphia. Dr. Randall Miller of St. Joseph's University aided me with his rich knowledge of the South, and Dr. Harry Silcox shared his research on urban leadership. Dr. L. A. O'Donnell of Villanova University helped me with his studies of Irish labor figures. Dr. Dale Light and Dr. Timothy Meagher provided acute interpretations of Irish-American social development, and Dr. Maureen Murphy of Hofstra University presented keen studies of Irish-American women for my benefit. To Mick Moloney, musicologist and friend, I am deeply indebted for his learning in music and folklore and for his research into the Irish tradition in many lands.

I cannot praise too highly the remarkable assistance afforded me by professional librarians and archivists at the fine regional collections in the Houston Public Library and the Denver Public Library. Without the extraordinary resources of the Van Pelt Library of the University of Pennsylvania and its efficient staff, and the unique archives of the Balch Institute for Ethnic Studies in Philadelphia, I would never have completed this work.

The transcription of the manuscript was the diligent task of Margaret Brennan who, while presiding over a busy household, sorted and typed everything from scrawled notes and scattered pages to computer print-outs and archival flitters. I owe her a salute of gratitude for every sentence typed.

My wife, Josepha O'Callaghan Clark, and my children, all distracted with their own urgent concerns, were steadily tolerant and forebearing of my chronic habits of composition. To my youngest daughter, Brigid, I proffer special thanks for her assistance in keeping my references and meandering lists together. May they enjoy the book and regale themselves in that rampant stream of delights and adventures, the Irish tradition.

INTRODUCTION

Every people must labor to understand those influences that have shaped its common memory. Where two people have interacted the task is made more complex, but also more urgent. Political and social responsibility, cultural clarity, and the support of humane values can only be maintained if people understand how they have arrived in their contemporary situation, and what forces have enabled them to function and progress from one generation to the next. The modern development of critical historical study has intensified the struggle to make the education of free men a process that refutes self-flattering illusions and distorting mythologies. Critical history, especially in the field of social history, seeks to examine the life of peoples in the fullest breadth and detail with the goal of enlightening our culture concerning what actually happened in the past and how what happened has affected life today.

Among the dramatic transformations of the modern world, none is more momentous than the transfer of millions of people from traditional, usually rural and more static societies, to the dynamic and rapidly changing "new" societies formed by exploration, technology, and the mingling of heretofore separate cultures. A fascinating example of this process has been enacted in the movement of millions of people from Ireland to America in the period since the sixteenth century. Propelled by a history of oppression, displacement, and rural collapse in Ireland, and attracted by adventure, economic gain, and new institutions in America, the flow of Irish population to the United States has constituted an archetypal series of immigration cycles and social interactions within the history of America.

This great Irish infusion into American life began, like America itself, with efforts of colonization and exploration, but it grew to embrace several of the fundamental movements that have animated the growth of the United States. It was from the outset an experience of the frontier. Frontier advancement across the continent was, as numerous historical works have shown, one of the central elements of American imagery and the self-consciousness that have formed the nation's character and outlook.

The Irish engagement with American life was thereafter also part of the technological expansion that opened the resources of the continent in an almost unbelievable revelation of ingenuity, wealth, and economic development. The Irish participation in this economic achievement was at first one of labor, then entrepreneurship, then bureaucratic ratification of the structures and processes involved. In this participation there was unfolded an ethnic history for the group that varied extensively according to the regional differences throughout the country. It was conditioned by the topography, climate, regional social patterns, and economic undertakings characteristic of the vast areas making up the diverse national landscape.

As the adaptation of the Irish proceeded, it blended the group's historical legacy, its emigration experience, and indigenous American patterns of social life. Sequences of development formed and were repeated with variations over and over again. The Irish population, and families within it, maintained a distinct identity while interacting with American education, professions, advanced occupations, and social mobility. From a minority status the Irish were at length transmuted into symbolic democratic representatives in the general culture.

The information presented in this study uses selected networks of dispersion, pioneer journeying, and canal and railroad construction to demonstrate the geographical distribution that was to be a key aspect of Irish passage into American life. The regional variations of this passage will be examined and the import of the interaction of the Irish with American institutions and culture will be evaluated, again using particular examples of social interchange. For those who deem the presentation as wanting in fuller detail, it is to be hoped that the endeavor will be accepted as a worthwhile scholarly pursuit and a valid departure from previous efforts. The analysis of regional characteristics and Irish-American relations to them is not likely to satisfy all partisans of regional identity, but it is proposed as a description of a process that was, and is, inescapable in a nation of great geographical expanses.

In order to provide more than a geographical dimension to the regional variations of Irish-American interaction with life in the United States I have relied especially on Raymond Gastil's *Cultural Regions of the United States*. Daniel Elazar's political science work, *Cities of the Prairie: The Metropolitan Frontier and American Politics*, has also been instructive with respect to variations and "culture streams" that have affected political behavior. The criteria used to discriminate among the physiographic, economic, and sociocultural areas of American life in a society increasingly influenced by mobility and mass media are bound to be controversial. Gastil's formulations are based upon an evaluation of studies and theories of settlement patterns, elites, traditional "borders," dialects, subregional areas, and historic aggregations of social experience. The framework he sets forth consists of eleven cultural areas, plus Alaska and Hawaii, that he maps across the continental United States. Each of these has distinctive cultural characteristics and provides a focus for assessing the penetration, adaptation, and persistence of the Irish in these regions. The cultural regions are New England, New York metropolitan area, Pennsylvania, the South, the Upper Midwest, the Central Midwest, the Rocky Mountains, the Mormon area, the Interior Southwest, the Pacific Southwest, the Pacific Northwest, Alaska, and Hawaii.[1] If this appears an elaborate division through which to pursue Irish experience, it is certainly no more elaborate than the experience itself in a nation with great distances and regions much larger than most European countries. American impatience with the distinctions history demands of us is one of the simplistic dispositions that we can no longer afford in a world of tremendous complexity, intermingling, and cultural pluralism.

Can a demarcation of various areas of the United States that is oriented toward contemporary patterns of culture be utilized to provided a frame of reference for historical interaction? Basic cultural areas must be defined in terms of their historical evolution. Culture is not instantaneous. It emerges, changes, and shapes its character in response to continuing trends and formative influences. Each of the cultural regions designated has a validity rooted in the terrain, economics, demography, events, and broad experiences that have informed its growth and special character.

The broad-ranging accommodation of the Irish to American mores and institutions was in itself a creative adventure, and it provided many areas of the nation's life with an energy, style, determined accomplishment, and timely contribution that offset the rejection, social disabilities, and failures that were also part of the Irish-American drama. There are very significant questions to be asked about this interlacing of an ancient people with a new land. Considering the triple handicaps of ethnic, religious, and social disabilities the Irish bore in the eighteenth and nineteenth centuries, how is it that they were able to penetrate the mainstream American culture that had originally reviled them? How is it that they were not permanently segregated, like Blacks, driven into the wilderness like Mormons, or gradually diminished like Indians? Although the Irish did not have dark skins, it is pertinent to recall that they were conceived to be a separate race, like Blacks and Indians, until the twentieth century. A knowledge of the rejection and contumely to which they were subjected, especially prior to the American Civil War, justifies our study. How is it that the group retained its identity despite the sharply different regional involvements that varied its continentwide dispersion? How is it that this group not only finally penetrated American circles of power and leadership, but came to be a key element in the accepted imagery of democracy and civil responsibility? These and other questions are the focus of this book.

We do not have a satisfactory examination of Irish-American history that would help us to respond to such inquiries for a number of reasons. The time span and scope of Irish-American engagement with America is daunting in itself. The record to be compiled and weighed is immense. From the earliest days and eventually in all areas of the country they have been present. Yet as a cultural group the Irish were themselves a people dispossessed, bringing to America only the fragments of their Gaelic heritage plus such versions of English speech and ways they could gather in Ireland amid oppression and successive national misfortunes. This left them with few resources to record and study what would become an enormous panorama of Irish-American activity. As a people with strong Roman Catholic or Protestant traditions, much of what was written about the group had a religious orientation that often could provide a misleading emphasis for reasons of church policy or simply religious self-justification. Of overriding importance was the influence of the dominant Anglo culture which harbored deep prejudices against the group and which was preoccupied for generations with presenting the history of Anglo elites, uncorrected by an exposition of minority participation in the social development of the country. The gentleman scholars and upper-class university dons prior to the university expansion of the second half of the twentieth century were not disposed to delve into the history of an ethnic group that had a negligible intellectual profile in their view.

Nor has there been major research sponsored from Ireland itself about the emigrant world. Having gained partial independence in 1921, Ireland was intent upon rewriting its own internal history. The emigrant phenomenon was not something regarded with pride by the learned class in Ireland. It was the poor who emigrated, and for those educated people who remained in the home island the emigrants were rather *déclassé,* estranged by a wide array of new ways and different perspectives. There was also in Ireland the influence of English models of scholarship and interest that detracted from any consistent devotion to American and Irish-American studies.

The deficiencies of Irish-American historical studies have been roundly criticized by Donald Harman Akenson in his sharply analytical book, *Being Had: Historians, Evidence and the Irish in North America.* He accuses historians of framing the story of the Irish in the United States on badly flawed evidence and a gross misreading of what valid evidence exists.[2] Overemphasis on urban experience and concentration on inaccurate census material has been matched, he asserts, by a reckless construction of poorly based conclusions. Akenson's criticisms should be well taken, although some of his corrective solutions, such as the use of Canadian census data which itself may be misleading, are problematical.

The most common approach to the story of the Irish-Americans ascribes the earliest role in pioneer and Revolutionary War times to Scotch-Irish Ulster Protestants, a partial view only.[3] The next theme treated tends to be the great famine immigration and its misfortunes of the 1840s and 1850s, but it is not usually followed beyond the Eastern seaboard cities and is rarely analyzed for its notable implications for American life. A succeeding theme emphasizes the success of the Irish as exponents of American life but rarely goes beyond extollation of prominent figures and statistics about occupational mobility. These themes are seldom dealt with to reveal the full continuity, creativity, and cultural impact of the Irish infusion. The achievements of the group in surviving as a recognizable ethnic element, in forming communal and interactive social structures across the continent, and in playing crucial roles in labor, social development, and political affairs, while generating important Irish nationalist movements linked to Ireland are all only superficially alluded to in most materials about them. To see the experience whole and in its true pervasiveness and extent is a historical imperative so that the validity and vitality of the subcultural life of the nation can be recognized for what it is, one of the major motive forces of American history.

In the last several decades there have been a number of specific works examining Irish-American history in various localities.[4] Many such studies are referred to in the course of this book, for they are rich with patient scholarship and insight. Of the books that seek to deal with the broadest outlines of this history, however, no one can be said to comprehend the extent and detail of the group's wide-ranging historical career. Lawrence McCaffrey's *The Irish American Diaspora* is reflective and strongly argued in its examination of the ideological influences shaping Irish-Americans, but it leaves the reader wanting an even fuller and more flexible exposition. William V. Shannon's *The American Irish: A Political and Social Portrait* is oriented toward political and cultural history, and it is full of admirable biographical summaries but, with the exception of a chapter on San Francisco, emphasizes the major Eastern cities.[5] For all of this scholarship we can be grateful. It keenly invites work toward synthesis and broader interpretations.

A statement is appropriate in this introduction as to just what the terms *Irish* and *Irish-American* imply. In the seventeenth and eighteenth centuries the designation "Irish" appears frequently in American documents. Commentators had no difficulty in recognizing those with ties of birth or relationship to Ireland, whether they were Protestant or Catholic. The Gaelic and Catholic Irish had a long and historic record of identity familiar to Englishmen and thus to Anglo-Americans. The politically troublesome Irish radicals, both Anglo-Irish and Scots-Irish as well as those of Gaelic background, who were such a disruptive influence in early modern Ireland, were especially prominent in America from 1750 onward. Those without particular political orientation nevertheless had characteristics that made them identifiable to the Anglo-Americans. Their speech was strongly influenced by Gaelic inflections and pronunciations, and peculiarities and terms not to be found in England or among Anglo-Americans. Indeed, for tens of thousands of Irish people Gaelic would have been the first language and English an acquired tongue. They also usually possessed a folk culture strongly marked by the customs and environment of Ireland. Whether Presbyterian or Roman Catholic, they bore a religious identity at variance with colonial America's mainstream Protestant heritage. Religious differences among the Irish, often bitterly antagonistic, still were not so decisively distinct that they caused Americans to exempt Irish Protestants from prevailing misconceptions about the group as a whole. For many, too, there may have been features of stature, build, and physiognamy fitting culturally familiar assumptions of how "Irish" people looked physically. Finally, for the preponderance of Irish people there was an antipathy toward England that was either readily expressed or never far below the surface, and this became a trait identified with them.

These social factors were perpetuated by continued immigration over such a considerable period that they became installed in American popular perception as recognizable marks of Irish and Irish-American identity. Even though they might diminish or disappear in a given family or community, they were so much a part of the social stereotyping and cultural identity system that they were maintained as part of general popular perception. The distinctive names deriving from Ireland, whether signified by the prefixes "Mac," "Mc," and "O" designating descent, or names familiarly Irish such as Kelly or Murphy, provided ready factors for identification of a great portion of the group. This identification, in turn, was quickly related to the other background indicators. Although some Irish changed their names, the vast majority did not, and hence they carried distinctive patronymic signs of their ancestry that were easily recognized.

The cumulative social experience and self-consciousness carried by the Irish through American life eventually led to the designation "Irish-American," which became current toward the end of the nineteenth century. "Irish-American" came to signify not only the factors noted above, but the legacy of historical roles played by major figures and the group as a whole in the military, political, religious, economic, and cultural life of the country. While assimilation and detachment went far to blur the connection with this tradition for many people, for multitudes of others the identity and tradition remained a notable formative and recollective social reality.

Kerby A. Miller, in his massively researched book *Emigrants and Exiles: Ireland and the Irish Exodus to North America*, concludes that the Irish were "unhappy exiles," brooding cultural cripples due to archaic attitudes and the misfortunes of history.[6] The initiative, zest for life, and social drive of the Irish recounted in the following chapters should provide at least one contrasting perspective to that somber view. To this author it seems evident that whatever their misfortunes, the Irish managed to respond to America with a heartening and creative vitality that befits their remarkable tradition.

NOTES

    1. Raymond Gastil, *Cultural Regions of the United States* (Seattle: University of Washington Press, 1975), pp. 29–45; Daniel Elazar, *Cities of the Prairie: The Metropolitan Frontier and American Politics* (New York: Basic Books, 1970), pp.156–174. A book rich in bibliographical reference and exposition of earlier views of American regionalism is Merrill Jensen, ed., *Regionalism in America* (Madison: University of Wisconsin Press, 1965).

    2. Donald Harman Akenson, *Being Had: Historians, Evidence and the Irish in North America* (Ontario, Canada: P.D. Meany, Publisher, 1984), pp. 37–39, 189.

    3. Older works like C.A. Hanna, *The Scotch-Irish*, 2 vols. (New York: G.P. Putnam's Sons, 1902), were excessive in their concentration on Scotch-Irish social and

political effects, but later books like J.G. Leyburn, *The Scotch-Irish* (Chapel Hill: University of North Carolina Press, 1962), are more balanced and critical.

4. Representative studies for major cities are R.A. Burchell, *The San Francisco Irish, 1848–1880* (Berkeley: University of California Press, 1980); Dennis P. Ryan, *Beyond the Ballot Box: A Social History of the Boston Irish, 1845–1917* (Rutherford: Associated University Presses, 1983); Dale B. Light, "Ethnicity and Urban Ecology in a Nineteenth Century City: Philadelphia's Irish, 1840–1890," Ph.D. diss., University of Pennsylvania, 1979. For smaller communities recent studies include Brian C. Mitchell, *The Paddy Camps: The Meaning of Community Among the Irish of Lowell, Massachusetts, 1821–1861* (Urbana: University of Illinois Press, 1986); Timothy J. Meagher, "'The Lord Is Not Dead': Cultural and Social Change Among the Irish in Worcester, Massachusetts," Ph.D. diss., Brown University, 1982; Stephan Thernstrom, *Poverty and Progress: Social Mobility in a Nineteenth Century City* (Cambridge, Mass.: Harvard University Press, 1964).

5. Lawrence J. McCaffrey, *The Irish Diaspora in America* (Bloomington: University of Indiana Press, 1976); William V. Shannon, *The American Irish* (New York: The Macmillian Co., 1963).

6. Kerby A. Miller, *Emigrants and Exiles: Ireland and the Irish Exodus to North America* (New York: Oxford University Press, 1985), p. 516.

Hibernia America

1 FACING FRONTIERS

A resplendent world of promise lay beyond the Atlantic Ocean as Ireland in the seventeenth century writhed in spasms of war, persecution, and conquest. England strove with fire and sword to impose her will on the ever refractory society of the Gaels even as that society lurched toward destruction. A Celtic way of life that had been ancient when Caesar first encountered it upon the plains of Gaul, and which had in Ireland persisted for two millenia lighted by successive bursts of literary and religious brilliance, was being fiercely reduced. Its soaring poetry was now turned to bitter political harangues. Its native law was being overturned. Its leaders were hounded across the sea in penury to European refuges. An ancient civilization was dying on the rack of English conquest.

As the Irish people sank before the armies and administrators, the confiscations and the proscriptions of English kings, there emerged from a mythic distance the first popular consciousness of the American alternative. Sailors, soldiers, freebooters, visionaries, imperial dynasts, and princes of avarice all bore tales of what was in the Western ocean. Land and the lure of unimaginable wealth at the edges of a thousand shining estuaries beckoned. As rumor turned to actual account and then to recounted first-hand experience, it was not just the calculating speculator and the baronial grandee who were beguiled, but the suffering religious dissident, the sulking and uneasy youth in the barnyard, the bone-weary ploughman in his rock-strewn field, and the girl shepherd on the mountain. To look at the sea that surrounded Ireland was to be made aware of the American possibility as ships in full sail moved to the horizon and beyond. The ravaging of Irish society had, as in the revelation of some mighty Gaelic epic, reached a climax just as the Western continent arose in the mind of the Irish victims as a dream of escape and redemption.

It is difficult for us to comprehend the emotions and anticipations that moved the first settlers to the American continent. Extraordinary perils faced them at sea and in the new country, but these were balanced by an all too real understanding of the misery and constraints that surrounded common people in Ireland,

England, and Europe in those times. A recollection of the legislation protecting the rural property of the ruling classes provides an almost incredible catalog of offenses that were hazards for impoverished country dwellers. Hunting and forest law, trespass law, game laws, fishing laws, and a whole complex of restrictions pertained to growing things that in America would not even be considered property. Wardens, underkeepers, bailiffs, deputies, justices, and informers tended the system with minute care so that deer stealing, rabbit poaching, and grazing violations were actively pursued. A vast thicket of medieval regulations had grown among England's forests and fields, and those who held power worked diligently to protect their interests. Natural products like berries, mushrooms, roots, bark, birds' eggs, and even the feathers of fowl were property and could not be removed from the demesne of the lord. Poaching, wood stealing, illegal trapping, or gathering were all dealt with to the extent that administrative action and rural surveillance would allow. Peat, dead trees, windfall wood, moss, ferns, and reeds were guarded by forest keepers, and severe penalties were inflicted on those daring to filch them. The taking of fauna from woods or fields was even more harshly treated.[1] Common people who came to America were by the single fact of emigration made almost entirely exempt from such laws and constraints.

Ireland in the seventeenth and eighteenth centuries was slowly being overlain with this web of English law. In previous centuries, while life was far from idyllic in the Irish countryside, there was far more latitude and freedom to rove among nature's scenery than in England, where law and the state were more comprehensively developed. It was this web of constriction confining everyday rural life that was of far greater moment for ordinary people than the transfer of titles and castles and seats in royal councils. The coming of the fullness of English law to Ireland was, it must be emphasized, a concomitant of conquest.[2] Therefore, enforcement was at once more severe and more erratic as a result. The colonization of Ireland under the English legal system was a forecast of English colonization schemes for America, but the immensity of America would at the outset make English law puny amid the teeming wilderness.

Hence, the confrontation of English and Irish people with the astounding resources of America would soon have had the most exhilarating effects. Here were whole forests beyond the reach of any lord. Wood, nuts, fruit, resin, flowerings, seeds, and the birds that abounded among them were all there for disposal. No conqueror, no bailiff or warden brooded over the endless expanses of this world. Game seethed at the watering places and gamboled in primeval abundance across countless clearings and mountainsides. The maddening codes and enactments that kept the poor, the hungry, the covetous, the greedy, and the adventurous from all such bounty in the Old World were instantly absurd in the New where no power could possibly oversee the awesome land.[3]

The contention that all early Americans regarded the forest as a "wilderness" and "desert" largely derives from the terms used by William Bradford to describe the outlook prompted by Puritan suffering in the godly isolation of early Massachusetts. This is understandable, but not representative of all colonies. The Puritans' antipathy toward the backwoods came in part from their own frustration in not having forest skills. Robert Beverley gave quite a different and more sanguine picture of Virginia in his descriptive work on its seventeenth-century aspect, referring to its "extreme fruitfulness" and its alluring abundance. The ultimate proof of the attitude of the new Americans toward the landscape is that within a century tens of thousands of families and individuals had settled in it.

The colonizing fever that swept English commercial and ruling circles in the sixteenth century did not begin to produce results until the seventeenth century. Sir Henry Sidney's schemes for plantation in Ireland after 1565 faced tough resistance. Queen Elizabeth frequently lost patience with the designs for Ireland. Her favorite, Essex, lost an army in the bogs and drumlins of Cavan and Monaghan. Sidney saw the Irish as pagans, descended from Asiatic Scythians, barbaric in their stubborn resistance to what the English considered to be their obviously superior ways. As Nicholas Canny has pointed out, the English suffered from a "blindness to reality" in their cultural conflict with the Irish, and this same kind of blindness was to deeply condition their relations with the Indians in their American undertakings.[4] Duplicity, repression, and extermination were to be regular features of the colonists' behavior in their long duels with the native American tribes and federations, a repetition of the record in Ireland.

The Irish colonial projects that were a prelude to American plantation did little to improve the basic military, legal, and social assumptions underlying English colonization efforts. Commercial motivation, religious justification, and royal approbation were the keys to the seaborne progressions to Virginia and New England. Inevitably the Irish were involved as factors in the American schemes. Usually they were included in a purely utilitarian fashion, to fill out crews, to make up quotas of migrants when others dropped out, and frequently as servants and indentured laborers to be placed at will on the far side of the sea. In 1621 Thomas Nuce was offering to plant 2,000 of them for the Virginia Company in one of the first large-scale plans to use them en masse. In 1653 the commissioners of Ireland sent out an order to generals in the occupying army to supply 250 "women of the Irish nation" and 300 men from Cork, Kinsale, Youghal, Waterford, and Wexford to be transported to New England.[5] In a mysterious plot worthy of Elizabethan theater, George Talbot, cousin of Lord Baltimore and relative of Richard Talbot, lord lieutenant of Ireland, contrived to obtain a charter for lands beside the Elk River in Maryland to form the basis for a colony to be called New Ireland. The Northeast River was to be rechristened the Shannon and lands were to be allocated to one Edwin O'Dwire and fifteen other Irishmen. George Talbot became involved in the murder of a royal revenue official. William Penn was greatly distressed by this rival activity on the border of his chartered lands, and political plotting in England and Ireland subverted the venture. Talbot had planned manors, a line of forts along the disputed area bordering Pennsylvania, and had extensive surveys under way. Some authors have argued that the Irish to be involved were Catholics, as the clan name O'Dwire suggests; others argue it was to be a Protestant colony. Whatever its religious color, the colony was one of the earliest attempts to move Irish people as such in a large group to American shores.[6]

These and other such ventures were a casting forth of stricken people into the forest frontier. The hagiography of America's first settlements does not contain any successful Irish Jamestowns or Plymouth colonies. The Irish would remain a subordinate element in the forest frontier, but that too would have its significance, for the ultimate American image of the frontiersman would not be one of a godly company but one of the solitary rover, the marginal man, the man on the edge of society.

It would be difficult to refute the fact that the Irish who came to the earliest white man's America were the poorest of the colonial immigrants. Bishop George Berkeley was to query in 1750, "Whether there be upon earth any Christian or civilized people so beggerly, wretched, and destitute, as the common Irish?"[7] With few exceptions in the first century of colonization, and even thereafter, "poverty" was synonymous with "Irish." A review of the lists of early settlers of Maryland shows few Irish as "immigrated," that is, paying their own passage. Scores of others, Kellys, O'Neills, and Murphys, were "transported" by having their passage paid or were brought as "servants."[8] But just as Englishmen coming to Maryland could become "gentlemen" by virtue of the voyage, so Irishmen would become landowners with alacrity on completing terms of service or by undertaking the labor of clearance and the building of rude domiciles.[9] Early land warrants in South Carolina show not only Irish servants, but Christopher Kelly, Thurloe Duffee, and Daniel Kellary with 500-acre allotments. James Mullrayne and his wife, Marie, held their 170 acres jointly, and Thomas O'Grady and four others settled on 350 acres in 1683. Brian Kelly held 300 acres in "Coleton" County forty miles beyond Charleston. These settlers not only owned but traded land. Mrs. Priscilla Burke sold forty-eight acres of land to Captain Florence O'Sullivan in 1672. O'Sullivan was the exceptional Irishman who arrived with an entourage of sixteen servants. Some immigrants like Galwayman Nicholas Lynch, his wife Alice, and his brother John, came by way of Barbados.[10]

The acquisition of land in such allotments, modest by American standards, was utterly beyond possibility in Ireland where both Catholics and Presbyterians were driven to desperation by the wholesale aggrandizement of the Crown and its clients. By the eighteenth century less than one-tenth of Ireland was owned by the Irish themselves. A Catholic could not be a physician, a soldier, or a lawyer; could not practice his religion; had to pay tithes for someone else's religion; could not deed land; and if he or she owned any or held it on short tenure, would be a fool to improve it. He lived under the "most compleat code of persecution that ingenious bigotry ever compiled," as the chief secretary for Ireland, George Macartney, put it.[11] A French traveler in Ireland wrote, "It is now almost destitute of trees; and when on a fine day in spring, it appears though bare, full of sap and youth, it seems like a lovely girl deprived of her hair." And now, here in America was not only land, but land overgrown with potential riches. The contrast of the woodlands of a place like South Carolina was hardly lost on those who moved inland from the coastal pine groves to the hardwood stands of the interior.

Pennsylvania was the true immigrant colony. Quakers who had sought refuge in Ireland from the blasts of religious intolerance in England brought Irish servants with them. Presbyterians from Ulster flocked to the loam-rich fields in the counties beyond Philadelphia. They forged into the mountain fastness. The good land in accessible areas southeast of the mountains was taken quickly. As word spread back to Ireland, the fact that settlement would be in the dark backwoods was either omitted or not understood. The Presbyterian bands had to hack their way to lonely homesteads and then brace themselves for Indian attacks. The tales of their hardihood were legendary by the time of the American Revolution.[12] Nor were they the only Irish frontiersmen in Pennsylvania. Captain Michael McGuire and others acted similarly, and one of the first Catholic churches in the Pittsburgh area was on land donated by McGuire. Among the Indian traders in the Upper Ohio Valley a "large number" were Irish in the 1750s with names such as Fitzpatrick, Kelly, and Obryan.[13] Often reports do not cite religion, because already that may have seemed irrelevant in the midst of the strenuous life of these forest dwellers. The lenient Quaker immigration policy brought thousands of Irish from all sectors of Ireland's life into the colony. Although some few married with other kinds of people, most married among their own ethnic group.[14] Family networks were the first seedbeds of American ethnic traditions, and it has remained so over the generations.

The enfilading of Pennsylvania with what William Penn's agent, James Logan, described as "bold and indigent strangers" would have a far-reaching effect on the shape of American events. As the American Revolution approached, these Irish and Scotch-Irish dissidents, with far less esteem for English institutions than their Anglo contemporaries, forced the issue of republicanism to the political forefront. In the state that was the keystone to the strategically paramount middle states, they exerted a critical influence that tilted the American cause decisively toward independence.[15]

The greater proportion of Irish Catholics came to America in the 1600s and 1700s as underlings, as servants and indentured laborers, both male and female. Their position was not enviable. They had the worst reputation of any group as servants and the highest record as runaways from indentured servitude. Bounties would be offered for them if they ran away and both courts and masters were likely to punish them harshly. Even as fugitives they were mocked, as an advertisement from 1769 in Lancaster County, Pennsylvania, illustrates:

Forty Shillings Reward
June 1769

Little Britain Township, Lancaster County
"Between the Sixth and Seventh Day,
Mary Nowland ran away;

> Her age I know not but appears
> To be at least full twenty years;
> The same religion with the Pope.
> Short neck, scarce room to fix a rope;
> She's large and round from neck to hips,
> Brown hair, red face, short nose, thick lips;
> Short, thick and clumsy in her jog
> As neat as any fatten'd hog.
> Upon her tongue she wears a brogue,
> And was she man would be a rogue."[16]

There were some unlikely success stories. Dubliner Daniel Dulaney, indentured to a Maryland magnate, married well and became a rich planter himself. Thomas Lynch did the same in Virginia.[17] For the most part, however, the route to success was escape from the indenture bondage. In a two-year sample of indentured servants, one study found that ten percent of the largely Irish indentured in Philadelphia ran away.[18] The cumulative effect of this flow of fugitives is an intriguing factor in early frontier life. Runaways were not likely to be casual about meeting people in their forest refuges. The places to hide were in the thinly settled mountains. It is notable that Appalachian mountaineers' characteristics of independence, guarded reception of strangers, and detestation of civil authority are all traits likely to be found among fugitive indentured people. If the Presbyterian homesteaders were marked by such traits, so were these former bonded people on the run. They did not bring clergymen with them, but eventually they raised up their own. Changing identities, names, and dwellings, at length they rooted themselves in the fastnesses beyond the Eastern seaboard. Their spirit persists until today from the Endless Mountains of Pennsylvania to the Ozarks, as does their vibrant legacy of Irish music. Newly free, they sang and played their racing tunes, poor perhaps, but safe in their mountain hollows.

There are truly extraordinary stories of the Irish penetration of this first American frontier. One of the most memorable is that of William Johnson. Born in Ireland to a family related to the Clan O'Neill, the old name of McShane was made into its English equivalent, Johnson. There is a suggestion of determined ambition in that act, a compulsion to beat the overlords at their own game. Johnson came to Boston in 1737 and in 1739 purchased 130,000 acres in New York State. Through carefully cultivating the fearsome Iroquois, he was able to extend his influence from his holdings near the Mohawk River. From a trader he became an Indian agent, a leader, a power, a force on the frontier whose name and words affected events from New England to Georgia. This man wielded influence in a territory as large as half of Europe. Knighted by the Crown, he never lost his Irish orientation. He imported a whole troupe of relatives to help manage his enterprises and, it was reported, was quite partial to Iroquois women.[19]

But destiny could frown as well as smile. A scholarly man from Galway named Mathias O'Conway journeyed to Spain in the late eighteenth century. Learned in Irish and the classical languages, he learned Spanish and sailed to

Havana and then New Orleans. His work as a teacher and translator was unprofitable. He moved to Philadelphia, and decided to study Indian languages to become a trader. An attempt to do this on the frontier beyond Pittsburgh failed. Back in Philadelphia, O'Conway struggled as a poor tutor, while unsuccessfully seeking to publish grammars in various tongues. As an old man he worked tirelessly on a huge glossary of his native Irish language. This, too, was never published. Mathias O'Conway died in poverty in Philadelphia after his sons had died before him serving with various revolutionary armies fighting for liberty in Latin America.[20]

Visions of power and glory easily deluded men who could ride alone for days across uninhabited territory that seemed to beg for a possessor. Dr. John Connolly and George Croghan schemed to set up a small empire beyond Virginia's farthest settlements in the 1770s. Dr. James O'Fallon, agent of the Carolina Company, dreamed of an independent state in Alabama and Mississippi and intrigued with Spain in 1789 to try to accomplish it. Harman Blennerhasset plotted with Aaron Burr from his island fort in the Ohio River for a similar goal, but ended with his mansion burned and his property seized by creditors. These were daring men taking perilous risks with the Indians and the twisting politics and statecraft of their day. Some failed, like Philip Nolan who traded with the Spaniards in the 1790s from Louisiana and was killed on an expedition into Texas. Some succeeded for a time, like Col. Daniel Mooney who was appointed in 1808 by the new American governor of Louisiana Territory to be governor of the wild Arkansas wilderness.[21] Indecision by British and American officials, the lure of the lucrative fur trade, and the drive for power all propelled such men into grandiose strategies to dominate territories that would dwarf ten times over a country the size of the island from which they sprang.

The fortunes of most of the Irish settlers were cast more modestly, however. They appear often in isolated situations, like John Kelly, the solitary attorney at the Isles of Shoals in Maine in 1647. Some loners isolated themselves from whites, like the man named Doherty who, a traveler related, took an Indian bride beyond the Allegheny. Charles McManus poled and floated his boat down the Ohio in the 1790s to join Hugh McGary's tough settlers in Kentucky. James McBride was the first white man on the Kentucky River and Michael Cassidy fought the Indians in that territory until more peaceful pursuits were possible. Rivers were the highways from the beginning. In 1793 John Moylan advertised in Lexington's *Kentucky Gazette*:

WANTED a number of hands to work my boats down to New Orleans; none need apply but such as can be well recommended and those will be preferred who have already been down the river . . . .

Moylan shipped flour, tobacco, bacon, whiskey, and furs in fifty-foot boats. James Hogan had ferry rights in Fayette County and built a warehouse there for such traders. The country may have been rude, but the trade was brisk.[22]

Other than sheer dispersion, these settlers signify a great diversity of roles. The various Irish listed in the 1790 census in North Carolina had gotten themselves into a variety of occupations. The 1800 census in Georgia shows Irish holding substantial acreage and numbers of slaves, and some of these Irish were themselves former convicts. The census in the same year in Kentucky lists Caseys and Cavanaughs, Doughertys and Dugans, McCaffertys and McCartys, O'Neals and Quinns, and William T. Barry would soon represent them in Congress, all as taxpayers. They were fewer in upstate Louisiana in the 1810 census, but Madame O'Donly in Lafourche Parish and John Hagerti in Attakapas Parish had Irish neighbors as well as the Cajuns. Boatmen, officials, Indian fighters, traders, plantation owners, saltmakers, lawyers, explorers, and whatever else made up frontier work life included Irish people in this busy and restless society.[23]

This dotting of the frontier with all kinds of Irish involved more than a simple presence. It made them part of a process of ambition, difficulty, and the eventual establishment of order shared with their non-Irish compatriots. They "cleared land, rolled logs, burned brush, blazed out paths from one neighbor's cabin to another, hunted deer, turkeys, otter and raccoon, caught fish, dug ginseng, hunted bees—and, lived on the fat of the land." But life among winding wagon tracks looked out on tree stumps and half-burned log piles, ramshackle corncribs and smokehouses, sleeping hogs, broken tubs and rainbarrels. "The frontier was one big rural slum saved by the fact that the open spaces were not far away."[24]

Civil order did emerge from all this with more rapidity than we would be disposed to believe. Old frontier hands like John Reily lived in Georgia and Kentucky, fought in the Revolution in North Carolina, and ended up in the Northwest Territory, where with one Judge Dunleavy he helped to organize the territorial courts.[25]

Local government and the early legal system involved almost everybody, so that while the quality of domestic and community life remained relatively unchanged for several generations, civil development was actively pursued. To the optimism and abundance of this way of life was added the local order that was to be the basis of America's settler society.[26] This was the first dimension of that long and creative Irish engagement with American politics that was to mark the group in U.S. history from the earliest period.

However, if order evolved in one place, the disorder of the rolling frontier continued ever westward. As Georgia settled down to taxpaying stability, General William Carroll fought desperately to save Andrew Jackson's troops in the Tennessee wars with the Creek Indians. And the civil organization of territorial units was itself often a fractious process. The Irish in the log town of St. Louis could toast the prospects of statehood at their St. Patrick's Day gathering in 1820, but their delegates Mathias McGurk, John O'Fallon, Daniel Murphy, and John C. Sullivan would be enmeshed in uproarious agitations to bring statehood to reality in the lands along the Mississippi.[27]

The older works on colonial and Revolutionary Irish-Americans are argumentative in behalf of two things: establishing the group as part of the American nation-founding process, and disputing whether Irish Catholics had a significant role along with Irish Presbyterians in that process.[28] It is manifest even from the sources cited above that Irish people of various backgrounds were part of the earliest frontier panorama. Audrey Lockhart states correctly that an accurate tabulation and full assessment of their role is not possible because of a lack of primary source material. David Doyle has revised upward the figures of Irish in the period largely based on research about indentured labor. Lockhart states that only eight percent of indentured servants seem to have made a stable adjustment. This suggests an early American liberation movement, a democratic voting with the feet, with extensive implications, only a few of which have been touched on here.[29]

The import of the early Irish distribution may not lie with these considerations, however. The broader issue is that recognizable, and by contemporaries recognized, members of this group, which was to play a massive role in immigration and in American life, were to be apprehended in all parts of the country during its early period of primitive settlement. In some places their presence was marginal, in others more substantial, but they did share and, indeed, helped to shape the frontier imagery of the nation. Their early dispersion made it impossible thereafter to confine them in any stringent way, as was done with Blacks, no matter how intense the hostility toward them. They were part of the country's original populist pantheon of the frontier, and the historical recognition of this fact, although it came late to academic historians, was a part of the local and family lore of the people even before the nation was founded.[30]

NOTES

1. E.P. Thompson, *Whigs and Hunters: The Origin of the Black Act* (New York: Random House, 1975), pp. 27–54; Douglas Hay, "Property, Authority and Criminal Law," in Douglas Hay et al., *Albion's Fatal Tree: Crime and Society in Eighteenth Century England* (New York: Random House, 1975), pp. 17–64.

2. Margaret MacCurtain, *Tudor and Stuart Ireland* (Dublin: Gill and Macmillan, 1972), pp. 69–72, 114–139.

3. It was English policy to seek to denude Ireland of forests that served to hide rebels. Ibid., 91. Rutherford Platt, *The Great American Forest* (Englewood Cliffs, N.J.: Prentice-Hall, 1965), pp. 19–20, tells of the forested land. The abundance of American natural resources and their initial impact on the minds of settlers is detailed in William Cronon, *Changes in the Land: Indians, Colonists, and the Ecology of New England* (New York: Hill and Wang, 1983), pp. 1–26. James Oliver Robinson, *American Myth, American Reality* (New York: Hill and Wang, 1980), pp. 16, 20, 38, 45–46, 115–117; Robert Beverley, *The History and Present State of Virginia*, Louis B. Wright, ed. (Chapel Hill: University of North Carolina Press, 1947), pp. 296, 298, 346.

4. Nicholas P. Canny, "The Ideology of English Colonization from Ireland to America," *William and Mary Quarterly* 30, no. 4 (October 1973): 575–598. Karen Ordahl Kupperman, *Settling with the Indians: The Meeting of English and Indians in the Cultures of America, 1580–1640* (Totowa, N.J.: Rowman and Littlefield, 1980), pp. 171–173,

notes that Ralph Lane, first governor of Roanoke with military experience in Ireland, "requisitioned" Indian food and kidnapped children as hostages.

5. Edward D. Neill, ed., *History of the Virginia Company* (Albany: Joel Maunsell, 1869), p. 178; Patrick Mahony, *It's Better in America* (Washington, D.C.: Institute for the Study of Man, 1964), p. 152.

6. Carl Ross McKendrick, "New Munster," *Maryland Historical Magazine* 35, no. 2 (June 1940): 147–159. In 1983 archaeological remains of a "New Connaught" section of this tract were uncovered by Mary Gowen in what she believed to be a farm settlement.

7. James Carty, *Ireland from the Flight of the Earls to Grattan's Parliament* (Dublin: C.J. Fallon, 1949), p. 109.

8. Gust Skorda, *The Early Settlers of Maryland* (Baltimore: Geneological Publishing Co., 1968), pp. 271–310.

9. William Reavis, "The Maryland Gentry and Social Mobility, 1637–1676," in John Lankford and David Reimers, eds., *Essays on American Social History* (New York: Holt, Rinehart and Winston, 1970), pp. 91–99. Land availability is described in Peter Wolf, *Land in America: Its Value, Use and Control* (New York: Pantheon Books, 1981), p. 32.

10. A.S. Salley, ed., *Warrants for Lands in South Carolina, 1672–1711* (Columbia: University of South Carolina Press, 1973), pp. 200, 323, 390, 418, 671; Agnes Leland Baldwin, *First Settlers of South Carolina, 1670–1680* (Columbia: South Carolina Tricentennial Commission, University of South Carolina Press, 1970), passim.

11. Carty, *Ireland from the Flight of the Earls to Grattan's Parliament*, p. 144.

12. R. Garland, "The Scotch-Irish in Western Pennsylvania," *Western Pennsylvania Historical Magazine* 6, no. 2 (April 1923): 65–105; James G. Leyburn, *The Scotch Irish: A Social History* (Chapel Hill: University of North Carolina Press, 1962).

13. Margaret E. Maloney, *Fág An Bealach: The Irish Contribution to America* (Pittsburgh: United Irish Societies of Pittsburgh, 1977), passim; John Arthur Adams, "The Indian Traders of the Upper Ohio Valley," *Western Pennsylvania Historical Magazine* 17, no. 3 (September 1934): 163–174.

14. *Names of Persons for Whom Marriage Licenses Were Issued in the Province of Pennsylvania Previous to 1790* (Baltimore: Geneological Publishing Co., 1963), pp. 139–140, 187–188.

15. Robert Kelley, *The Cultural Pattern in American Politics* (New York: Alfred A. Knopf, 1979), pp. 72–75.

16. *Pennsylvania Gazette*, June 29, 1769.

17. J.C. Furnas, *The Americans: A Social History of the United States, 1586–1914* (New York: G.P. Putnam's Sons, 1969), p. 108.

18. Dennis Clark, *The Irish Relations: Trials of an Immigrant Tradition* (Rutherford, N.J.: Fairleigh Dickinson University Press, 1982), pp. 19–23, n. 10.

19. James Sullivan, ed., *The Papers of Sir William Johnson*, 14 vols. (Albany: University of the State of New York, 1921), vol. 1, xxxiv; James Thomas Flexner, *Lord of the Mohawks* (Boston: Little, Brown and Company, 1959), pp. 233–234.

20. Lawrence F. Flick, "Mathias James O'Conway: Philologist, Lexicographer and Interpreter of Languages," *Records of the American Catholic Historical Society of Philadelphia* 10, no. 4 (December 1899): 385–422.

21. George Croghan, Irish-born friend of William Johnson, was Connolly's uncle. Francis S. Philbrick, *The Rise of the West, 1754–1830* (New York: Harper and Row, 1965), pp. 40–41, 184–185; Furnas, *The Americans*, p. 288; Robert Ferris, *Founders*

and Frontiersmen (Washington: U.S. Department of the Interior, 1967), p. 313; Richard Bartlett, *The New Country: A Social History of the American Frontier, 1776–1890* (New York: Oxford University Press, 1974), p. 85; Thomas Wuttall, *A Journal of Travels into Arkansas Territory, 1819* (Norman: University of Oklahoma Press, 1980), p. 101; Reuben Gold Thwaites, *Early Western Travels, 1748–1846*, 32 vols. (New York: AMS Press, 1966), vol. 31, 306–307, lists many other Irish frontier figures.

22. Wilbur Spencer, *Pioneers on Maine Rivers* (Baltimore: Geneological Publishing Company, 1973), p. 55; Clarence W. Alvord and Lee Bedgood, *The First Explorations of the Trans-Allegheny Region by the Virginians, 1650–1674* (Cleveland: A.H. Clark Co., 1912), p. 91; M.J. Spalding, *Sketches of Early Catholic Missions in Kentucky* (Louisville: D.J. Webb and Brother, 1844), p. 35; Mary Verhoeff, *The Kentucky River Navigation* (Louisville: John P. Morton, 1917), pp. 50, 173.

23. *First Census of the United States, 1790, North Carolina, Heads of Families* (Washington: Government Printing Office, 1908), cf. alphabetical listings for Brenans, Caseys, Farly, Kelly, O'Daniel, O'Farrell, O'Herne, O'Neal, O'Quin, Sullivan. G. Glenn Clift, *Second Census of Kentucky, 1800* (Frankfort: Privately published, 1954), cf. listings for Casey, Cavanaugh, Connolly, Daily, Donaghue, Dooley, Dougherty, Dugan, Dunaghy, Farral, Finn, Flanagan, Foley, Gallagher, Kain, Kavanaugh, Kelly, Kinney, McBride, McCafferty, McCarty (15 pages of names beginning with "Mc," some of course clearly Scots), Mullins, O'Donald, O'Hara, O'Neal, Quinn, Reily, Riley, Sullivan. John C. Linehan, "Irish Pioneers and Builders of Kentucky," *Journal of the American Irish Historical Society* 3 (1900): 78–88. Frank Parker Hudson, *An 1800 Census for Lincoln County, Georgia* (Atlanta: R.J. Taylor Foundation, 1977), pp. 51, 54, 66. Ronald Jackson, Gary E. Teeples, and Donald Shaefermeyer, eds., *Louisiana 1810 Census Index* (Bountiful, Utah: Accelerated Indexing Systems, 1976), listings for Foley, Gallaghan, Hagerti, McClusky, McGuire, Morphy, Nugent, O'Conner, O'Donly, O'Relly.

24. Furnas, *The Americans*, p. 259.

25. Jacob Burnet, *Notes on the Early Settlement of the Northwest Territory* (Cincinnati: Derby, Bradley Co., 1847), p. 469.

26. Malcolm J. Rohrbough, *The Trans-Appalachian Frontier: People, Societies and Institutions, 1775–1850* (New York: Oxford University Press, 1978), pp. 406–407.

27. Michael Paul Rogin, *Fathers and Children: Andrew Jackson and the Subjugation of the American Indian* (New York: Random House, 1976), p. 155; Floyd C. Shoemaker, *Missouri's Struggle for Statehood: 1804–1821* (New York: Russell and Russell, 1916), pp. 96–123.

28. Michael J. O'Brien, *A Hidden Phase of American History: Ireland's Part in America's Struggle for Liberty* (New York: Dodd, Mead and Co., 1920), pp. 38–53, 287–288.

29. Audrey Lockhart, *Some Aspects of Emigration from Ireland to the North American Colonies between 1660 and 1775* (New York: Arno Press, 1976), pp. 149–159; David Noel Doyle, *Ireland, Irishmen and Revolutionary America, 1760–1820* (Cork, Ireland: The Mercier Press, 1981), pp. 51–93. In the early Midwest where the plantation and slavery system was posed against freeholding small farmers, the Irish usually voted for freeholding: John D. Barnhart, *Valley of Democracy: The Frontier versus the Plantation in the Ohio Valley, 1775–1818* (Bloomington: Indiana University Press, 1953), pp. 111, 153, 156, 184, 207–208.

30. By 1850 the Irish were distributed in a pattern generally similar to that of the total

population. After that a historic pattern of concentration prevailed dictated by later immigrant settlement traditions. This analysis applies only to the Irish-born population. Morton D. Winsberg, ''Irish Settlement in the United States, 1850–1980,'' *Eire-Ireland* 20, no. 1 (Fall 1985): 7–14.

2 DIGGERS

What could have been a more prophetic act than for the Americans to actually inscribe upon the vast landscape of the New World the channels that would open up its treasures? God-created rivers were the first routes into the forested and prairie heartland, but that was not access enough. New waterways would be cut through the terrain on a scale that no Pharoah, no emperor had ever dreamed possible. Great water roadways for the flow of commerce and people as the first man-made integrated transport system in the nation were to be gouged out of hundreds of miles of countryside. Having hacked through the woodlands and struggled over the mountainsides and found that the land was rich in thousands of minerals, creatures, trees, plants, and quarries of stone, the settlers were compelled to find ways to gather and transport these things and to distribute the labor to do it. The mightiest teams of beasts could not haul forth this bounty over the rough land. Only on water could it be serenely floated to become processed, sold, and used, and roads of water had to be constructed for the task. Rivers were too devious, rock-strewn, untamed, and uncontrollable except for the very largest which flowed majestically above all obstacles,—the Delaware, the Susquehanna, the Hudson, the Ohio, and that ultimate continental artery, the Mississippi. Only canals could be managed to flow with precision from town to town. There had to be canals, and there had to be men to dig them.

In 1807 the U.S. Senate, in response to demands for internal improvements, requested Secretary of the Treasury Albert Gallatin to examine the problem of means for national communication and transport. In 1808 he reported on "Roads and Canals," proposing a canal network along the Eastern seaboard that would reach back into the hinterlands in a gigantic effort to tap the nation's potential. But Gallatin's report came a whole generation after the first canal plans in the country. A young George Washington had surveyed for canal building beginning in the 1750s. Early charters for the James River Company and the "Patowmack" Company were granted for canal plans in the 1780s. Washington was president of the company beginning the waterway that would grow to be the Chesapeake and Ohio Canal. By 1808 when Gallatin issued his report, sixteen canals in eight states were already in operation, about 115 miles of locks and channels altogether. Before 1850 the mileage of canals in the country would grow over thirty times this total to sprawl 4,000 miles across a land area that reached into the country's prairies adjacent to the Mississippi. From the Atlantic to Illinois, America would freight its wealth through gurgling channels of commerce.[1] But in the seventy-five years after the Republic's founding, an epic of labor would be expended, and the chief labor force in this Herculean dig through thousands of miles would be Irish. This great Irish dig, immense even by twentieth-century standards, was a prelude and a complement to industrialization. It would set the terms of trade, the fortunes of cities, and the orientation of the country's commercial life in the Republic's formative decades.[2]

River rafting had been tried before the canal era and was found to be inadequate to transport cargoes. Then a plan for "The National Road" was announced. A thousand Irishmen were given the task under Mordecai Cochran, Philip Mc-Ginnis, Tully Gallagher, and Thomas Monaghan to tear a path through the thick forests from Braddock's Grove to Uniontown, Pennsylvania, and on into Ohio. With a fury of athletic effort they set to the job and did indeed chop, dig, and grade a path through the wilderness.[3] But the spring rains, winter mud, and accumulated wagon ruts made for a very poor road indeed. The wretchedness of the early roads convinced leaders that it was canals that were needed. The early Virginia and Maryland canals had shown that they were workable. These and other pioneer canals had the same characteristics as much of the early industrialization of the country. They were adaptable, they could be used inten-sively, and they could be manned by labor that was itself flexible and interchangeable.[4]

Historian Richard Bartlett calls the Irish the "canal and railroad builders of America."[5] They gained their experience early. The workmen on the Chesapeake and Delaware Canal, completed after years of effort in 1829, dug across the peninsula between the Delaware and Chesapeake bays to join those two major bodies of water. It was difficult for the Maryland farmers to take kindly to the footloose Irish diggers. Accommodations in nearby towns were hard to find and canal men fought pitched battles with townsfolk in Elkton. The pattern for living quarters for digger gangs was already set. They lived in companies of fifteen or twenty in shanties. If there were Blacks who shared the work, they lived similarly, but segregated from the whites.[6]

The work to be done was extraordinarily difficult. Early America was used to hard labor. Farmers cleared fields and dug drainage ditches, but canal work required clearing, leveling, and banking the land in the route, and then excavating it to the proper depth. Portage paths, aqueducts, sluices, dams, reservoirs, dikes, diversion channels, tunnels, slips, and docks all had to be dug out before the canal and its locks could function.[7] Ploughs and scrapers could be used for some of this work, but usually it was axe, pick, shovel, and barrow that were the chief tools. The country was chronically short of labor, especially for brutal labor like this, so recruits were sought directly from Ireland.[8] When they arrived, they were put to the task, and it is a tribute to their persistence that they were able for it. Three Irishmen finished three rods of the Erie Canal four feet deep in five and a half days in December weather in 1817 for $1.80 a day.[9]

Not only was the work fearfully hard and the living arrangements terrible, but the work could stop without warning. A man could travel hundreds of miles to the canal dig, begin work, and then be laid off. James Cochran, contractor on the Washington Canal, abandoned his digging crews after one year of construction when money ran out in 1810.[10] Many of the canal schemes were speculative, ill-conceived, or outright frauds, so when accounts tell of Irish workers rioting, as on the Chesapeake in 1832, it was not usually just exuberant Irish spirits. Pay cuts, bankruptcies, shutdowns, strikes, and the setting of one group on another in promoter-fomented labor competition were all involved.[11]

On the 147-mile canal to Lynchburg, Virginia, two-thirds of the laborers were Irish. They engaged in a strike in 1838 to raise their wages. The heat in May and June was intense, and some died of heat stroke. The heat became so bad that 200 quit the job and migrated north to hunt for other work.[12] Cholera was one of the great scourges of this labor in steaming swamps and lowlands. Typhoid fever, malaria, and in the winters typhus, pneumonia, and frostbite took a very heavy toll. Although the men lived partly as migrants, they often had families back in the seaboard cities or in towns along the completed canal sections. Mathew Carey in 1831 described their unfortunate state in his *Address to the Wealthy of the Land*, one of the finest American pleas for social justice ever penned. The men could make ten to twelve dollars a month in summer, but only five dollars in winter. Some worked only for food. With the earnings of wife and children, a family in good health with arduous effort could make $136 in a year. Carey gives a budget for such a family, an annual minimal budget based on his familiarity with his fellow Irishmen in canal work:

Rent	26.00
Adults' shoes, clothes	24.00
Two children's shoes, clothes	16.00
Washing	6.50
Soap, candles	3.12
Fuel (.15 a week)	7.80
Food	87.60
Total	$171.02

On an annual wage of $136 this left a deficit of $35.02. It is little wonder that Carey termed canal work "an unholy and ungodly employment." In an earlier pamphlet, Dublin-born Carey recounted how 700 men worked for a contractor for 15 months and got nothing because the finances of the Chesapeake and Delaware Canal were so chaotic.[13]

The harsh record was much the same in New England. In 1826 the Irish were brought to Worcester, Massachusetts, to dig the Blackstone Canal. Irish diggers on the Suffolk Canal in East Cambridge, Massachusetts, were housed in tents and shacks. Cardinal O'Connell of Boston would recall that in the 1840's they were "herded in a quarter of the town and told to stay there like Jews in the Ghetto, and these outer portions of the village were designated Dublin or Cork in derision."[14] The men hired to work on the canal at Sault Ste. Marie in northern Michigan in 1854 were described by a contemporary as "sick, starved, lean, lank, slim, light of build, about half of them weigh under 100 pounds. They look as if they had come from abroad or an emigrant ship lately."[15] These half-starved famine refugees were put to a labor that would stagger the strongest of men, and the result was that they died by the thousands. On all the tributary canals of New York—the Chemung Canal, Crooked Lake Canal, Oswego Canal, Chenango Canal, and Genesee Valley Canal—and the Delaware and Hudson the story was the same. The work was driven at enormous human cost. The "aliens" were transported throughout the state, which observers found "striking beyond all reason."[16]

The more skilled work was often performed by English or Welsh masons and miners, as on the 3,000-foot Paw Paw tunnel of the Washington Canal, where the Irish did the digging. On the Brunswick Canal in Georgia, slaves were used at first to excavate, but they were unequal to the work, so Irishmen were recruited in Boston and brought south. A writer in the South noted that "the niggers are worth too much to be risked here; if the Paddies are knocked overboard or get their backs broke, nobody loses anything."[17] Especially in the South manpower shortages were acute. The first Alabama canal was delayed for years by lack of workers. Workers taken to the New Basin Canal near New Orleans, who had been hired in Philadelphia, found deplorable conditions and exploitation and went on strike.[18]

Although some canal works failed due to economic depression, such as the Winnipiseogee Canal in New Hampshire, others failed simply because they were wild land speculators' schemes, the mere rumors of which would increase land values. Government aid to the projects depended on the stage of development of the area, geographical obstacles, and availability of private capital.[19] In the Midwest land speculators promoted the Wabash Canal, the Illinois and Michigan Canal, and the Fox and Wisconsin Canal, all of which drew Irish workers and all of which failed in early stages. In Ohio, however, the canals produced an economic boom. The Sandy and Beaver Canal was begun in 1834. Irish families had settled as early as 1812 in New Lisbon, Ohio. On the canal project, James Kelly was the contractor. The men lived in shantytowns near Dungannon, Ohio, and a Corkman named James McIntire led the crew through the hard rock boring of the Dungannon tunnel. The canal boats were pulled through the tunnel by chains when operation commenced. The boats moved at two miles an hour on such canals. The Ohio canal network was enormous, reaching north and south through the state from Cleveland to Portsmouth and from Toledo to Cincinnati.[20]

The population effects of this canal activity were prodigious. The economic stimulus attracted throngs of people westward and intensified the life of the more developed seaboard areas. In Pennsylvania in 1832 the Lehigh Canal shipped 75,000 tons of coal. By 1855 it carried 1,276,000 tons, and the state's other canals promoted similar shipping increases.[21] With such growth came more opportunities for workers. Although some Irish were involved in canal surveys and engineering, like James Riley who surveyed the Maumee River basin in 1820, most were part of only the unskilled digging force.[22] As the canals were completed, however, the Irish moved into the ranks of the boatmen—semi-itinerant, hard-living "river rats." By 1818 there were already 2,000 boatmen on the Ohio River "ferocious and abandoned in their habits." Scores of Irishmen bought and operated canal boats by 1850.[23]

Herman Melville described the Erie Canal workers in the fulsome terms in which the men of his age saw them:

For three hundred and sixty miles, gentlemen, through the entire breadth of the state of New York; through numerous populous cities and most thriving villages; through long, dismal uninhabited swamps, and affluent, cultivated fields, unrivalled for fertility; by billiard room and bar room; through the holy-of-holies of great forests; on Roman arches over Indian rivers; through sun or shade, by happy hearts or broken; through all the wide contrasting scenery of those noble Mohawk counties . . . flows one continual stream of corrupt and often lawless life . . . the Canaller would make a fine dramatic hero, so abundantly and picturesquely wicked he is.

Still others became steamboat captains, those skillful scions of thousands of journeys who appear memorably in the works and recollections of Mark Twain. From the Great Lakes to Texas they guided their tall river craft leaving long plumes of smoke to the horizon. The canal boats themselves became a way of life for families who worked them. The keelboat had originated from the French trapper's *bateaux-plats*, and its centerboard, rudder, and sweeps evolved to fit local conditions.[24] For many of the Irish, however, such as those who founded Akron, Ohio, in 1825 after completing the Beaver Canal, more settled conditions were preferable.[25]

The Illinois and Michigan Canal eventually had a potent impact on the area around Chicago, setting off land booms and settlement through a wide area. Begun in 1836 but interrupted by bond sale failure, politics, and economic recessions, the project was not completed until 1848. The canal was the brainchild of Dr. William Egan, a County Kerry man who was involved in the feverish land dealing in the Chicago vicinity. The Illinois legislature in 1843 finally voted funds to enable contractors to complete a shallower canal than originally planned. These contractors included immigrant entrepreneurs Patrick Casey, William B. Snowhook, Thomas Lonergan, Owen McCarthy, and Edward Cullerton, all of whom became prominent in business and politics in Chicago. The diggers themselves formed part of the booming Chicago Irish population. The canal was an important factor in retaining the northern part of Illinois in that state's territory rather than joining it to the new state of Wisconsin.[26]

The canals, of course, were for the purpose of getting the products of the earth and the workings in the hinterlands to the trading centers, and the ore and coal of the early mining operations were eagerly transported by a peculiar and ingenious linking of mechanical and hydraulic devices. The Delaware and Hudson Canal is a good example. Desperate to get anthracite coal out of the Pennsylvania mountains, entrepreneurs failed repeatedly using rough river rafts. In 1823 the Pennsylvania General Assembly granted a charter to build a canal from Honesdale in the mountains east of Scranton to the Delaware River at Port Jervis, then northeast to the Hudson River, thus gaining access to the New York City market. The twenty-foot-wide ditch and an aqueduct across the Delaware were built against extraordinary obstacles of rugged terrain, forests, lakes, and rocky ravines. Boats loaded with forty tons of coal passed through seventy-six-foot locks in 1828. Two of the leading engineers for the project were Edward Sullivan and Col. John L. Sullivan, who had worked on the Erie Canal.

The Irish workers on the project performed remarkable labors of excavation, embankment, and stone slab construction. They left their names on the canal locks and stations: Foley's, Jack McCarthy's, Joe McKane's, Pat Gannon's, Billy O'Brien's, Mike Connor's, Hennessey's, O'Han's, and McKahill's. In 1829 the Pennsylvania Coal Company built the first locomotive railroad in America from a point near Pittston to meet the canal south of Honesdale. This wild route was mainly a gravity railroad, combining stationary steam engines, tracks, water flumes, inclined planes, and a mechanical jamboree of contrivances up hill and down dale, but it worked. Coal was freighted out to New York and Philadelphia in thousands of tons, and timber and stone as well. The canal was widened in 1850. When the rail line was being built there was much rivalry with the canal workers. For the rail labor to proceed at some places required stopping canal traffic. That meant lost wages. Rail men and canal men fought it out. The rail men won, and for a time the canal traffic had to be halted under the threat of violence.[27]

If the Irish were the country's diggers on the surface they could easily be put to digging underground. From canal to mine was a downward descent in every sense. Mines were even more dangerous than canals. Rock falls and cave-ins, flooding, explosions, and all kinds of hazards to the lungs were daily perils, and the mining camps and company towns were polluted and jerry-built. Still, it was work in America, even if it was work under America—under its ground, under its society, under its exploitative mine owners—so in all the locales where earth veins were to be dug the Irish went down into the holes. From the bog iron mines of southern New Jersey in colonial times to the lead mines in Galena, Illinois, they dug ore. In the 1750s Irish-born Robert Coleman was smelting at his Cornwall Furnace in Pennsylvania. In the earliest coal diggings the Irish were black with the dirt in the tunnels. From Pennsylvania's hard coal region in Schuylkill County to coal holes in the Kentucky mountains they did the work the more experienced Welsh and Cornish miners avoided.[28] Dig, dig, dig was the labor of their days, and the canals brought their production to markets and cities.

For the Irish this involvement with the country's first great transportation system was a further diffusion throughout the land. Along with the earlier rovings of frontiersmen and settlers it placed Irish people in a very wide array of American situations. Their employment as miners began a long record of Irish immigrant servitude in mineral industries that would last into the twentieth century. The canal era was a period of mobility for the group. Even before the great famine refugee influx of the 1840s they were distributed deep into the interior of the nation. A far-reaching negative feature of the canal experience, though, was that the group was identified with the degraded work that the canals entailed, and the stereotype of Paddy the digger would have long-lasting implications for Irish-American social position and imagery for a century. More positively, the canal labors accredited to the Irish one more achievement in the drama of American development, a credit not to be lightly weighed in a nation that was intent upon glorifying its own growth as the nineteenth century progressed. Thus the Irish became a further part of the American scene from New England to Virginia to Georgia, Alabama, and New Orleans and into the prairie states of the interior through the sheer use of Hibernian muscle and sinew.

NOTES

1. Richard G. Waugh, Jr., "Canal Development in Early America," in Thomas F. Hahn, ed., *The Best from American Canals* (York, Penn.: The American Canal Society, Inc., 1980), p. 3.

2. J. Douglas Porteous, *Canal Ports: The Urban Achievement of the Canal Age* (New York: Academic Press, 1977), pp. 1–40. The numbers of immigrant workers were estimated on the larger canals to be Erie Canal: 3,000 (1818); Ohio canals: 2,000 (1825); Pennsylvania canals: 5,000 (1828); Chesapeake and Ohio Canal: 3,100 (1829); James River and Kanawha Canal: 3,000 (1837). George Rogers Taylor, *The Transportation Revolution, 1815–1860* (New York: Harper and Row, 1951), p. 291.

3. Carl Wittke, *The Irish in America* (Baton Rouge: Louisiana State University Press, 1956), pp. 32–33.

4. Carl Siracusa, *A Mechanical People: Perceptions of the Industrial Order in Massachusetts, 1815–80* (Middletown, Conn.: Wesleyan University Press, 1979), p. 17.

5. Richard Bartlett, *The New Country: A Social History of the American Frontier, 1776–1810* (New York: Oxford University Press, 1974), p. 151.

6. Ralph D. Gray, *The National Waterway: A History of the Chesapeake and Delaware Canal, 1769–1965* (Urbana: University of Illinois Press, 1967), p. 53.

7. Noble E. Whitford, *History of the Canal System of the State of New York* (New York, 1905), vol. 1, pp. 50–80.

8. Carter Goodrich, *Government Promotion of American Canals and Railroads, 1800–1890* (New York: Columbia University Press, 1960), p. 78.

9. Archer Butler Hulbert, *The Great American Canals* (Cleveland: A.H. Clark Co., 1904), vol. 2, p. 122.

10. Ernest H. Schell, "Tiber Creek to Murder Bay," in Hahn, *The Best from American Canals*, pp. 56–57.

11. Goodrich, *Government Promotion of American Canals and Railroads*, p. 78.

12. Wayland F. Dunaway, *History of the James River and Kanawha Company* (New York: AMS Press, 1969), p. 131.

13. Mathew Carey, *Address to the Wealthy of the Land* (Philadelphia: William Geddes, 1831), pp. 4–7; Mathew Carey, *Exhibit of the Shocking Oppression and Injustice Suffered by John Randel of the Chesapeake and Delaware Canal* (Philadelphia: Mathew Carey, 1825), pp. 1–11. For Pennsylvania canals see Dennis Clark, *The Irish in Philadelphia: Ten Generations of Urban Experience* (Philadelphia: Temple University Press, 1973), p. 66; Elizabeth G. C. Menzies, *Passage between Rivers* (New Brunswick, N.J.: Rutgers University Press, 1976), p. 40.

14. C.E. McGuire, ed., *Catholic Builders of the Nation: A Symposium of the Catholic Contribution to the Civilization of the United States* (Boston: Continental Press, 1923), p. 224; Francis Christie, "An Historical Footnote to Cardinal O'Connell's Recollections," *New England Quarterly* 8, no. 2 (June 1935): 258–259.

15. John N. Dickinson, *To Build a Canal: Sault Ste. Marie, 1853–1854 and After* (Columbus: Ohio State University Press, 1981), p. 81.

16. Whitford, *History of the Canal System of the State of New York*, p. 890.

17. Thomas F. Hahn, "The Paw Paw Tunnel," in Hahn, ed., *The Best from American Canals*, pp. 40–41; Rowland Berthoff, *An Unsettled People: Social Order and Disorder in American History* (New York: Harper and Row, 1971), p. 168.

18. L.W. Richardson, "The First Alabama Canal," in Hahn, ed., *The Best from American Canals*, pp. 42–43; Richard Niehaus, *The Irish in New Orleans, 1800–1860* (Baton Rouge: Louisiana State University Press, 1965), p. 45.

19. Goodrich, *Government Promotion of American Canals and Railroads*, pp. 165–191; Paul W. Gates, "The Role of the Land Speculator," *Pennsylvania Magazine of History and Biography* 66, no. 3 (July 1942): 314–333.

20. R. Max Gard and William H. Vodrey, *The Sandy and Beaver Canal* (East Liverpool: Ohio Historical Society, 1952), pp. 59–68; Frank Wilcox, *The Ohio Canals* (Kent, Ohio: Kent State University Press, 1969), Figure 1.

21. C.P. Yoder, *Delaware Canal Journal* (Bethlehem, Penn.: Canal Press, 1977), Table III, p. 241.

22. Charles E. Slocum, *History of the Maumee River Basin* (Defiance, Ohio: Published by the author, 1905), pp. 546–547.

23. Mary Verhoeff, *The Kentucky River Navigation* (Louisville: John P. Morton, 1917), p. 98; Jane Curry, *River's in My Blood* (Lincoln: University of Nebraska Press, 1983), passim; John Brendan Flannery, *The Irish Texans* (San Antonio: Institute for Texas Cultures of the University of Texas, 1980), p. 122; Richard Garrity, *Canal Boatman: My Life on Upstate Waterways* (Syracuse: Syracuse University Press, 1977), p. 1; Hahn, ed., *The Best from American Canals*, p. 27; *Pleadings and Testimony: The Delaware and Hudson Canal Co. vs. The Pennsylvania Coal Co.*, 8 vols. (New York: W.C. Bryant and Co., 1858), vol. 6, p. 3665; Herman Melville, *Moby Dick or, The Whale* (New York: Random House, 1950), pp. 250–251.

24. Henry E. Chambers, *Mississippi Valley Beginnings* (New York: Putnam's Inc., 1922), pp. 23, 363–364.

25. Richard Lingeman, *Small Town America: A Narrative, 1620 to the Present* (Boston: Houghton-Mifflin Co., 1980), p. 161.

26. John Kelly, "I. and M. Canal Ensured Irish Role in Chicago's Development," *Sceal* (Newsletter of the Chicago Irish Folklore Society) 3, no.1 (Spring 1983): 1, 8.

27. Edwin D. Le Roy, *The Delaware and Hudson Canal* (Honesdale, Penn.: Wayne County Historical Society, 1950), pp. 11–30, 79–80. Two generations later the Irish were still the majority of boatmen on the canal. Also Philip Faherty, "The Irish and the Delaware and Raritan Canal," *The Beacon* (Lambertville, N.J.) (June 28, 1984).

28. Robert P. Howard, *Illinois: A History of the Prairie State* (Grand Rapids, Mich.: William B. Eerdman Publishing Co., 1972), pp. 165–171; Robert Coleman Papers, Grubb Family Papers, Brinton Collection, Historical Society of Pennsylvania, Philadelphia; *Catholic Star Herald* (Camden, N.J.) (March 16, 1968); William A. Gudelmas and William G. Shade, *Before the Molly Maguires: The Emergence of the Ethno-Religious Factor in the Politics of the Lower Anthracite Region, 1844–1872* (New York: Arno Press, 1976), pp. 10–50; Verhoeff, *The Kentucky River Navigation*, p. 173.

3 STEEL RAIL MEN

If canals were the country's mechanism for penetrating the hinterlands, railroads were its means to dominate the American land mass completely. Railroads were forty percent cheaper to build than canals. Construction was faster, but not necessarily less laborious, and there was ultimately much more of it, since the railroads would reach into all corners of the United States. At first the technical problems were difficult. How to construct an efficient steam engine was an elusive art for years, with all kinds of experiments going wrong and with boilers blowing up with disturbing regularity.[1] When that problem was solved, however, the same work force that had built the canals found jobs with railroad companies. In some cases the railroad companies grew out of canal enterprises and the work force was shifted en masse.[2] By 1850 some 4,000 miles of canals had been built. The initial railroad expansion was even more rapid. In 1830 there were only seventy-three miles of rails. By 1860 there were more than 30,000 miles of railroad, with the decade after 1850 being the one of greatest construction. By 1860 over 36,000 workers were employed by railroads.[3]

For the Irish the railroads were central, and some would say indispensible, to their adjustment to America. As the largest economic enterprises of the nineteenth century, the railroads were a crucial instrument of industrialization upon which the livelihood of millions of immigrants would depend. As the primary network for the social unification of the country, they were also the primary medium for the distribution of the Irish at a time when the immigration of that group surged by the hundreds of thousands at mid-century. Not only did the labor needs of the rail system coincide with the flood of Irish immigration, but the dispersion of Irish people through the system relieved the urban ghetto confinement and ostracization that attended heavy immigrant arrivals at a time when religious and social hostility toward the group was most intense. Further, there was a romance to the railways in the 1800s. They were a technological wonder—swift, a force representing modernization and daring achievement. For young men from rural backgrounds to be able to identify themselves with this work after the construction phase was over was to share the victory over distance and backwardness.

In 1830 Henry O'Reilly wrote a history of Rochester, New York, and foresaw the tremendous impact that rails, cars, and locomotives would make upon communities like his own.[4] But the railroad age was also to continue the infamous suffering of workers as the forging construction proceeded. The speculative recklessness of the canal era was repeated, and the exploitation of labor was unabated. No labor unions, no watchful government, no sympathetic public opinion tempered the cruelty of the early rail-building campaigns. As early as 1837 the Irish diggers were militant as their employers set groups of Germans and Yankees against them to cut wages.[5] The Baltimore and Ohio construction in 1829 was being "prosecuted with energy." A cave-in killed four Irish laborers and injured others. There were numerous quarrels between laborers and contractors and among the hard-driven workers themselves. Liquor in the work camps added to the problem. The laborers were owed more than $9,000 in back wages. The railroad executives took out a riot warrant but could not raise a posse. Hugh Reily, leader of the workers, sent the railroad officials back to Baltimore for the wage money, but they returned with soldiers to break the strike.[6]

This same scenario was to be reenacted countless times where the government would be used to enforce the injustices of the railroad heads. Twenty-five years later the very same behavior is documented on the North Eastern Railroad in South Carolina. The victims are, as usual, Irish seeking a $1.25 a day wage. Instead, twenty-three strike leaders got $5 fines and two-month prison terms, a disaster for men whose families already lived on the edge of destitution.[7] The dirt, disorder, danger, and exploitation of the railway labor jobs prevailed wherever the lines were being built. It was the same on the Philadelphia and Reading, the Erie, the New York Central, and all the way south to the Opelousas and the Pontchartrain railroads. Irish workers recruited in New York even went to the fever jungles of Panama to build the line across the isthmus.[8]

Wherever this trail of travail was acted out there is comment about the violence of the work force. The Irish had little experience with such slave-driving work previously in Ireland. Though poor to beggary, their rural labor had been agricultural, hard but familiar, and fitted into centuries-old planting and harvesting custom. Ireland had few railways till relatively late.[9] The male emigrants in America were often single young men. When all-male groups gather anywhere they are likely to be boisterous, cocky, and given to roughhouse antics that easily turn into brawls.[10] At least that was true in the America where men were hardened by tough physical labor and looked on punching frays as mere sport. Add to this the real tensions involved with the migrant railroad work and the provocations of evil promotion schemes and living conditions, and the violence is explicable. Still, its frequency added to the detractions and distorted public perception of the Irish from one locale to another and, indeed, added to the nationally accepted stereotypes of the group.

In 1841 Charles Dickens passed through upstate New York and saw the railroad labor in its domestic squalor:

clumsy, rough and wretched . . . hovels. . . . The best were poor protection . . . the worst let in the wind and rain through wide breaches in the roofs of sodden grass . . . some had neither door nor window; some . . . were imperfectly propped up by stakes and poles; all were very . . . filthy. Hideously ugly old women and very buxom young ones, pigs, dogs, men, children, babies . . . all wallowing together in an inseparable heap . . .

A French traveler heard of an Irish pick swinger having a letter written for him to his family in Ireland and expressly instructing the writer to say he was having meat three times a week. The writer reminded the man of the fact that he sometimes had meat three times a day, bad though the stew might be. "Sure, if you wrote that, they'd never believe it," said the railway digger.[11] Terrible though American work might be, it was work, while in Ireland, as one man said, "starvation was the chief occupation."

By 1860 twenty railroads stretched lines that wended from the Atlantic to beyond the Mississippi. The rail leap across the geography of settled America was astonishingly rapid. By 1835 railroad expansion had opened up 1.8 million acres of public domain in Michigan alone. With return on capital in 1846 at 8.7 percent, the frenzy to build farther and farther was unabated. When the money ran out the rail companies paid their Irish labor in scrip. They also paid in land, crops, worthless paper, and whiskey. Some of these workers were so green to the country that they could strike for a raise of "a shilling," as they put it, above their seventy-five-cent-a-day current wage.[12]

As the railroads moved into the Midwest the Irish went with them. They became part of a railway lore and, for many Americans, synonymous with the country's transport network.[13] The stories about them were as colorful as the Irish were ubiquitous. Tom and Pat Mortagh were brothers who were rivals as enginemen for the Illinois Central. Tom ran a beautiful Norris Company engine, "The Crescent," while Pat guided one called "The Black Prince," also built at the famous Philadelphia Norris works. Engine efficiency, measured by the number of miles per cord of wood, was hotly debated by the two. They vied with one another to make records, and both got eighty-five miles to a cord in their engines with five-and-a-half-foot driving wheels.[14]

In 1876 when the Minneapolis and St. Louis Railway was competing with others for the right of way near Fort Dodge, the line was required to get a vehicle across the county line on its rails at fifteen miles an hour. One Billy O'Brien in an heroic performance preserved the railway's legality by pumping a handcar in excess of that speed across the county line.[15] Railroading was still a highly dangerous field of work. There was little standardization of equipment, and weather frequently caused perilous operating conditions. A thousand things could and did go wrong, and railroaders left widows in droves. It was the most dangerous work system in the country.[16] There were sensational rail calamities, such as the collapse of the bridge at Ashtabula, Ohio, in 1876 where thirty-four died, and where Dan Maguire, the engineman, barely escaped with a flying leap. Often trouble resulted from poorly trained workers as in the song called "O'Shaughnessy":

> O'Shaughnessy it is me name,
> The truth I will relate to ye:
> I worked upon the section line,
> I am a decent Irishman.
> A conductor came to me one day
> And to me these words did say:
> "Ye must drop your shovel right away
> And go braking on me train."
>
> He took me up to the railroad yard,
> He put in my hand a big time-card;
> He said that braking wasn't hard
> If I was only game.
>
> He put on me head a railroad cap,
> And said it was wore by all our crap,
> And this by a decent Irish chap,
> While braking on a train.
>
> They sent me out on the Number Tin,
> And then, my boys, me trouble begin;
> One would send after a pin,
> The other would fire me back agin,
>
> They kept me running from ind to ind,
> While braking on a train.
>
> I swung the lantern over me head,
> It was a signal, so they said,
> For the ingineer to go ahead,
> And then I were to blame.
> Then I forgot to t'row the switch,
> The cars uncoupled and went into the ditch,
> The conductor called me a son of a bitch,
> While braking on a train.
>
> The cars uncoupled, came down the hill,
> The conductor said that I was a gill
> For smashing the property of Jimmy Hill,
> While braking on a train.[17]

From the East into the Far West the lowly track gangs remained mostly Irish. General John Casement and his brother, Dan, one of the big contractors for the Union Pacific, employed 10,000 men at one point, mostly Irish and many Civil War veterans. He also employed 2,500 Chinese in 1865.[18] The worst of the railway work was so bad that the builders had to reach all the way to the Orient to find among the coolies of Asia a labor supply as depressed as the Irish. One reminiscence tells of track layers standing in the moaning prairie wind waiting for orders in the frozen winter. The gang boss named Pat "wrapped in a bearskin cloak that reached to his galoshes, and with a beehive fur hat on his head, walked up and down the track." Afraid of freezing without some activity, one worker said, "We're getting paid for doing nothing." "It's the only rest we get," his companion responded.[19] The work of keeping switches unfrozen and the track clear of snow was a dreadful, laborious task, and excuses didn't count if it was not done. As the rails moved west, the living quarters, which could hardly get worse, rarely got better. An old photograph of the Kilpatrick construction crew grading the Burlington and Missouri line in Nebraska in the 1880s shows a disheveled scene of men, women, children, horses, and track on the lonely flatlands.[20]

Beyond the growing Midwest toward the western horizon, into Indian territory, and right up to the spectacular heights of the Rocky Mountains the surveyors' lines directed the steel rails. From Minneapolis they reached toward the forbidding Dakotas and Montana with James J. Hill's Great Northern route. From the huge web of lines reaching west from Omaha and Kansas City the rails of the Union Pacific, the Denver and Rio Grande, and the Atchison, Topeka, and Santa Fe were set on ties across the seemingly endless prairies. From New Orleans to Dallas and on to El Paso the Southern Pacific and the Texas Pacific rails burned in the sun amid mesquite and tumbleweeds. In all this awesome space, only parts of Iowa, Missouri, and Louisiana had more than an average of 2.25 persons per square mile in 1860.[21] But at the leading edge of the ever-growing rail system were the Irish digger gangs, struggling at the labor, winter and summer, bound to the railway system, the greatest transport network ever made by man.

A notable study of the Atchison, Topeka, and Santa Fe work force from 1869 to 1900 by James H. Ducker gives a detailed look at the rail workers of this great road that ran from Kansas City to Albuquerque. In the 1870s the A.T. and S.F. track gangs were largely Irish, and they were an accepted part of a rowdy tradition of men called "boomers."

Restlessness was a trait of many Santa Fe railway men. That of the boomers was displayed in boozing, brawling, and roaming ways. Old-timers also had an eye out for their big chance and some showed an eagerness to quit railroading for other work. This restlessness was a product of some discontent with railroading coupled with an awareness of the opportunities offered in an expansive, fast-developing society. Moreover, railroaders' adventurousness resulted in part from a reputation that fed on itself. Many railway jobs were known as exciting and dynamic and, therefore, they attracted young men ready to work hard, accept responsibilities, travel, take risks, and break old emotional ties. Maturity and growing families eventually made men more conscious of the need for steadier habits. However, even this did not tame all restlessness, because a process of natural selection dictated that railroading attracted more than its share of adventurous American youth.[22]

By 1881 these crews had laid rails from Colorado into New Mexico and south along the Rio Grande River, and plans were being made to lay rail across Arizona to San Diego. Track washouts, blizzards, drunken riders, train robberies, and landslides made the job of keeping the right of way open a continual battle. Track workers would quit en masse when their hours were cut. Tom Foley got drunk, recruited three tramps as passengers, and roared an engine out of La Junta, Colorado, at full steam for a joy ride. Mickey Brennan discovered his engine was expected to pull eighteen loaded cars, more than the engine could manage, and created a furor until one-third of the cars were dropped. Other employees, however, were almost mechanical men living by railroad time and railroad rules. Patrick Reagan worked the shops and yards for thirty years, and Patrick Walsh was a baggage master for fifty years.[23]

For years the responsibility of driving engines was far above most of the Irish. As one commentator noted with some prejudice, "In the early days on the Boston and Lowell only Irishmen were employed as firemen, for the characteristic reason that when they once learned to fire, they were satisfied to work in that capacity as long as they lived."[24] The payroll of the Hartford and New Haven showed teams and pairs of brothers and groups of relatives—"Brasills, Kellys, Murphys . . . and Sullivans"—in the work force. In 1860 among Philadelphia Irish railwaymen, thirty-five percent were laborers, and their status there got worse in 1870 and 1880 when thirty-eight and then forty-eight percent of the Irish were listed as laborers. By 1880 there was at least some mobility, however, with Irishmen moving into skilled trades and lower management in the rail yards. Whether this was due to less discrimination and rigidity in the system or to the sheer weight of Irish numbers is hard to calculate.[25]

After a full generation of railroad work the Irish at last began to move up the occupational ladder in the rail system. Payrolls from 1869 for the Great Northern–St. Paul and Pacific Railroad show Irishmen as rodmen, chainmen, firemen, and flagmen—all relatively unskilled jobs. By 1878, while there are still McGintys, McNarnys, and Kehoes listed as laborers and flagmen, and plenty of Irish as brakemen earning $25 to $52 a month, P. Finnegan was a yard master making $85 a month and J.C. Brinnen earned $64 a month as a foreman, while J.P. Farley was general manager. There were even some instances of men with experience on Ireland's small railroads working for the St. Paul, Minneapolis, and Manitoba Railway. William Johnston had been a telegraph operator in County Monaghan and was a station agent in 1882 on the Breckenridge Division. Paralleling the occupational improvements, though, was the continuation of the toll taken by the work. Northern Pacific files list the deaths of workers in accidents, some attributed to a lack of "firmness" and lax discipline on the part of employees.[26]

Almost without exception, references to the living conditions of the laborers continue to include comments on the shanties that were their abodes. On the Denver and Rio Grande in Colorado in the early 1880s, however, the Irish were found not only as laborers, switchmen, brakemen, and firemen, but also as engineers, yard foremen, superintendents, and auditors in Leadville, Durango, Pueblo, and Colorado Springs and for them living conditions were somewhat better.[27]

Women appear as railroad employees with the title of "boarding boss," that is, manager of a railroad boarding house. Wives and widows of rail men, they set hardy tables and kept order in boisterous towns like Navajo, Sherwood, and Crevasse where the boarding bosses were Mrs. Nolan, Kate O'Brien, and Mrs. Jerry McCarthy. When officials such as Richard J. McCarty, vice president of the Kansas City and Southern, and Charles McCormack, telegraph superintendent of the Chicago and Eastern Illinois, journeyed west, the boarding bosses would spare no effort to put forth great feasts of venison, Rocky Mountain trout, and homemade breads, for there was a tradition of mutual entertaining among the elite of the railroad personnel.[28]

The administrative activity involved in organizing railroad construction and maintenance involved a formidable interaction of unskilled and skilled labor, technology, engineering, timing, and procedural regulation. The Union Pacific work at divisions at such places as Platte, Colorado, and Cheyenne, Wyoming, in 1869 brought together Irishmen who were coal heavers, wood loaders, laborers, train mechanics of various trades, electricians, switchmen, teamsters, well diggers, machinists, clerks, and telegraphers, in addition to the locomotive enginemen, firemen, and brakemen who ran the trains.[29]

As all this monumental construction proceeded it was inevitable that certain men would advance far above others to positions of leadership. Litton Shields came to America from Ireland in 1866 and joined the gold rush to the Black Hills of South Dakota. He became an engineer and construction supervisor with Foley Brothers, contractors, and worked on the Northern Pacific route west of Mandan, North Dakota.[30] There were scores of such rising and ambitious men, and one of the most successful was John Scullin, "the great American tracklayer." His rise was hard. As construction boss for the Missouri, Kansas, and Texas Railway he pushed the road through Kansas at the rate of a mile a day. His driving teams were famous as they came into Indian territory. The goal was to link up the army posts that were spread among restless Cherokee and Chetopa tribes. Scullin and his men had to literally battle rival railroad work crews to the Oklahoma Indian territory border. Scullin later founded the Scullin Steel Company of St. Louis and made the rails he was famous for laying.[31]

Success was a fickle goddess. Peter Donahue, an engineer, built a gunboat in New Jersey and sailed it to Peru. He went to California in 1849 for the gold rush there. From his machine shop he became related to the San Francisco and San Jose Railroad, and he completed the road for Charles McLaughlin for a fortune of $2 million. Contrast this success with Michael J. Farrell who planned the Nevada Railway from Carson City, but after years and years of work, the road was never built.[32]

The headaches of these railway building barons involved everything from work gang battles to financial intrigues with Wall Street and frontier banking buccaneers. James J. Hill's Great Northern empire was kept out of Seattle for years until he worked with Tom Burke, an influential lawyer of that city, to assemble the needed land for access. J.W. Gilluly put together endless deals to build the Rio Grande and Southern Railroad. Wilson McCarthy arranged the final takeover of the Denver and Rio Grande after absentee Eastern ownership had controlled it for 60 years. Texas railroad building after 1870 brought to the fore C.H. Higgins, Frank P. Killeen, John J. Moran, John Thomas Brady, and George Sealy who were involved with such roads as the Gulf, Colorado, and Santa Fe and the Missouri, Kansas, and Texas.[33]

The tremendously powerful Pennsylvania Railroad stretching from Philadelphia to beyond St. Louis was credited in 1874 with the "opening of gas and coal mines . . . the utilization of remote forests, the immense production of oil," and creating "home markets for products of the farm, the forest, and the mines all along its lines."[34] There were 6,615 miles of the Pennsylvania in 1875. It was an empire with its own regulations, legislatures it controlled, laws it created, "coal and iron police," an entire system of oversight and a domination that ruled cities, states, and the lives of farmers, miners, mill hands, and businesses across the Eastern lines it conducted. It was only one of the powerful rail empires that warred among themselves. If there were some Irish railroad heads, they tended to be from the West. In the East there were practically no Irish railroad barons.[35] No matter who headed the railroads, the capitalism of the day was designed for polarization of owners and workers.

The Irish who had seen the great famine of the 1840s, had lived through the mortality of the emigration to America, had seen their men caught up in the military bloodbath of the Civil War, and had struggled through the railroad building boom were struck hard by the economic depression of 1873. In that economic collapse, the railroads cut wages, laid off thousands of workers, closed mines and shops, and generally sharply reduced the nation's largest business. The rights of capital had long been clear. There was no apology for the drastic measures that wiped out legions of jobs. Unfettered company power was rampant legally and in the ideology of the time. In 1860 the annual report of the Delaware and Hudson stated that the company would "resist to the end, and at any cost, every attempt, by combinations of working men, to dictate the manner in which its business shall be conducted."[36] In 1873 and 1874 eighteen railroads faced strikes by engineers, firemen, brakemen, track hands, and laborers resisting wage cuts and breaches of employment contracts. There was intermittent violence and widespread labor collaboration in boycotts and retaliations against the rail companies.[37] This was just a prelude to a much greater railroad strike wave and violence in 1877. Beginning in Martinsburg, West Virginia, on the Baltimore and Ohio Railroad, the strikes and disorders, including bloody clashes with troops, arson, and rioting, spread to Chicago, Philadelphia, St. Louis, and rail centers across the country. The Irish were involved on both sides, being numerous as police and soldiers as well as among rail workers. Franklin B. Gowen of the Philadelphia and Reading Railroad had already shown what could be done against militant labor by having Irish "Molly Maguires" hung in Mauch Chunk in what was probably the largest civilian execution not involving slaves in the country until then. The labor uprising on the nation's railroads in 1877 was just one episode, though a spectacular one, in the enormous struggle between working people and a rapacious railroad leadership.[38] For the Irish such experiences continued to build a cadre of radical labor militants, and for the rank and file workers, a deepening commitment to labor organization as a defense against exploitation and occupational insecurity.

The implications of this engagement with the American system of rail transport and resource recovery were momentous for the Irish. It involved them with the chief medium of mobility of the age. The mobility attained was both geographical and occupational. Irish representation with rail enterprises made socially manifest their full kinship with the American drama of continental occupation and economic growth. Their placement throughout the country provided the basis for participation in regional affairs that would itself further mingle them with the nation's history. The long hardships with railway labor and its auxiliary trades and occupations rooted the Irish-Americans in the work culture of the country and gave the group the character that was to be its distinguishing social feature during the nineteenth and most of the twentieth centuries, identification with the working class and the common people of the democracy.

For the group itself, the railway experience abetted the process of survival as a subculture in America. For a people without an independent country, with a calamitous recent history, and with low social status in the United States, involvement with America's greatest economic enterprise gave assurance to the Irish of their utility and, indeed, necessity in the new land. The railroads were the country's primary communication system, and the Irish on them, in an informal but very real bonding, related to one another across great distances. The steel rail men would be part of a broader network of Irish affiliations to come that would have all kinds of ramifications for the group's interaction and self-development. Finally, these decades of railway association would extend over more than one hundred years and would enhance the group's image of itself as one of historic and expansive participation in the American cavalcade of national achievement.

NOTES

1. Bruce Sinclair, *Philadelphia's Philosopher Mechanics: A History of Franklin Institute, 1824–1865* (Baltimore: The Johns Hopkins University Press, 1974), pp. 171–173.

2. This occurred, for instance, on the Brunswick Canal in Georgia when workers were transferred to the Savannah and Albany Railroad. Thomas F. Hahn, "The Paw Paw Tunnel," in Hahn, ed., *The Best from American Canals* (York, Penn.: The American Canal Society, Inc., 1980), p. 40.

3. George Rogers Taylor, *The Transportation Revolution, 1815–60* (New York: Harper and Row, 1951), p. 291.

4. Alvin F. Harlon, *The Road of the Century* (New York: Creative Age Press, 1947), p. 56.

5. Richard B. Morris, "The Measure of Bondage in the Slave States," *Mississippi Valley Historical Review* 41, no. 2. (September 1954): 219–240.

6. Edward Hungerford, *The Story of the Baltimore and Ohio Railroad, 1827–1927* (New York: G.P. Putnam's Sons, 1928), pp. 66, 119.

7. Richard B. Morris, "White Bondage in Ante-Bellum South Carolina," *South Carolina Historical and Geneological Magazine* 49, no. 4 (October 1948): 195.

8. Carl Wittke, *The Irish in America* (Baton Rouge: Louisiana State University Press, 1956), pp. 36–41; Richard Niehaus, *The Irish in New Orleans, 1800–1860* (Baton Rouge: Louisiana State University Press, 1965), pp. 46–47.

9. J.C. Conroy, *A History of the Railways in Ireland* (London: Longmans, Green and Co., 1928), p. 48.

10. Hungerford, *The Story of the Baltimore and Ohio Railroad*, pp. 66 and 119. Wittke, *The Irish in America*, pp. 36–41.

11. J.C. Furnas, *The Americans: A Social History of the United States, 1586–1914* (New York: G.P. Putnam's Sons, 1969), p. 384.

12. Robert J. Parks, *Democracy's Railroads: Public Enterprise in Jacksonian Michigan* (Port Washington, N.Y.: Kennikat Press, 1972), p. 43; Fred A. Shannon, *The Farmer's Last Frontier, 1860–1879* (New York: Harper and Row, 1945), p. 41; Richard C. Overton, *A History of the Burlington Lines* (New York: Alfred A. Knopf, 1965), p. 8.

13. Harlon, *The Road of the Century*, p. 427; Frank P. Donovan, *Mileposts on the Prairie: The Story of the Minneapolis and St. Paul Railway* (New York: Simmons-Boardman, 1950), p. 28; Walter Licht, *Working for the Railroad: The Organization of Work in the Nineteenth Century* (Princeton: Princeton University Press, 1983), p. 148; Time-Life Books, *The Railroaders* (New York: Time-Life Books, 1973), p. 113.

14. Carlton J. Corliss, *Main Line of Mid-America: The Story of the Illinois Central* (New York: Creative Age Press, 1950), pp. 182–83.

15. Donovan, *Mileposts on the Prairie*, p. 55.

16. Roger Lane, *Violent Death in the City* (Cambridge: Harvard University Press, 1979).

17. Stewart Holbrook, *The Story of American Railroads* (New York: Bonanza Books, 1947), pp. 283, 437–438.

18. Oscar Osburn Winther, *The Transportation Frontier: Trans-Mississippi West, 1865–1890* (New York: Holt, Rinehart, and Winston, 1964), p. 107.

19. Richard Reinhardt, ed., *Workin' on the Railroad: Reminiscences from the Age of Steam* (Palo Alto: American West Publishing Co., 1970), pp. 221–222.

20. Overton, *A History of the Burlington Lines*, Plate 7.

21. Winther, *The Transportation Frontier*, p. 9.

22. James H. Ducker, *Men of the Steel Rails: Workers on the Atchison, Topeka and Santa Fe, 1869–1900* (Lincoln: University of Nebraska Press, 1983), p. 68.

23. Ibid., pp. 61–63.

24. Licht, *Working for the Railroad*, p. 148.

25. Ibid., p. 50, Table G–1, p. 223.

26. Engineer's Payroll, First Division, St. Paul and Pacific Railroad, April 1869; Payroll Amount Book, First Division, St. Paul and Pacific Railroad, September 1878; personal record of William Johnston, St. Paul, Minneapolis, and Manitoba Railway, Vol. 1, February 13, 1882; letter from T.F. Oakes to H. Haupt, June 17, 1882, New York,

Northern Pacific Railroad Company; letter from Frederick P. Leavenworth to his father, January 1, 1859, St. Paul, Minnesota. Archives of the Northern Pacific Railroads. Archives and Manuscripts Division, Minnesota Historical Society, St. Paul.

27. Company roster, Denver and Rio Grande Railroad, November 15, 1887; lists and biographical notes by Jackson Thode, former Denver and Rio Grande official; letter from J. Thode to D. Clark, December 27, 1983.

28. Ibid. Lists and biographical notes.

29. Payroll Book, Cheyenne Division, September 1869, pp. 837–857, and Platte Division, September 1869, Stations Department Nos. 5019, 5027. Archives of the Union Pacific Railroad, Union Pacific Museum, Omaha, Nebraska.

30. *Mandan Pioneer* (Mandan, South Dakota) (June 9, 1933); Public Relations and Advertising Department, Archives of the Northern Pacific Railroad, Archives and Manuscripts Division, Minnesota Historical Society, St. Paul, Minnesota.

31. V.V. Masterson, *The KATY Railroad and the Last Frontier* (Norman: University of Oklahoma Press, 1952), pp. 33, 66–67, 124–125.

32. Gilbert Kneiss, *Bonanza Railroads* (San Jose: Stanford University Press, 1941), pp. 35, 105–107.

33. O.M. Wilson, *The Denver and Rio Grande Project, 1870–1901* (Salt Lake City: Howe Brothers, 1982), pp. 57 and 64; Albo Martin, *James J. Hill and the Opening of the West* (New York: Oxford University Press, 1976), p. 392; Mallory Hope Ferrell, *Silver San Juan: The Rio Grande and Southern Railroad* (Boulder, Colo.: Pruett Publishing Co., 1973), p. 361; Robert A. Le Massena, *Rio Grande to the Pacific* (Denver: Sundance, Ltd., 1974), p. 119; John Brendan Flannery, *The Irish Texans* (San Antonio: Institute for Texas Cultures of University of Texas, 1980), pp. 124–127.

34. *Report of the Investigating Committee of the Pennsylvania Railroad, Annual Meeting, March 20, 1874* (Philadelphia: Allen, Lane and Scott, 1874), p. 3.

35. Thomas C. Cochran, *Railroad Leaders, 1845–1890: The Business Mind in Action* (New York: Russell and Russell, 1965), passim. One exception was Samuel Sloan, a partner of Commodore Vanderbilt.

36. G. Talbot Oliphant, *Annual Report to the Board of Managers of the Delaware and Hudson Canal Company for 1860* (New York: Nathan Lane, 1861), p. 4.

37. Herbert G. Gutman, *Work, Culture and Society in Industrializing America: Essays in American Working Class and Social History* (New York: Vintage Books, 1977), pp. 295–322.

38. Philip S. Foner, *The Great Labor Uprising of 1877* (New York: Monad Press, 1977), pp. 7–32, 86–87, 110, 145–46, 173, 179, 226; "Report of the Committee Appointed to Investigate the Railroad Riots of 1877," Legislative Document No. 29, Senate and House of Representatives of the Commonwealth of Pennsylvania (May 23, 1878), pp. 468–469.

4 YOKED TO YANKEES— NEW ENGLAND

The area of the Atlantic coast and the hinterland from Philadelphia to Maine dominates the early history of the nation. The littoral of Virginia with its contribution of surpassing talent in the founding era produced extraordinary leadership and intellectual inspiration but was soon overshadowed by the broader democracy and wealth of the states to the north. They did not bear the mordantly compromising institution of slavery. Their society had fewer pretensions to aristocracy, and their development of popular institutions was more energetic and extensive.

New England and its history is, even today after many revisions of earlier versions of America's past, still the primary focus of what most people in the United States think of as the matrix of the country's beginnings. In the catalog of ideas that is mixed confusedly with the sentiments of American patriotism, the New England heritage of religious independence, individualism, achievement amid frugality, and Anglo-American thought about law, family, and community are all in the forefront of the national experience.

Middle-class farmers, artisans, and tradesmen were the great mass of founding emigrants in New England, and indentured servants were fewer than in Maryland and Virginia, Samuel Eliot Morison tells us.[1] The more affluent families assumed leadership in church, town meeting, and social relations. This oligarchy quickly dominated the region's chief city of Boston and contrived to set itself up as a righteous elect, a special elite, controlling the trade and opinion of New England life.[2] The rate of population growth was great as the hardihood of the people sought to match the Biblical injunction to multiply. In Connecticut the population doubled every twenty-five years for several generations after the first settlement. The solidity of the small freeholders and the temperate nature of the social outlook provided a balance for the personal idealism and religious rigor cultivated in the chill of the Atlantic seaboard and the rocky fields of the New England interior. What evolved was a conservative, individualistic culture—cautious, introverted, acquisitive, and skeptical of grand designs. The propertied and intellectual leadership of this New England society, with its self-justifying myth of Hebraic religious precedence, was part of the American cult of toughness that would fight for independence and also fight any threat to its dominance. The smaller folk were content to work hard for sufficiency, well-tutored as they were in thrift. In Ireland Benjamin Franklin would extol the ''happiness of New England where every man is a freeholder.''[3] To the Irish the prospect at the time would have seemed delirious.

Although property may have been available to the Protestant Puritan elect and those they favored, the Irish who came to New England in the seventeenth and eighteenth centuries were not accorded religious tolerance and barely managed civil existence. The fact that one Irishwoman, Granny Glover, was to become a victim of the infamous Salem witch trials, probably because her Gaelic was mistaken for some Satanic expression, is symbolic of the hazards the Irish suffered in a hostile society. While the New Englanders were cultivating their keen and integrated cultural identity, the Irish among them were part of a sub-culture of rejection over that long period prior to the American Revolution, and indeed well into the nineteenth century. Religious animus, alien status, and mutual antagonism were the marks of the relationship. The earliest versions of the disadvantaged status of Irish-Americans which was to form the longest record of white minority rejection in American life were forged in this New England. The exception was on the frontier, where the canons of religious and social election were less operable. In New Hampshire strong Scotch-Irish colonies in the Merrimack Valley were built in the first half of the eighteenth century and constituted perhaps ten percent of the population.[4]

One estimate for the 1790 census period gives Irish and Scotch-Irish enu-meration for New England states as Maine, 10,000; New Hampshire, 10,000; Vermont, 5,000; Massachusetts, 15,000; Connecticut, 6,000; and possibly 5,000 for those parts of New York in the upstate areas.[5] Once again the accurate numbers are not available. What is available is a broad record of Irish presence.[6] As for the distinction between Irish Catholics, Irish Anglicans, Scotch-Irish Presbyterians, and other Irish of whatever persuasion, such differences were of little significance to the righteous Anglo believers of New England. Irish of whatever kind were anathema. As in Ireland, many Irish people were motivated to deny Irish lineage and to characterize themselves with new Anglo names.[7] It can be assumed with some assurance that in New England the group, despite being subject to active hostility, was in an early position to play a modest role in the life of the region simply because of distribution throughout it, but the role would be won in a hard contest.

The major historical experiences shaping the New England tradition were the religious and social formation of its original community life, the American Revolution and its heritage, industrialization, and the eventual compact of plu-ralism that changed the political base of the area. With respect to the foundation of the New England moral and social constitution, as has been indicated above, the Irish had little to do. They did influence it sharply in the nineteenth century by challenging its assumptions and practices, perhaps helping to make it even less tractable than it originally was by ardently and stubbornly opposing its leadership and political dominance.

The conceptual basis of the American Revolution derived largely from English and French thought, but the Irish as disaffected antagonists, or at least skeptics, about British rule did become strong protagonists of the American cause. The death of Patrick Carr in the disorders of the Boston Massacre is a token of that lower-class discontent that matched the disillusion of intellectuals and merchants and the rebelliousness of backwoodsmen in generating the war against England. David Doyle has skillfully shown that the Irish patriots were a forcefully active rebel element, but less so in the leading dissident state of Massachusetts than elsewhere. That the Irish did enter the American army in disproportionate numbers seems clear, since as servants, former servants, footloose immigrant males, and aspiring adventurers they were more easily recruited than sober land-owning farmers. The strenuous efforts of Michael J. O'Brien to place the Catholic Irish in the forefront of the Revolution along with the more fully evident Scotch-Irish Ulstermen can be taken as a salutary corrective to previous discrimination that undervalued their admittedly minor role.[8]

General John Sullivan, one of Washington's most battle-hungry but difficult officers, was the chief New England Irish protagonist of the cause. The mischievous venom of the Irish contribution is caught in the barbed poem about the British retreat from Concord to Boston:

> By my faith but I think ye're all makers of bulls,
> With your brains in your breeches, your guts in your
>   skull.
> Get home with your muskets, and put up your swords
> And look in your books for the meaning of words.
> Ye see now my honies, how much you're mistaken,
> For CONCORD by Discord can never be beaten.
>
> How brave you went out with muskets all bright,
> And thought to befrighten the folks with the sight;
> But when you got there how they powder'd your bums,
> And all the way home how they pepper'd your bums,
> And is it not, honies, a comical farce,
> To be proud in the face, and be shot in the arse.
>
> How come ye to think now, they did not know how,
> To be after their firelocks as smartly as you.
> Why ye see now, my honies, 'tis nothing at all,
> But to pull at the trigger, and pop goes the ball.
>
> And what have you got now, with all your designing,
> But a town without victals to sit down and dine in;
> And to look on the ground, like a parcel of Noodles,
> And sing, How the Yankies have beaten the Doodles.

I'm sure if you're wise you'll make peace for a
    dinner,
For fighting and fasting will soon make ye thinner.[9]

Thus, in the hagiography of New England patriotism a grudging place had to be made for Irish-American participants. Although this place would be veiled by Anglo-American presumptions and ethnocentricity, it could not be denied, and it would have implications for the evolution of pluralism in the future.

The increase in the Irish-born Catholic population in New England in the 1820s was to be a culture shock for the intently Protestant region. The disabilities, social difference, and partisan spirit of the immigrants alarmed and deeply distressed the leaders of the area. By 1850 one-fifth of the population of Irish-born in the United States lived in New England. Many had come from Canada and the Maritime Provinces to Portland and Boston, having been brought simply as a substitute for ballast in lumber ships that had taken the great tree trunks of the northern forests to Britain. Through their work in the lumber industry, thousands of Irish families learned and invented techniques for the wildly athletic rafting of timber down the rivers of Maine and New Hampshire to the coast.[10] Boston was the focus of the disturbances that this great influx produced. Endemic poverty, famine, and social deterioration in Ireland seemed to send an unending cavalcade of affliction to the proudly Protestant city that saw itself as the intellectual and civic capital of the country.

Oscar Handlin vividly portrayed the crisis in Boston's life that this immigrant population generated. So great was the privation of the newcomers that it is a mystery as to how they at first subsisted. Forty-eight percent of the males were common laborers. Exploitation of the group was unremitting. Socially ostracized, vulnerable, and slow to adapt to a strange urban setting, the immigrants had "escaped into a way of life completely foreign and completely unfavorable to them."[11] Handlin's picture has been criticized as too pessimistic, but his book, first published in 1941, has been widely influential in projecting an interpretation of Irish-American experience. Later works provide more emphasis upon regional differences in opportunity, economic mobility, and the internal resources of the Irish, but Handlin's book correctly confirms the aggravated reaction of New England society to the tragedy of Irish emigration.

And Boston was to be the cockpit of Yankee-Irish conflict as the newcomers sought to break the cycle of ostracism, exploitation, and disability that afflicted them. A full century of antagonism and political combat would ensue. What Handlin calls a "continuity of adjustment" was to come into effect whereby persistent immigration from Ireland added to the social cohesion and improvement designs of the group and formed the structures for a strong subculture that animated political and social change.[12] Education, property, and family precedence sustained the Boston Brahmins and Yankee worthies as the elite strengthened its own economic position. Intermarried Amorys, Appletons, Jacksons, Lawrences, Lees, and Lowells faced the Irish invasion in the security that they

controlled Massachusetts railroads, textile mills, banks, and insurance companies.[13] The Irish for their part built a network of schools, social organizations,
and improvement media that became the staging areas for political penetration
of the city's life. The Irish Emigrant Society, the Home for Destitute Irish
Children, the House of the Guardian Angel, the House of the Good Shepherd,
Saint John's Grammar School, a Diocesan Teachers' Institute, hospitals, and
charitable service societies all confirmed the separation between Irish and Yankees. The Catholic network was not without failures. St. Mary's Infant Asylum
in the 1870s had an almost unbelievable mortality rate among foundlings. Irish
girls by the score became prostitutes. The Catholic schools for decades were
weak in faculty preparation and informed leadership. But the foundations had
been laid to preserve identity, promote advancement, and confront community
responsibilities.[14]

In terms of power sharing, Boston had from its founding never been a democratic city. Merchant aristocrats and later industrial magnates dominated Massachusetts and the city.[15] The Irish problems of the 1840s and 1850s and afterward
created an ethical conflict for men such as James Russell Lowell and Charles
Eliot Norton. The assumption that the "intelligent and propertied classes" should
stabilize democracy was upstaged by the Irish pressure to relieve social grievances
through a process that would provide jobs, influence, and political machine
perquisites. Henry Adams would lament that "poor Boston has fairly run up
against it in the form of its particular Irish maggot, rather lower than the Jew. . . . ''[16]

In the period after the Civil War, the Boston Irish not only built political
muscle, but through the Boston *Pilot* newspaper became the tribunes of Irish-
American Catholics. John Boyle O'Reilly's poetry recalled the American commitment to inclusive democracy and social justice. Patrick Donahoe and James
Jeffrey Roche were liberal voices in active dialog with Boston's more tolerant
Protestant leadership. Literary leaders and ward bosses, unlikely allies, were
nevertheless linked. Their advocacy paid off. In 1886 Boston elected its first
Irish Catholic mayor, Hugh O'Brien, and later Patrick Collins, a Harvard graduate. The deal had been made. The Brahmins and Yankee politicians had acceded
to the rising power of the immigrant and his children. Harsh feelings did not
disappear, but hard bargains were struck, and the Irish became the leaders of
the Democratic party, which reigned in the city.[17] The elect of the Puritan
geneology would henceforth have to deal with the exiled children of Erin.

The conflict of the Boston Irish and the Yankees has been presented as the
archetypal Irish-American experience.[18] This has been and is quite misleading.
Bigotry, unfair discrimination, mutual hostility, competition, and social distance
there certainly was, but all of these things existed in other Eastern cities as well.
Boston had Irish Catholic mayors in the nineteenth century. Philadelphia did not
have one until the 1960s. The Draft Riots in New York in 1863 and the anti-
Catholic and anti-Irish riots in Philadelphia in 1844 had no real Boston counterparts on the same violent scale. Other cities had huge Irish slums and dreadful
exploitation of immigrants. Why was the Boston experience accorded such a

reputation for intensity when anti-immigrant attitudes and behavior were wide-spread for much of the country's history?

The answer lies partly in Boston's distinctive characteristics. It was a city with a more integrated leadership class than others. This class included a self-conscious intellectual component that, as with most intellectual groups, tended to overdramatize its sufferings, and the Irish were seen to be a form of suffering. The length of dominance of this class made any challenge to it seem outrageous, since it had held sway for over two centuries when the Irish assault on it occurred in the 1870s. Boston was not only more pivotal to its region's economy and leadership than other Eastern cities, New England had no other city to match it. It was one of the few large American cities that was also a state capital. The political rewards were thus enhanced in Boston, for both local and state patronage were electoral prizes. Certainly religion, too, held a special eminence in Boston, and the Irish Catholic dissent from Protestant codes evoked a mournful disappointment. Many of Boston's leaders, as thinkers and reformers, had especially intimate ties with England, and the animus of anti-Irish prejudice was easily transmitted to them from its historic nurturing places in English culture.

Oscar Handlin's pioneering study of the city's reaction to the Irish immigration appeared before there were many other studies of Irish presence in different localities that would show the parallels and contrasts to the history in Boston. But Boston's distinctiveness was partly due to the fact that it absorbed an especially heavy proportion of Irish into a less diversified economy and social structure than other cities. However, the conflict generated does not seem on balance to have been any more fierce than that attending the Irish infusion in such places as the mining areas of Pennsylvania or the smaller cities throughout the Northeastern region. The conflict was long and hard almost everywhere, whether against Philadelphia railroad tycoons, Pittsburgh steel magnates, or Connecticut mill owners. Old-line Bostonians simply felt they had been singled out by their stern God to specifically endure the Irish epidemic. In Boston the arena was made to seem narrower due to the city's own preoccupation with itself, its past, and its pretensions.

The arrival on the Boston scene in 1899 of the astonishing rascality of James Michael Curley, elected to various offices for a period of fifty years thereafter, was a denouement, then. He was the apotheosis of the Boston Irishry, but the actual conquest had been earlier. He was its celebration. The novels of Edwin O'Connor have enshrined the raucous humor, winsome deviousness, cynicism, and intractable spirit of it all. But beneath the political posturing there were intermittent revivals of the bitter conflicts with the unforgiving Yankees and generations of Irish rancor that led a minority of the group into bigotry, rabid isolationism, and willful obstructionism in local and national affairs.[18] Curley's theatrical style, his bombastic and erratically expressed partisanship in behalf of the poor, and his lack of personal wealth at life's end emphasized the distinctiveness of his approach to popular politics. Although the rhetorical style and antic spirit of Irish politicians has been potently characteristic of American politics generally in all regions of the country, Curley's version was more irrepressible, inventive, and locally flavored than that of others. His first public office as a Boston city councilman at the turn of the century arose in the period when actual street violence still characterized much of America's local voting. As a four-term congressman and four-time mayor of Boston he was *the* Irish pol of prodigious talents. But, as William V. Shannon has written, Curley never transcended the boundaries of Boston. "He exploited the sufferings and the inexperience, the warm sentiment, the fears, the prejudices of his own people to perpetuate his personal power. He solved nothing. . . . "[19] His career, strongly localized, signified the broader fact that the great majority of the Irish-Americans in the first half of the twentieth century remained stuck in the difficulties of working-class status no matter how colorfully successful their political idols became.

The careers of John and Robert Kennedy were spawned by Curley's Irish Boston but were not spun of its fiber. Jack Kennedy as a playboy politician assumed the leadership of the older politicos, one of whom was his grandfather John F. "Honey Fitz" Fitzgerald, but transmuted the shabby mantle into a regal robe with the aid of his father's wealth and the new vehicle of mass media politics. Kennedy's presumed Boston Irish affiliation is assessed well by Gary Wills who rates it as political theatrics. Kenneth O'Donnell and David Powers, two friends of JFK, were much more rooted in the Irish social context of Boston than were the rich Kennedys. Below the high profile of Kennedy success was a Boston world of work and of petty scrounging, competition, and pathology memorably portrayed in the novels of George V. Higgins.[20]

At Kennedy's inauguration to the presidency Robert Frost advised him to "be more Irish than Harvard" in his orientation, but this simply was not possible. The Kennedys were too cosmopolitan, too broadly connected to wealth and internationalism, too imprinted with the attitudes and assumptions of Harvard elitism. They did not have the substantive feel of Irish-American associations, but they could appeal brilliantly to the group's conscience and hunger for full recognition. The shocked realization of the Kennedy brothers when they confronted the poverty of mountain West Virginia was a revelation of how insulated they had been. The poverty areas of old Irish neighborhoods throughout the country were equally distant from them. In the panorama of victory, power, and Camelot dreaminess of the Kennedy administration, the Irish connection became little more than a minor fetish to be skillfully flourished on appropriate occasions. The connection had been artfully magnified for John F. Kennedy's career, but no more so than the more sophisticated factors of Eastern establishment Harvard, ties to upper-class Britain, the perilous internationalism of the Bay of Pigs and the Vienna meeting with Khrushchev, and the media settings arranged by eager advance men as theater for American domestic life. "Glamour overshadowed quality" in the Kennedy career, and the glamour was not compromised by much indulgence in the Irish tradition that could summon too many harsh realities from its recollection. The Kennedys lacked the working-class association, the social views, and the more parochial ethnic consciousness of most of their contemporary Irish-Americans. Their emergence from a regional base to national power dictated this. But as exponents of a narrow echelon of successful Irish-American achievers in New England, they transformed their careers and family affairs into a popular national legend with climaxes of the most moving and morbid tragedy, a legend with exaggerated attributes of Irishry that could only produce confusion when set against the ethnic realities.

Outside of Boston the Irish experienced a somewhat more diversified social geography, but many of the same inhibitions and repressions surrounded them. Cardinal William O'Connell remembered the prejudice he grew up with in Lowell in the 1870s as a child taught by Yankee women who held a "bitter antipathy, scarcely concealed, which nearly all these good women . . . felt toward those of us who had Catholic faith and Irish names." By 1860 the cotton mills of Lowell were thoroughly dependent on Irish women who worked up to seventy-five hours a week for wages only half of those paid men. The social pressures within this laboring population produced angry assertions of grievances, but the Yankees were unyielding. The result was social withdrawal and antagonism.[21] In Worcester the Irish lived an almost secret existence until after the mid-nineteenth century. In Quincy when the Irish gained control of the town meeting in the 1880s, the Yankee majority promptly voted the town meeting out of existence.[22]

The slow solvent for eventually relieving such tensions was the industrial revolution that would over a century change work life, expand towns, and create a society too complex for overt control by one group. The capitalists at first sought paternal control, then repressive control of the new mill and factory environment. Workers sought their own form of control by determining the number of people at the labor sites and in trades.[23] Both groups were outpaced by the changes inherent in the new order. In the mill towns of New England the Irish lived through exploitation as early fodder for the unsafe and brutalizing factories. Then came cycles of militancy, displacement, depressions, unemployment, and the gradual erosion of the region's original economic base of manufacturing and commerce.

Fairly typical of the regional Irish participation was that enacted in the Connecticut "Brass Valley" of the Naugatuck River where the metal was forged and milled that would shine all over the country as bar rails, doorknobs, train fittings, and ornate bedsteads. Torrington, Watertown, Waterbury, Ansonia, and Derby shared the brass-making task. English and Yankee skills founded the industry, but the Irish came early to it. The first Irish Catholic mayor of Ansonia was elected in 1894. A "workingman's mayor," Jack Meade, was elected in 1920, when there was still much anti-Catholic and anti-Irish sentiment in the town. From the work force dependent almost entirely on brass foundries and mills, strong labor leadership arose that could improve working conditions, but which was powerless to stem the decline of the brass industry in the area.[24] As other immigrants entered the valley in the twentieth century, the Irish were pressed into occupational stalemate in a declining industry, and this was all too common in the entire region.

The same basic conditions pertained to those cities in the New England cultural hinterland that extended into upper New York State, such as Troy and Syracuse. The mid-nineteenth-century exploitation prevailed, and the economic position of the great majority of families was fragile even after the worst misfortunes of emigration and poverty were overcome. This was as true in Troy and Syracuse as it was in Lowell and Lawrence.[25]

Stephan Thernstrom in his study of the economic mobility of the Irish in Newburyport, Massachusetts, found a shifting instability accompanying what economic progress there was. "It is evident that Newburyport did not develop a degraded proletarian class with fixed membership in the 1850–1880 period." Rather, it developed a pattern of labor turnover and expendability through which families had to maneuver in the mills, day laboring, and marginal jobs available. Many moved on, seeking a more permanent way of life. Others stayed in the town and developed a hard-won enclave of minimal sufficiency as wage earners.[26] This pattern of insecurity pertained to mill towns like Holyoke and Naugatuck where cotton manufacturing and rubber fabrication dominated. In Malden the rubber factories hemmed in the lives of vocationally static males for two generations, and only their women moved to white collar occupations. In these smaller towns, labor unions were quite slow to emerge and even when they did evolve depressions and strikes continued to ruin family hopes for improvement time and again.[27]

Rhode Island provides other examples of the digressive character of early Irish presence and the emergence of a later parochial solidarity. When the Irish Brigade in the service of France came to aid George Washington's army, the Irish debarked at Newport. The state's first permanent Catholic parish in Pawtucket was in a state where only 600 Catholics lived among 97,000 Protestants in 1829. In the 1840s the anti-Catholic Thomas Dorr led a voter rebellion that set up property barriers to Irish voting. Bishop Bernard O'Reilly, derided as "Paddy the Priest," defended his nuns from bigoted mob menaces in 1855. The problem of harmonizing the Irish church, built against hostility, with French, Portuguese, and later Italian Catholics took a century. It was not until 1972 that a French-American became a bishop among the Rhode Island Irish. It was a small world in a small state led by nineteenth-century manufacturer Joseph Banigan and political figures like Charles Gorman, Edwin McGuinness, and James Higgins who built machines that dominated the state after the 1930s.

At the beginning of the twentieth century there occurred throughout New England a rise in tension between the Irish Catholics and the French-Canadian Catholics. Disputes over church leadership arose in Connecticut, Massachusetts, Vermont, and especially Maine. The right to use the French language in church and school, the appointment of French-speaking bishops and pastors, and the formation of "French" parishes caused difficulty for the dominant Irish. The

Irish churchmen, however, responded with considerable managerial tact, and a sharing of church facilities and leadership was worked out.[28]

The result of this ill-adapted social situation was that the Irish immigrants and their descendents composed for themselves a system of tolerance and motivation that was in many ways as individualistic as that of the crusty Anglo New Englanders. The escape from Ireland's ancient poverty placed them in a more economically competitive New England where subsistence was better than Ireland, but their progress was slow, interrupted, and plagued by the neglect and contractions of laissez-faire economy and ideology. Largely excluded from economic power, the group used politics to try to correct the worst abuses, but they could make no real structural changes from a minority position beset by lingering distrust and prejudice. An urban subsystem of neighborhood, labor union, parish church, intra-ethnic ties, and fraternal association constituted their network for mutual social support and educational advancement. One student found that assimilation into heterogenous social life and popular mainstream folkways of the general culture greatly reduced Irish-American consciousness in the twentieth century, for smaller cities often lacked the resources for ethnic groups to maintain traditions that had been important to previous generations.[29]

The process of ethnic reduction was accomplished in many communities more through internal change than through the efforts of assimilationist reformers or hectoring critics. An Irish response to the prevailing American cult of patriotic self-glorification at the beginning of the twentieth century produced two somewhat paradoxical folk ideologies: one focused on Irish ethnic traditions rooted in the old country, the other on a cult of religious and patriotic sentiment about Irish achievement in America. The "old country" cult worshipped the church and Ireland's past. The perfervid Catholic Irish patriotic testimony featured such elements as chauvinist Americanism, "lace curtain" values of propriety and social aspiration, a horror of socialism, and cordial but guarded relations with other ethnic groups. The latter cult carried the day and became dominant, even as the swift changes of the 1920s loosened the ties of young people to ethnic traditions across the country.[30]

Another influence prompting religious and patriotic responses among Irish-Americans was the realization that America had stark limitations for this group in the early twentieth century. However, sentiment will not be denied. A compensating affirmation of religious and patriotic commitment in the Irish-Americans was inspired. This commitment, triumphal in religion and bombastic in patriotism, formed a rhetorical frame of reference that satisfied their need for self-justification and social definition. The exaggeration of the cult overrode the realities of social failure, economic limitation, and ambiguous identity. It was this psychological adjustment that was perhaps responsible for the lack of occupational motivation and attainment uncovered by Thernstrom in his study of the Boston Irish.[31] The Irish aligned a set of values for themselves that offset vocational blockages and inspired within the group a sense of self-worth and pride that was relatively independent of extensive economic and social mobility. Their values of family, religion, and acclaim of Irish-American institutional and political accomplishments satisfied their need for a social perspective and an intelligible Americanized tradition.

The Irish never did come to terms with the educational and intellectual heritage of New England. Thoreau lamented their miseries, James Russell Lowell tried to reform them, and Alice James supported their campaign of nationalist agitation, but clerically dominated people in both the Anglo and Irish spheres were unable to fuse their traditions of thought. Eugene O'Neill, deeply sensitive and keenly aware of the New England Yankee tradition, felt snubbed by the Protestant "old money" of New London. "Resenting the WASP elect, O'Neill pretended to embrace its opposite," the misfits, failures, and down and outs, drunken sailors, and broken wage-slaves. O'Neill wrote, "One thing that explains more than anything about me is the fact that I'm Irish."[32] The cultural gap, even for such cosmopolitan and creative personalities, was broad and difficult to bridge. The Irish heritage was one of uncountable injuries fiercely borne, and an elan that dramatized melancholy as well as victory. The Yankee was taut with inherited custom and steeped in the pride of Pilgrims who averred that their tradition alone should prevail. Only the amplitude of a slowly emergent American pluralism would permit the two groups to adjust to one another.

New England's insistence upon cultural conformity shaped its beginnings. "Sequestered from foreign influences," the people exhibited a distinct character for a century and a half. The Irish reaction to this social matrix produced not only their political zeal, but an intellectual formulation of their own expressed by James Jeffrey Roche, John Boyle O'Reilly, and others in the 1880s and 1890s. It was a modest copy of New England's own tidy outlook and reform ideals. New England's views colored it deeply, so that in addition to Catholic Boston College, many Irish Catholics matriculated at Harvard or Yale, not Notre Dame. The successful Irish of New England, in accent, style, and aspiration, partook of the codes and outlook of the region in a clearly conformist manner.[33]

The New England experience of the Irish was not prototypical for the nation, but it was a deeply rooted record within the nation's historic Eastern heartland. As Thernstrom notes, "Newburyport was perhaps more representative of the nineteenth century American city than New York. In 1850 only a seventh of the American urban population lived in cities as large as 250,000. . . . "[34] And the record of social debility for the Irish in Newburyport was long. In such New England towns there was a cultural struggle, and at length the Irish altered the civic compact of the area through their demographic presence, their political style and victories, and their assertion of pluralist values and aspirations. Where the first permanent settlements of the United States were made in New England the Irish became an occupational, social, and ultimately a leadership element that expanded the region's life and made it fulfill democratic promises in spite of itself.

NOTES

1. Samuel Eliot Morison, *The Oxford History of the American People* (New York: Oxford University Press, 1965), p. 70.

2. Bernard Bailyn, *New England Merchants in the Seventeenth Century* (Cambridge: Harvard University Press, 1955), p. 168; George F. Willison, *Saints and Strangers* (New York: Time-Life Books, 1945), pp. 273–293; Kenneth A. Lockridge, *A New England Town: The First Hundred Years* (New York: W.W. Norton, 1970), pp. 57–78.

3. Louis Hartz, *The Liberal Tradition in America* (New York: Harcourt, Brace, and World, 1955), p. 81.

4. Jere R. Daniell, *Colonial New Hampshire* (Millwood, N.Y.: KTO Press, 1981), p. 141; Charles Mason, *The History of Dublin, New Hampshire* (Boston: John Wilson and Son, 1855), p. 7. Names that would be identified with Irish Catholics are hard to find in the 1790 census. *Heads of Families at the First Census of the United States in the Year 1790* (Washington: U.S. Government Printing Office, 1907), p. 131.

5. Lester J. Cappon, ed., *Atlas of American History: The Revolutionary Era, 1760–1790* (Princeton, N.J.: Princeton University Press, 1976), p. 66.

6. The general character of the immigrants from Ireland in the first half of the nineteenth century is shown by Cormac O'Grada, "Across the Briny Ocean: Some Thoughts on Irish Emigration to America, 1800–1850," in T.M. Devine and David Dickson, eds., *Ireland and Scotland, 1600–1850* (Edinburgh: John Donald Publishers Ltd., 1983), pp. 118–130; G.F. Donovan, "The Pre-Revolutionary Irish in Massachusetts, 1620–1775" (Ph.D. Diss., St. Louis University, 1931); M.L. Hansen, "The Second Colonization of New England," *New England Quarterly* 2, no. 4 (1929): 539–560; Michael J. O'Brien, "Irish Settlers in Connecticut in the 17th and 18th Century," *Journal of the American Irish Historical Society* 24 (1925): 125–141; R.J. Purcell, "Rhode Island's Early Schools and Irish Teachers," *Catholic Educational Review* 32 (1934): 402–415; James O'Beirne, "Some Early Irish in Vermont," *Vermont History* 28, no. 1 (January 1960): 63–70; Michael J. O'Brien, "The Early Irish in Maine," *Journal of the American Irish Historical Society* 10 (1911): 162–170.

7. *List of Persons Whose Names Have Been Changed in Massachusetts* (Baltimore: Geneological Publishing Co., 1972) shows almost invariable changes from Irish to Anglo names. John O'Donovan noted the same process in Ireland in 1837. Rev. Michael O'Flanagan, *Letters of John O'Donovan Containing Information Relative to the Antiquities of Londonderry* (Bray, Ireland: Michael O'Flanagan, 1927), pp. 181–259. This is a further reason for the inaccuracy of statistics about the Irish.

8. David Noel Doyle, *Ireland, Irishmen and Revolutionary America, 1760–1820* (Cork, Ireland: The Mercier Press, 1981), pp. 112, 142; Michael J. O'Brien, *A Hidden Phase of American History: Ireland's Part in America's Struggle for Liberty* (New York: Dodd, Mead and Co., 1920), pp. 38–53.

9. "The Irishman's Epistle to the Officers and Troops at Boston," *The Pennsylvania Magazine* (Philadelphia) 1 (May 1775): 232.

10. David Ward, *Immigrants and Cities: A Geography of Change in Nineteenth Century America* (New York: Oxford University Press, 1971), p. 63; Joseph A. King, *The Irish Lumberman-Farmer: Fitzgeralds, Harrigans and Others* (Lafayette, Calif.: Joseph A. King, 1982), pp. 127–142.

11. Oscar Handlin, *Boston's Immigrants: A Study of Acculturation* (New York: Atheneum, 1968), pp. 55–86.

12. Oscar Handlin, *The American People in the Twentieth Century* (Boston: Beacon Press, 1954), p. 76.

13. William H. Pease and Jane H. Pease, "Paternal Dilemmas: Education, Property and Patrician Persistence in Jacksonian Boston," *New England Quarterly* 53, no. 2 (June 1980): 147–167.

14. Dennis P. Ryan, *Beyond the Ballot Box: A Social History of the Boston Irish, 1845–1917* (Madison, N.J.: Fairleigh Dickinson University Press, 1983), pp. 21–40, 57–81; Mary J. Oates, "Learning to Teach: The Professional Preparation of Massachusetts Parochial School Faculty, 1870–1940," Working Papers Series, Series 10, no. 2 (Cushwa Center, University of Notre Dame, Fall 1981), pp. 1–10.

15. Howard Zinn, *A People's History of the United States* (New York: Harper and Row, 1980), pp. 47–48.

16. Barbara Miller Solomon, *Ancestors and Immigrants: A Changing New England Tradition* (New York: John Wiley and Sons, 1956), pp. 1–15, 37.

17. Arthur Mann, *Yankee Reformers in the Urban Age: Social Reform in Boston, 1880–1900* (New York: Harper and Row, 1954), pp. 24–48; James J. Hennessey, *American Catholics: A History of the Roman Catholic Community in the United States* (New York: Oxford University Press, 1981), p. 178; Murray B. Levin, *The Compleat Politician: Political Strategy in Massachusetts* (Indianapolis: Bobbs Merrill Co., 1962), pp. 32–43.

18. Edwin O'Connor, *The Last Hurrah* (Boston: Little, Brown and Co., 1956); John F. Stack, Jr., *International Conflict in an American City: Boston's Irish, Italians, and Jews, 1935–1944* (Westport, Conn.: Greenwood Press, 1979), pp. 50–77.

19. William V. Shannon, *The American Irish: A Political and Social Portrait* (New York: The Macmillan Co., 1963), pp. 201–213, 231; Charles H. Trout, *Boston: The Great Depression and the New Deal* (New York: Oxford University Press, 1977), p. 41.

20. Herbert S. Parmet, *JFK: The Presidency of John F. Kennedy* (New York: The Dial Press, 1983), p. 353; William G. Carleton, "Kennedy in History," in James B. Walsh, ed., *The Irish: America's Political Class* (New York: Arno Press, 1976), pp. 277–299; Gary Wills, *The Kennedy Imprisonment: A Meditation on Power* (Boston: Little, Brown and Co., 1981), pp. 61–83.

21. Solomon, *Ancestors and Immigrants*, p. 47; Brian C. Mitchell, *The Paddy Camps: The Meaning of Community Among the Irish of Lowell, Massachusetts, 1821–1861* (Urbana, Ill.: University of Illinois Press, 1986), pp. 1–40.

22. Allan R. Whitmore, " 'A Guard of Faithful Sentinels,' The Know-Nothing Appeal in Maine, 1854–1855," *Maine Historical Society Quarterly* 20, no. 2 (Winter 1981): 151–197; Vincent Powers, "The Invisible Immigrants: Pre-Famine Irish in Worcester" (Ph.D. diss., Clark University, 1976), pp. 1–50; Solomon, *Ancestors and Immigrants*, p. 29.

23. Irwin Yellowitz, *Industrialization and the American Labor Movement, 1850–1900* (Port Washington, N.Y.: Kennikat Press, 1977), pp. 13, 99–103. Irish labor militancy was a strong factor in the Knights of Labor in the 1870s in towns such as Lynn. Alan Dawley, *Class and Community: The Industrial Revolution in Lynn* (Cambridge: Harvard University Press, 1976), p. 190.

24. Jeremy Brecher, Jerry Lombardi, and Jan Stackhouse, eds., *Brass Valley: The Story of Working People's Lives and Struggles in an American Industrial Region* (Philadelphia: Temple University Press, 1982), pp. 1–41.

25. Daniel Walkowitz, "Working Class Culture in the Gilded Age: The Iron Workers of Troy, New York and the Cotton Workers of Cohoes, New York, 1855–84" (Ph.D.

diss., University of Rochester, 1972), p. 275; John A. Beadles, "The Syracuse Irish, 1812–1928" (Ph.D. diss., Syracuse University, 1974), pp. 1–40; Michael Frisch, *Town into City: Springfield, Massachusetts, 1840–1880* (Cambridge: Harvard University Press, 1972), p. 196; Tamara K. Haraven and Randolph Langenbach, *Amoskeag: Life and Work in an American Factory City* (New York: Pantheon Books, 1978), p. 98.

26. Stephan Thernstrom, *Poverty and Progress: Social Mobility in a Nineteenth Century City* (New York: Atheneum, 1969), pp. 17–31, 85. Forty-five percent of the laborers' families in the town in 1850 are not even listed in the directories that are a key element for this research (p. 31). For comparative family data see Albert G. Mitchell, "Irish Family Patterns in Nineteenth Century Ireland and Lowell, Massachusetts" (Ph.D. diss., Boston University, 1976).

27. Constance McLaughlin Green, *American Cities in the Growth of the Nation* (London: John DeGraff, 1957), pp. 79–99; Richard Klayman, *The First Jew: Prejudice and Politics in an American Community, 1900–1932* (Malden, Mass.: Old Suffolk Square Press, 1985), pp. 56–59.

28. Kenneth B. Woodbury, Jr., "An Incident between the French Canadians and the Irish in the Diocese of Maine in 1906," *New England Quarterly* 40, no. 2 (June 1967): 260–269; Michael Guignard, "The Case of Sacred Heart Parish," *Maine Historical Society Quarterly* 22, no. 1 (Summer 1982): 21–36.

29. Marjorie Fallows, *Irish–Americans: Identity and Assimilation* (Englewood Cliffs, N.J.: Prentice-Hall, Inc., 1979), pp. 49, 74–76.

30. Timothy J. Meagher, " 'The Lord Is Not Dead': Cultural and Social Change among the Irish in Worcester, Massachusetts" (Ph.D. diss., Brown University, 1982), pp. 545–608.

31. Stephan Thernstrom, *The Other Bostonians: Poverty and Progress in the American Metropolis, 1880–1970* (Cambridge: Harvard University Press, 1973), pp. 132, 169, 259.

32. Brendan Gill, "Philip Barry," *The New Yorker* (September 5, 1975): 42; Louis Shaeffer, *O'Neill: Son and Playwright*, 2 vols. (Boston: Little, Brown and Co., 1968), vol. 1, p. 10.

33. John Gorham Palfrey, *The History of New England during the Stuart Dynasty*, 3 vols. (New York: AMS Press, 1966), vol. 1, p. viii; Dixon Ryan Fox, *Yankees and Yorkers* (New York: New York University Press, 1940), pp. 2–3; E. Digby Baltzell, *Puritan Boston and Quaker Philadelphia* (Boston: Beacon Press, 1979), pp. 428–430.

34. Thernstrom, *Poverty and Progress*, p. 204.

5 EAST SIDE, WEST SIDE— NEW YORK

New York City—gargantuan, inimitable, the ultimate crescendo of American urban life—began as a tiny Dutch village. The deft colonial displacement of the Dutch by the English removed a small nation from the chessboard of imperial rivalry in North America. It could hardly be foreseen that two centuries later another small nation, Ireland, would have its sons and daughters and their progeny preside over a New York transformed into a vast center of power surpassing that seat of empire, London.

In the Atlantic world of contending royal obsessions, imperial scheming, and mercantile contention in the seventeenth and eighteenth centuries, the realities of New York's advantages were clearly recognized. The dramatic beauty of the Hudson Valley, its rich, wooded terrain and Manhattan's extraordinarily fine harbor, made the island the object of throngs of ambitious men. This superbly sited harbor city was not only strategically placed to be the entrepot of the Great Lakes hinterlands, but it would soon dominate all American shipping. By so doing it would assume a position of surpassing importance in Ireland's history of ties with America. Not only would wave after wave of emigrants sail to it, but its wonders, its lifestyle, its affairs, and even its gossip would be the common currency of Irish people for over a century, and this would be true not only for emigrants and those who returned to Ireland, but for whole villages of people who would never even see New York. More than the city of Dublin, which would retain a largely alien caste of civic and government leadership well into the twentieth century, New York would represent the opportunities and achievements of the common people of Ireland, the democracy, and, further, the achievements of those who had been rejected by the putative leaders of their own country.

The city was not, of course, any hospitable and bucolic retreat. It was at first a tough seaport, a roughly competitive hive of artisans, merchants, and intriguers. It had in its body politic the anti-Catholic virus common to all the colonies. The Scotch-Irish had to strenuously affirm their repugnance of Catholicism as they moved to the rude interior that would become Ulster County. The Irish Catholics

had to comport themselves cleverly to avoid conflict, for even rumor and suspicion could be deadly. The "New York Conspiracy" of 1741 gave ample
evidence of the dangers. At that time there were in the city about 2,000 slaves.
A robbery occurred at the house of one Robert Hogg at Broad Street and Jew's
Alley (now William Street). Blacks were suspected. An Irishwoman named
Peggy Kerry was accused of receiving the stolen goods. Before the tempest could
be contained, numerous Blacks were decried as plotters of a slave revolt in
concert with an Irish dancing master, John Corry, and a group of soldiers, Andrew
Ryan, Edward Kelly, Edward Murphy, and Peter Connolly, and a peddler, John
Coffin. A conspiracy of Blacks and Irish Catholics was imagined out of "the
holy hatred of Roman Catholics that was inculcated by Church and State."[1]
Before the affair ended, thirteen Blacks were burned at the stake, sixteen hanged,
and others transported. In one of the earliest examples of Irish negotiating skill
in the city, all the Irish people involved were released. Thus the turbulent
character of the city was demonstrated early, and all could be forewarned that
New York's opportunities were hedged around by incalculable furors and grim
penalties for those who might fall as random victims.

Colonial New York was to quickly assume its historic role as a polyglot port
of entry for immigrants. In 1755 a regular packet service to England was established. The result was an increase of Irish as well as other immigrants. "Foreign
invasions of Beggary and Idleness" created a chronic condition whereby asy-
lums, relief expenditures, and the Poor House, Work House, and House of
Correction were overwhelmed by the indigent. Funds were voted to pay return
fares for immigrants, but the problem was insuperable. The city's predicament
was typical of the inability of American centers to organize themselves in any
rational way to deal with immigrants. The concepts of government were too
limited, the flow of immigrants too great, and the alienation of the newcomers
too pronounced to permit the orderly reception and adaptation of the incoming
tide.[2]

In 1784 when New York had 12,000 people, one estimate calculated that
1,000 families were supported by public and private charity. Jobless immigrants,
widows, orphans, the sick, aged, and insane were the worry of the commissioners
of the Alms House. The swift growth of New York population from 33,000 in
1790 to 60,000 in 1800 produced a chaotic social situation for the poor. Perhaps
one-third of the population of New York was composed of poor people. The
discord resulting from competition for employment, street gang clashes, and
political haranguing began the long, long sequence of street violence and public
controversy involving the Irish.[3]

In this city where the poor thronged in lower Manhattan in jerry-built hovels,
a mile above the stone fort at the Battery the wide streets leading off Broadway
were lined with stately mansions and dignified churches. Beyond the city proper
the DeLanceys, Clintons, Hogelands, and other baronial families had their great
mansions. Henry Knox on his way to Ticonderoga found them proud and con-
ceited and objectionable in their "profaneness which is intolerable, in the want

of principle which is prevalent, and in their Toryism which is insufferable.''[4] Thus, New York was early to display one of its most enduring characteristics, a sharp contrast between the rich and the poor. One of the earliest successful Irishmen, Dominick Lynch, was also one of the elegant set that flaunted wealth in the city. Educated for a time in France, Lynch introduced choice French wines to the country and also brought the first grand opera, ''The Barber of Seville,'' to America by personally recruiting an entire company from Europe.[5]

The dispute with Britain over trade and political status grew as the colonists contested such measures as the Stamp Act. In January 1770 British soldiers shot and killed a New Yorker, the first person to be killed in the revolutionary struggle. In April 1774 the port had its own tea party, pouring British tea into the harbor, and in May 1774 the fifty-one-man Committee of Correspondence of New York called for a Continental Congress. But pro-British sentiment was strong in New York and in the fall of 1776, as Washington retreated southward, the city was occupied by General Howe's British garrison and hemmed in by his powerful fleet.

Irish-Americans are fond of recalling the Irishmen who served with George Washington. They are more reticent about those who were set against him. These included not just agitated men like John Kain in New York, but rich men like Thomas Lynch, who lost over $100,000 in property that the rebels confiscated, a tremendous sum at that time.[6] Circulating among the loyalists was Washington's extremely brave spy, Hercules Mulligan, and he had much to do. William Smith and perhaps one-third of New York's Ulster Presbyterians did their utmost to counter the American rebel endeavors.[7]

When the Revolution was won, as Edmund Morgan notes, ''the fact that the lower ranks were involved in the contest should not obscure the fact that the contest itself was generally a struggle for office and power between members of an upper class; the new against the established.''[8] Still, when the Constitution was ratified, 4,000 New York artisans and mechanics marched with floats and banners feting the nation's charter of government and liberties.[9] Small property owners had a stake in this new order, and those who had no property were lifted by the hope that they would have, and this was a basic nourishment of the spirit of New York henceforth.

The Federal period in New York brought about an intensification of all that went before—population increase, commerce, physical expansion, and a restless surging of promotion and energy. For the Irish the decades after 1800 would establish that powerful local subculture that would provide the metropolis with an indispensible labor supply for over a century as immigrants took jobs at whatever wages they could get on the docks, in the lofts, and in the ditches of the city. In the nineteenth century America built a vast infrastructure for its urban growth through a system of labor capitalization. Cheap labor built the sewers, water lines, tunnels, streets, and foundations that would underly the city buildings and traffic and bear the weight of an amazing new technology. And it was the Irish who were the chief excavators, haulers, and lifters in this ceaseless urban effort. Machines at the time were still unequal to the task, and the most arduous and perilous jobs fell to the immigrant poor in the labor of building for the comfort and utility of New York's population. When the Erie Canal was begun in 1817, thousands of Irish went off to dig it, but thousands more arrived in succeeding years to take up the shovels the others had left.

In the areas of lower Manhattan where the Irish population was concentrated, the density per block rose from 94.5 in 1820 to 163.5 in 1850. In the Tenth Ward the density rose to 170 per block in 1840, and this was before the great influx of the famine era. Overcrowding, outrageously bad sanitation, and the effects of malnutrition created an annual cycle of epidemics. In the Sixth Ward an epidemic of typhoid fever broke out in 1837, typhus in 1842, and cholera in 1849. Infant mortality took as many as one-third of the children of immigrants. Cellar dwelling was rampant, and even hospitals were dangers to those who fell ill. By mid-century 85 percent of all those admitted to Bellevue Hospital were Irish-born. In 1858, of 2,000 prostitutes examined at the Penitentiary Hospital, 706 were Irish-born.[10] Add to this the catalog of Irish who were born in the United States of Irish parents and the descendents of other Irish caught in the web of poverty, and the social impression conveyed by the group was horrifying to those unacquainted with its history and the reasons for its condition. Among the newcomers crime, despair, insanity, alcoholism, and helpless rage were the lot of tens of thousands. The toll taken by this passage of literally hundreds of thousands of Irish through the nether world of urban misery will never be fully known, for they perished anonymously in the brick hovels and shanty towns of New York, but the pride of America must be stringently corrected by the recollection of their fate.

This inpouring of Irish and its attendant suffering could not but produce political effects. In the slum wards of the city the pressure for improvement became intense. Even the promise of improvement held forth by some mountebank was enough to generate neighborhood mobilization for polling purposes. Cadres of artisans and mechanics with laborers and apprentices as adjuncts called themselves "Workies" and sought abolition of debtors' prison, free primary schools, and control of local public works jobs. Most Americans are unaware of the fact that much of the country's first century of voting had more to do with street combat and intimidation than with the free exercise of democratic franchise, and this is how New York's mass balloting proceeded. Gang clashes at election time were standard local voting behavior.

The elections of the 1830s brought out Anglo-American and Scotch-Irish voters in the American Republican party and similar groupings to furiously oppose Irish-Catholic adherents of Andrew Jackson's Democrats. The Whigs and Federalists gathered the older Anglo leaders. However, both Democratic and Whig leaders in this period were monied and of upper-class background. In Jacksonian times the Irish were definitely at the bottom of the political pyramid in New York. One estimate calculates that ninety percent of the Irish Catholics were Democrats by 1844.[11] Anglo-Roman Catholics were dismayed by the immigrant

Irish cleaving to one party. The Protestant voters were split in various ways, so that the Democrats had an increasing advantage as more immigrants were naturalized to vote each year or simply voted illegally without naturalization. New York leaders as well as those in New England and elsewhere feared by 1830 that the half million Irish in the United States would form a permanent alien element and would never participate intelligently in American politics. The "values, beliefs, attitudes and ways of life" of the Irish and Anglo-Americans clashed fiercely. "Antagonisms in non-political spheres" polarized electoral activities. The cultural conflict that would change the popular basis of American politics was joined.[12]

It is important that political conflicts in the 1840s usually attributed largely to religion be seen as more complex and the result of a broader cultural antagonism. The immigrant Irish had a whole set of specific grievances that paralleled, or perhaps were prior to, religion. These people were trying to survive as individuals, as families, and as an ethnic group amid a deeply disorienting experience of emigration and urban novelty. The volatility and bitterness of their responses derive from this primitive consideration. When this dynamic became involved with local politics the effects were intensely partisan.

Thus, the rise of the Nativist party in New York is partly attributable to raging fights over patronage jobs as well as religious antagonism. In 1843 not only were there conflicts over the Board of Education and its endorsement of the use of the King James Bible in the public schools, but when the Democrats won control of the city government from the Whigs, they worked diligently paying off political debts with jobs and contracts. Food market licenses were multiplied to increase the Irish dealers in provision and grocery businesses. Immigrants have always played a key role in food processing and distribution in our major cities, and the Irish through their work on the docks and railroads and canals were naturally widely related to the function of providing the city with its daily fare. Native Americans had dominated this activity previously and reacted vigorously to the threat to their dominence by Irish meat and vegetable merchants.[13]

Into this unsettled political and social situation there came between 1846 and 1855 a vast confluence of famine refugees from the poorest, most Gaelic areas of stricken Ireland. From the dead fields and rock-strewn mountains of Donegal, Sligo, Mayo, Clare and Kerry, West Cork and Waterford, from Galway, Leitrim, and Roscommon flooded a seemingly endless exodus of people—dressed in rags, weak with hunger, and numb with the fresh memory of corpse-filled workhouses, skeletal children, and tales of cannibalism. Inheritors of the powerful Celtic traditions reaching to the pre-Roman world, they were now homeless, nationless, and all but hopeless after a grim sea passage to an unwelcoming land. For the most part English-speaking, politically defeated in a generation of campaigns under the oracular Daniel O'Connell, steeped in a folk Catholicism, this outcast group had to acclimate to the revolutionary world of burgeoning American urbanism as they entered New York.

Despite all the disabilities the group bore, the very scale of its displacement was itself a strength. Communal by social disposition, the Irish retained a strong sense of family and group attachment. The awakening of nationalism in what was a conservative rural population on the western rim of Europe animated them toward political effort. The catastrophe of the Potato Famine of 1846–47 broke old molds. Paradoxically, what almost wiped out this group also sent them to America as an emergent people ready to take up new ways and ideas.[14] Patterns of chain migration, prepaid passages, family, and occupational connections would emerge that would greatly stimulate American life and change the history even of the nation's most powerful city.

New York, despite all its shortcomings as an organized civic and social community, was "a city built on motion and on the hope of improvement." It required a new class of opportunists "with a passion for humanity and comradeship" to lead a disorderly community of free men. It found these leaders among the Irish.[15] The first to emerge was John Kelly, who spent ten years as sheriff of the city. He replaced William Marcy Tweed as Democratic leader of the Tammany Hall brotherhood in 1868. Married to a niece of Cardinal John McCloskey but a man of limited education, he nevertheless represented the rising power of the Irish middle class. From the 1860s onward, as Seymour Mandelbaum has asserted, there was only one way New York could be "bossed" and that was by a devious and flexible alliance of political duchies. This alliance was the only defense of local order amid the turbulence of an awesome polyglot metropolis, and it could be financed only from the public coffers.[16]

Thus there emerged that behemoth of democracy's politics, the urban machine. The Irish had arrived in great numbers just when America was seeking a way to broaden political participation in response to popular pressure and grievances. The framers of the Constitution had no concept of political parties and their utility as electoral mechanisms. With mass populations unsettling the country, parties and their functions became crucial to political stability. They were the means of relieving tension, changing public agendas, and exchanging power. And the Irish became the most artful practitioners of party management with New York as the paramount demonstration.

The political bosses of the city served both rich and poor throughout the new metropolis. The Northeastern financial interests led by August Belmont needed political spokesmen and acolytes, just as the slum dwellers needed patrons and agitators in their behalf. There arose phalanx after phalanx of such men. They served and they stole in riotous corruption, but they took the places of more ethical leaders who disdained to serve. From the teeming East Side came Charles Murphy to deal with and dominate Daniel F. McMahon of the West Side, Lewis Haffen of the Bronx and the bosses of Brooklyn. In fealty to them was Daniel M. Donegan, collector of millions of dollars for Tammany war chests. Richard Croker was perhaps the most unrestrainedly larcenous of the group and after fleeing from prosecution died in Ireland, having provided to have himself buried in Glasnevin Cemetary in Dublin with his favorite race horse on one side and his mistress on the other. The succession of the Tammany Irish leadership reached up to and past John F. Hylan, the Brooklyn Democrat who was New York's mayor after World War I.[17]

These political dynasts arose in the age of the robber barons, those masters of capital manipulation who controlled in corrupt and irresponsible networks the railroads and basic industries of the new industrial America. The urban machine bosses were the political counterparts of these economic buccaneers. Frequently crude and graceless men, they came from a crude and graceless urban background, and they were just what a raw and petulant citizenry needed to gain at least some hold on the boisterous city, to give at least some relief to the poor, and to create an ethnic system for protection and advancement. Otherwise, they were immoral thieves.

The deeply perceptive research of David Hammack has revealed what took place amid the smoke and fury of political battle from 1880 to 1910. The Tammany machine was intermittently allied with economic elites in the early part of this period, but disputes about their opposing interests vitiated the effectiveness of these wealthy and traditionalist leaders. The professional politicians, led by the Irish allied with labor groups and a spectrum of ethnic elements, moved to positions of greater power to replace them. Hammack finds the Irish leaders "remarkably cosmopolitan." The wealthy " 'swallowtail Democrats' abandoned their policy of cooperating with Irish Catholics and failed to reconcile themselves to the increasing cultural heterogeneity of the metropolis." By the 1890s Boss Croker could rely on Daniel McMahon, Charles F. Murphy, George Washington Plunkitt, John C. Sheehan, and Thomas J. Dunn, contractors and saloon keepers connected with huge networks of followers, to run the machine and guide public works in a shrewd and somewhat less corrupt fashion than was the style under Boss Tweed earlier in the century.[18]

The progress of the poorest among the Irish and other groups, however, was quite slow. Although power was dispersing in the city, and although labor obtained greater leverage, unorganized workers and those most deprived remained on the edges of political power. The Irish were distributed throughout Manhattan broadly enough so that they were the controlling factor in numerous electoral districts, but even on the West Side, the upper East Side, and in Brooklyn, what could be controlled was not sufficient to really alter economic and social circumstances for the disadvantaged. Even the most successful of the Irish could not "join in social competition at the top levels of wealth." As late as 1900 just over ten percent of the Irish had risen to higher white collar occupations, and in 1910 they controlled only five percent of the city's mercantile, manufacturing, and private banking firms.[19] They had constructed a great pluralist political engine since the Civil War, but it was not powerful enough to lift a major portion of them out of the tenements, warehouse and gashouse areas into which they were crowded as hundreds of thousands of other immigrants poured into the mazes of New York.

Still, beneath the carnival of political maneuvering and peculation, a deeply significant process of ethnic creativity was taking place. It would result in the construction of a social model for minority group behavior in American life that would be imitated by a whole array of different groups seeking security in the midst of oppressive and disorganized conditions. The earliest Irish version of this pattern of adjustment was basically an adaptation of folk networks to the American scene. Family ties, fellowship based on specific locales and interests in Ireland, and ingenious reproduction in the American context of Irish customs and activities formed a cultural substructure for the group. Celebrations, informal social interaction, musical gatherings for traditional playing, singing and dancing, parties to greet new arrivals and say farewell to those headed elsewhere all were interwoven with the daily obligations of work and family care. Mutual identification and attachment were thus cultivated on a very broad scale. This was a central factor in the perpetuation of ethnic ties and the building of political structures.

Even a cursory review of the Irish newspapers indicates the complex web of business and organization links promoted by this social base. By 1860 there were over 200,000 Irish-born people in New York City and Brooklyn. This population's needs and preferences were served by a host of Irish businesses: hotels, restaurants, dry goods stores, food stores, bootmakers, tailors, sellers of music and books, travel agents, importers and makers of shirts, liquor, and household furniture.[20] Organizational formation was so rapid that printers advertised that they specialized in constitutions and by-laws. Thirty attorneys advertised in one Irish newspaper alone in 1883, and events were reported for the Celtic Musical Union, The Thomas Moore Centennial, the Hibernian Rifles, the United Irish Societies, and scores of fraternal and Irish nationalist groups. And these were only the events reported in the Irish press. There was a whole dimension of activity that was not reported because it was casual, impromptu, too small, or too intimate. There was also a realm of secret labor and nationalist groups whose doings went unreported. The reported activities alone show a very high level of social interaction.[21]

William H. Russell, correspondent for the *Times* of London, found the spreading Irish civic presence in 1861 to be impressive. "In New York there is scarcely a situation of honour or distinction, from the chief magistrate down to the police, that is not filled by the descendent of some Irishman who lived in savage hatred of England beyond the pale! . . . " He witnessed that year's St. Patrick's Day parade in Union Square and found the participants and Irish observers "decently dressed and comfortable . . . and proud of the privilege of interrupting all the trade of the principal streets, in which the Yankees most do congregate." More than 10,000 marching men took part "and all as noisy as music and talking could make them." He also noted that on other days the Irish could be seen "engaged in all the humbler occupations from shouldering the hod to rag-gathering."[22] Charles Dickens found those who were in the police force admirable, but regretted the "stupendous" corruption in public funds.[23]

After the Civil War the outlying neighborhoods of the city began to be built up extensively. In 1870 the Flatbush section of Brooklyn became heavily Irish and was to maintain this character for a century. A great many people from County Clare settled in this area, and it was not unusual to have various neighborhoods represent concentrations from given areas in Ireland. These areas usually had Irish dance halls, Ancient Order of Hibernians halls, church halls, and Tammany Hall outposts. Yet the semirural landscape in such areas as Flatbush gave immigrants an anomalous opportunity to perform agricultural work in the truck farms of the area in the 1870s and 1880s.[24]

Indeed, the diversity of the city distributed the Irish widely. Since most of the women and many of the men were engaged in service occupations, they went wherever employers bade them. Construction work took males to all corners of the region, as did work on the transportation lines. The ubiquitous boardinghouse made reasonable lodging available wherever they went; still, many remained confined to tenements. Charlotte O'Brien described the tenements in which they lived in Manhattan in the 1880s "as absolutely dark at midday . . . stifling" and wondered if a "more frightfully unwholesome system" could be imagined.[25]

Although oral tradition was strong in the group inspiring a continuing effusion of gossip, story telling, recitation, and more formal oratory, the new intensity of city life readily dictated more elaborate communication techniques. Irish and Catholic newspapers met part of the need. But the city itself was a theater of information and instruction, an enormous daily tutoring mechanism, fast-paced and repetitive, that substituted an entire new use of time, energy, and intelligence to suit the new milieu. The slow-talking Kerryman, the ingenuous girl from Mayo, the Cavan farmer who had worked alone in the fields—all were now caught up in a concourse of urban activity that changed their outlooks and personalities. The urban Irishman had been formed, half a century before James Joyce would delineate him and a century before he would become a major social reality in Ireland itself.

Rising out of this cultural base and interacting with it was the ceremonial, educational, and social service development of the Roman Catholic church. Irish Protestant congregations—being smaller—evolved more slowly, were more dispersed, and did not have the same kind of mass population base or ecclesiastical interrelationships that Catholics had. In the first half of the nineteenth century the Irish did not participate heavily in formal religious life in Ireland. After centuries of persecution the church structure and modalities were simply not there to permit them to do so. In addition, their religion was fundamentally a composition of folk beliefs and simple traditional practices, including a heavy quotient of superstition. Perhaps twenty-five percent of the people were related in a definitive practicing way to the official ceremonial life of the church. Even in New York where communications and freedom to participate were greatly improved, only about half of the mid-nineteenth-century Irish were related to parishes.

With the leadership of priests drawn directly from the people and with the acquisition of poor but serviceable church buildings, the desire for religious organization flourished. Parishes grew to an average size of 10,000 people in the city. The devotional spirit fostered within a Victorian code of discipline and observance surged. The bonds of group support formed by a highly active commitment to works of charity and mercy for the sick, the homeless, the bereaved, and the poor were confirmed in an ascending pride of achievement. Social problems abounded, but the gritty Irish perseverance that was a traditional factor in the group's heritage was strongly pitted against them. Something quite new had been created by this group—a kind of Catholicism that did not exist elsewhere. While the church was losing the allegiance of workers in Europe, the American Catholics led by the Irish had created a democratic Catholicism with popular support, financial and social, for what would become the country's largest religious establishment. True, the European organization of the church with its antique hierarchical structure contradicted democratic forms, but the Irish were able to blend a spirit of camaraderie, solidarity, and administrative flexibility with that structure to maintain popular participation. No government, no noble families, no church ownership of vast tracts of land supported this edifice. It was democratically financed by popular subscription. "Brick and mortar" clerics, not too different from their construction contractor brothers and cousins, built an unprecedented chain of educational and social service facilities throughout the city as an example of the strongest display of practical religious initiative that the country had seen since the institutions established by its colonial religious founders.[26]

One of the most prominent features of the identity and expression of the New York Irish was the pattern of nationalist activities for which the city served as a national and international focus. A complex of conditions assigned to New York the role of the overseas capital of Irish nationalist agitation and mobilization. The massive Irish-born population of the city and their descendants formed a sympathetic opinion base for Irish nationalist agitation. Further, a strategic segment of the Irish population was more than a sympathetic element for this agitation; it was a committed, talented, and volatile creative minority that had a passionate devotion to the liberation of Ireland from English rule. This cadre of editors, organization heads, ideologues, and exiled agitators was the inspirational and motivational heart of the Irish nationalist movement in America, quickly responsive to events in Ireland, keenly attuned to American politics, and related by powerful emotional bonds to the sentiments and outlook of the Irish in the country. This group was able to cultivate an opinion base in New York and elsewhere that could be maneuvered for nationalist purposes.[27]

This opinion bloc reflected the history of English misrule in Ireland. It had a folk legacy of deep antagonism toward England, and this emotional dynamic was enhanced by a sense of deliverance and a growing consciousness of peoplehood as a result of emigration to America. The great catalog of grievances against English rule, the organizational experience of nationalist activity in Ireland, the especially significant resentment against British repression of Catholic religious development in Ireland, and direct family traditions of misfortune attributed to

British rule all combined to form this opinion bloc. These views were invested with American beliefs about the superiority of popular democracy, of republican institutions, and rejection of colonial empires. America as a haven for the oppressed loomed large in the minds of those who had come to New York from other countries. Through a full annual cycle of nationalist observances, protests, organization programs, and publicity efforts this opinion force was maintained and guided in New York and from New York to constitute an influential factor in American politics and in Irish ethnic life.[28]

The absence of censorship in American life permitted the free expression of ideas that, were they spoken or printed in Ireland, would have resulted in imprisonment and the shutting down of any newspaper daring to print them. Agitator-editors like John Devoy, John Mitchel, Patrick Ford, and others, then, did not hesitate to take advantage of this liberty to print a steady barrage of news coverage, editorials, articles, and subscription forms highly critical of England. This journalism was a basic resource of the nationalist network, but since New York was also the mecca of American publication and journalism in the second half of the nineteenth century, the Irish were in a very advantageous position to influence the general press. Irish journalists often gave a strong pro-Irish bias to published materials dealing with Ireland. Hence, the nationalist publicists and those they could influence had a far-reaching voice that echoed throughout the country. The correspondence columns of their publications were filled with letters and pledges from Irish people in all corners of the nation decade after decade. All of this Irish communication and interest was concentrated in New York and augmented the nationalist base of the city itself.[29]

As the pole of one end of the transatlantic connection, New York was a beacon to those political fugitives who had to flee the homeland. As a result the Irish lecture circuit in the United States was rarely without some notable former felon or refugee. These men tended to be the center of public attention at least for a short time, but if they were outstanding personalities like the indomitable Jeremiah O'Donovan-Rossa, he whom the British prison masters had forced to eat off the floor in manacles, they became relentless activists on the New York scene. The location of New York also made it the center for information from Ireland and England and Europe, so that political commentary and analysis were steady fare that could be transmitted to the Irish in other areas.

The sinews of this nationalist body politic were the organizations that grew from the work of individual leaders, from nationalist campaign demands, and from domestic needs of the immigrants themselves. Daniel O'Connell's Repeal drive to sever Ireland's constitutional ties with England in the 1840s; James Stephens' Fenian Brotherhood full of burning purpose in the 1860s; its successor, the *Clan-na-Gael* (children of the Gael), secret and disposed toward terrorism; the mighty Land League of the 1880s; and the later Irish National League and the groups supporting twentieth-century Irish revolution all arose and throve in New York. Behind them were fraternal groups like the Ancient Order of Hibernians, the United County Societies, and an extensive interlacing of religious societies and Irish-controlled labor organizations. Fractious, stubborn, parochial, and mercurial, these groups were difficult to coordinate, but they were a force. Together with the families whose members supported them, they were the most successful minority transatlantic resource of the period before World War I. They were an instruction for Cubans, Jews, and Armenians. They were acutely important at particular junctures in their impact on Ireland's history, and they were the social ligaments of that Ireland outside of the home island itself.[30]

The evolution of New York's powerful Irish Catholic community would have far-reaching effects beyond the concerns of the group for local political and religious influence and for Irish nationalist undertakings. In the 1880s, desperate for some Irish movement toward social reform on the local scene, a significant following was organized for Father Edward McGlynn, a disciple of Henry George and his theory of the "Single Tax" to transform economic life. This radical doctrine contradicted the tenets of the capitalist order in the most definitive sense, and the reaction of Irish bourgeois leaders like Charles O'Conor and James T. Brady was one of studious avoidance or opposition. Father McGlynn's campaign for mayor in 1886 proved effective enough in rallying Irish Catholic discontent so that James Cardinal Gibbons in his plea to the Holy See not to condemn legitimate labor union participation by Catholics cited the McGlynn experience as evidence that social unrest must be dealt with by providing organizational alternatives to radicalism. The resultant tolerance of labor organization by bishops was a historic development for the United States.[31] The heavily Catholic working class was diverted from the socialist doctrines that had such a widespread impact in Europe. The stimulus of the New York Irish radicals of the 1880s had caused an epochal shift in the outlook of Catholic leaders toward moderate reform policies. The Irish in New York and elsewhere were by 1900 in an important position to take part in the social reform politics of the Progressives, and although their participation was hampered by the anti-Catholic sentiments of some of the key Progressive elements, it was still the largest political opportunity for reform of labor and social conditions opened to the group until that time.

In the cauldron of slum life the reformers had to contend with the ferocity of the underworld as well as the depredations of a labor system still unreformed. That system continued to use immigrants and the less mobile working population as the underpaid work force for marginal and exploitative industries such as garment manufacture, food processing, and laundry service. Males were involved still with a brutal world of port labor and the heavy tasks of building the underground facilities and subways beneath the city as well as the perilous iron construction work high above the streets as the skyline of New York was built higher and higher. Although the Irish served as intermediaries for Jews, Italians, and others seeking to adjust to city politics and institutions, ethnic conflicts and street brawling were often rife in local neighborhoods. In the underworld of professional violence the combat was even more murderous. The Brooklyn gang wars between Italians and Irish became legendary as an episode in the inter-ethnic killing that accompanied the decline of Irish domination of the urban crime world. Conflict between Blacks and Irish seemed an accepted social folkway, and such events as the race riot of 1900, which began at McBride's Saloon on West Forty-first Street and was the biggest Black-versus-Irish violence since the Draft Riots of 1863, really did not greatly disturb New York's opinion or leadership.[32]

Above this level of primitive encounter, the duel of the Irish with the monied elite of old family New Yorkers also continued. As John Higham has noted, for members of ethnic groups, successful assimilation can be viewed as betrayal of the inherited identity. New York was never lacking in upper-class detractors of the Irish and Anglophile imitators of aristocratic demeanor from Mayor William J. Gaynor, a true Victorian autocrat, to Walter Hines Page, who could pronounce: "We Americans have got to . . . hang our Irish agitators and shoot our hyphenates and bring up our children with reverence for English history. . . . " Theodore Roosevelt in 1882 wrote of the Irish in the New York legislature: "The average Catholic Irishman of the first generation, as represented in this Assembly, is a low, venal, corrupt and unintelligent brute."[33] Such statements, while irksome, could be treated with contempt by the newly wealthy Irish who came to prominence in the twentieth century. Thomas E. Murray, a utility magnate and inventor, James McDonnell, stock market tycoon, and Anthony Nicholas Brady, head of an electrical power combine, were counterparts of the Boston Kennedys and the Chicago Cuddihys. Successful beyond the dreams of most Americans, they formed an Irish Catholic social set who intermarried and maintained a very wide social distance from the Irish working people of the city.[34] They created a separate world for themselves and carried on their intense and pragmatic financial dealings with unremitting absorption, while leading a social life imitative of the wealthy Knickerbokers whose fortunes permitted them luxurious preserves exempt from the roiling disorder and insecurity that were the lot of the greater proportion of the city's inhabitants.

Economic and educational progress had also enabled thousands to ascend to higher income levels and move to better housing in the Bronx, Queens, and the far reaches of Brooklyn by the end of World War I. Some became middle class. They had moved into teaching, the law, and white collar positions in legions, but always there were, as there had been for a century, more immigrant Irish arriving with limitations that retarded mobility. The emergence of an Irish wealthy elite and a comfortable Irish middle class did not fundamentally change the exploitative process that grasped each generation of immigrants. Improvements in working conditions and social services might relieve the distress somewhat, but the reality of this immigrant cycle could not be offset by counting the survivors and the small rich group of superachievers. Its reality was to be measured in the massive record of pathology and the shortened lives of a myriad of victims for whom the American dream became a dreadful fantasy amid the ineluctable social processes of the metropolis. It was better than Ireland in that the toll and the casualties were fewer, but the toll was still of tragic proportions.

Yet, one generation after another, the Irish could in no way be dissuaded from pouring into the city. Why? Part of the answer has to do with the possibility of improvement the city offered over the penury of Donegal or the isolation of the Sligo mountains. But the magical attraction was also due to the contrast and drama the metropolis promised. By its sheer concentration of physical construction and the diversity of its social fabric, by the excitement of its daily movement and affairs, by the amazing variety of occupations and the conveniences the city held the immigrants were persistently attracted. The freedom to develop one's personality without conservative rural constraints was a subtle lure, too, for the immigrants were usually young and still striving for their personal adult status of independence.[35] No other place became such an institutionalized destination as New York, where patterns of ethnic acceptance, association, and subcultural affiliation had long ago become traditional. The experience of emigration itself and all that went with it had become a central feature of New York life, just as it had in Ireland.

New York City was so powerful in its influence that it was its own cultural region. Its attraction for trade and commerce, its political leverage, its leadership in one area after another oriented literally thousands of communities in its hinterlands toward it. Brooklyn, Newark, and Jersey City all had large Irish communities that maintained separate identities while still rotating in the orbit of Manhattan's magnetism, and cities as distant as Rochester and Buffalo related to New York City as well. Upstate Democrats from Utica nominated Francis Kernan for governor in 1872, the first Irish Catholic to be so designated since Thomas Dongan had held the office in colonial times. Kernan was defeated, but the Irish in upstate cities slyly copied Tammany tactics and bided their time.[36] In Albany the machine of Dan O'Connell arose that would utilize the Yankee image of revered Erastus Corning to maintain sway for forty years.

The state capital of Albany was a world of its own. The Irish had a community there in the eighteenth century, but the second half of the nineteenth century saw a stampede of political operators to the city. Whether full-time lobbyists or part-time representatives of Tammany in New York City, they were hardy political animals. Dan O'Connell's local machine in concert with the old Yankee Erastus Corning was an enduring construction lasting two generations. William Kennedy's widely hailed novels portray the seamy life of the city's down-and-outers in unforgettably melancholy terms.[37]

In smaller New York cities like Poughkeepsie the Irish lagged behind in the confusing elaboration of industrial skills needed for family income improvement. Those who were artisans after 1850 faced a diminished chance for self-employment, competition from factory-made goods, and constraints on mobility. In Poughkeepsie three out of four Irish in 1850 were unskilled, but one of every two American-born Irish males was skilled soon after. "For the Irish in the second generation, overwhelmingly sons of unskilled workers, the factory levelled up and so did opportunities in certain building and metal trades." In Buffalo the "leveling up" was slower and the Irish remained on the bottom of the occupational ladder even after decades of residence in the city. It was in the city of Troy where similar conditions existed that socialist James Connolly sought to advance the fortunes of hard-pressed workers, while his own family shared the poverty of the Irish mill district families who did not "level up." Socialist organizing was so unrewarding that Connolly returned to his revolutionary's doom in Ireland in the failed Dublin uprising in 1916. Workers might "level up" in mills and factories, but immigrant Irish were all but excluded from white collar occupations until the end of the nineteenth century.[38]

Northern New Jersey's canals and railroads brought the Irish to the hilly areas beside the Delaware, the flatlands to the south, and the sandy seashore. The model town of Paterson, Alexander Hamilton's dream of a capitalist showplace, was a nineteenth-century community of artisans and textile industry, but the coming of ever more immigrants and the railroad induced larger industry and brought contentious change. The depression of 1873 caused hard times, and workers in the mills went on strike. Joseph P. McDonnell, an Irish-born socialist, came from New York and successfully led the strike. Herbert Gutman has given evidence that more-traditional local businessmen opposed the new big factory owners and were sympathetic toward the strikers. Local political structure was not polarized on a class basis, for local conditions were too complex to permit that.[39]

In Jersey City the anti-Irish sentiment of nativists and Irish conflicts with Germans delayed the immigrants' rise to political power. Between 1857 and 1869, however, Irish-born aldermen took power in the city. Their rule was upset by middle-class Irish reformers, largely American-born, and also Republican native Americans in the 1870s. But Robert Davis, an immigrant from Ireland, led the Democrats until 1911 after that. Then Frank Hague took over and his regime lasted until the 1940s. Jersey City was a classic case of a satellite city long corrupted by railroad and business interests that cultivated the worst kind of ethnic political chicanery. The machine was the instrument not only of greedy ward bosses, but more fundamentally, the corrupt entrepreneurs who could not abide responsible government and law enforcement.[40] In Newark the situation was much the same. Immigrants and native-born working people were family-centered and not civically involved. Family and respite from work superseded politics in the nineteenth century, as consumerism did in the twentieth.[41] Christopher Norwood's judgment on Paterson applies to most industrial satellites of New York: " . . . its history—the neglect, the powerlessness, the corruption, the injustice toward its residents and people and itself as a city—is the history of urbanism in the United States. It would be futile to pretend that this heritage of anomaly, violence and alienation can be erased."[42]

The years after World War I saw the moderation of the Protestant codes that had enfolded American behavior, and nowhere was the "flapper age" released more gaudily than in New York. Prohibition, Jimmy Walker, the "Playboy Mayor," Irish boxers and celebrities, and a whole reckless spirit provided the imagery that glittered above the more homely working-class habits of the city. New York was the nation's entertainment center, and the Irish troupers who had toured for decades were a reservoir of talent for the musicals of George M. Cohan as they had been for those of Victor Herbert. Whole families played the vaudeville and legitimate theater circuit—the Foys, the Fays, and dozens of others. The strictly Irish melodramas and comedies of Dion Boucicault and others were replaced by ''Abie's Irish Rose'' and the new plays imported from Ireland's soaring literary renaissance.

The Irish nationalist organizations were furiously active at this time. Ireland itself was roaring with revolution in its struggle for independence, and an ardent and talented array of Irish-Americans orchestrated an exhilarating campaign to finance, publicize, and take part in the great Sinn Fein struggle for Irish independence. Judge Daniel Cohalen and Judge John W. Goff organized one fund drive after another; tried to advise Eamon de Valera, head of the infant Irish government; and tried to generate sufficient national political pressure to force a reluctant President Woodrow Wilson to recognize the new Irish government. Ancient John Devoy, like an implacable ghost from the haunted Irish past, was still active—agitating, publishing, intriguing, pressing his Fenian dream of the 1860s forward to victory in the 1920s. Because of its money, its still-huge Irish population, and its position at the apex of communications for the country, New York continued to be the culminating point of the American Irish nationalist campaign, but the inevitable factionalism of the complex effort tended to undercut its leadership.

As the automobile came into common use the old ethnic neighborhoods began to filter away. Irish parishes that had been fortresses of faith for a hundred years yielded their populations to the suburbs and the newer areas of the city. The city's Irish, still numbering in the hundreds of thousands, were by now as much a standard part of the city as Central Park and the Chrysler Building. Had they not labored to build the Brooklyn Bridge, the technological symbol of the nineteenth century in the city? Had they not dug its tunnels, policed its streets, sung in its cafes, paraded, danced East Side and West Side, and commanded its political legions for decades? Of all the groups in the city's melange, the Irish saw themselves as preeminent New Yorkers. ''We built it. We won it. We run it!'' was their slogan.

The career of Alfred E. Smith faithfully represented the neighborhood and homely working-class roots of the Irish adjustment to New York. His political ability, his reform of state government, and his espousal of child labor laws strengthened the hold of the Democratic party on lower-class voters and formed a prelude to the New Deal coalition that emerged in the crisis of the Great Depression. Smith could not reconcile Yankee and Protestant opinion with Irish concerns for parish schools, the repeal of blue laws and the rejection of Prohibition. In the 1928 campaign the old gulf between the Catholic Irish and the traditional Protestantism of the country was unbridgeable. New York and Al Smith were too Irish in their urban speech, their association with hordes of immigrants, and their raucous engagement with the cosmopolitan metropolis.

Thomas Wolfe would react to the Hibernian presence in New York as did many visitors viewing "the brutal, heavy figures of the Irish cops, and their beefy faces, filled with the stupid, swift and choleric menaces of privilege and power, shining forth terribly with an almost perverse and sanguinary vitality among the swarming tides of grey faced people."[43] This kind of reaction was scorned, however, by the Irish leaders whose aplomb often verged over into arrogance.

The high tide of Irish power in New York was during the 1920s. Each of the teeming boroughs had an Irish boss: John McCooey in Brooklyn, Maurice Connolly in Queens, Ed Flynn in the Bronx, and George Olvany in Manhattan. The stakes in political dealing were tremendous. Mayor John Hylan fought Governor Al Smith over a $300 million bond issue to eliminate railroad grade crossings, and this was only part of a larger financial and political warfare among Democrats. John J. Glynn, Smith's nephew, and a cavalcade of show business people like composer George M. Cohan, producer James P. Sinnott, and actor William Halligan added flair to the campaign of Jimmy Walker, and the playboy lawyer became mayor in 1926, only to leave office amid indictments for thievery and tales of personal folly.

New York was the perfect reverberation of the Roaring Twenties, and it drew its luminaries from all over the country. Jack Kearns brought Jack Dempsey to town to prepare for the championship fight at Boyle's Flats over in Jersey. John McGraw presided over epic baseball teams at Coogan's Bluff. Texas Guinan ran the hottest night club in town. Detective Johnny Broderick stalked Legs Diamond there after Diamond threatened to kill him. Storied saloons like Shannon's at Seventy-sixth Street and Third Avenue and McSorley's near the Bowery had to close during Prohibition, but speak-easys quickly opened everywhere. One newspaperman wrote that "the old days when father spent his evenings at Cassidy's with the boys are gone . . . since prohibition mother goes down with him." Catholic newspapers complained of jazz dancing in which " . . . the music is sensuous; the embracing—the female is only half dressed—is absolutely indecent."[44]

One effect of the 1920s was to further exorcize Irish-American cultural conservatism. The wilder spirits held in check by priest and propriety were set free amid frenzied prosperity and publicity. The old country ways had to coexist with the new excitement. Bernarr McFadden's lurid *True Story* magazine titillated millions, while John McCormack sang decorously at Carnegie Hall. The radio voice of Graham McNamee reported gangster crime daily, while stock manipulator Michael Meehan conducted RCA stock from 85 to 549 in one year. Newspapermen like Clarke Fitzpatrick and James J. Cain recorded the gossip and raucous energy of it all. The panorama was bizarre and irrepressible as it headed for the disaster of the Wall Street Crash of 1929, and the Irish were part of the zany circus at every level.

The decrease of immigration in the 1920s and the stifling effect of Prohibition on Irish associations whose functions featured drinking were harbingers of decline. The Depression of the 1930s dashed the hopes of thousands of families and further eroded neighborhood life. Multitudes of Irish were still caught in low-level jobs, such as the Transport Workers' Union members led by fiery Mike Quill who were still battling for a forty-hour week in 1950.[45] The economy revived during World War II, but the old sovereignty of Irish politics, church, and organizational life was coming apart. In the great migration to New Jersey, Long Island, and the counties north of New York City, new associations of Irish would be formed in the 1950s and 1960s, but the old mold was broken. Carmine De Sapio in Manhattan, Meade Esposito in Brooklyn, and Mayor John V. Lindsay would lead politics away from Irish dominance after Mayo-born Mayor William O'Dwyer had to take himself to Mexico to avoid prosecution for irregularities during his term in office. The precincts over which Ed Flynn had presided in the Bronx became increasingly the turf of Blacks and Puerto Ricans. The Irish grudgingly withdrew. The demographic process that had provided the Irish power base initially was now working against them as other multitudes took their place.

The decade of the 1970s saw the working out of those turbulent trends that eroded the social basis on which the New York Irish community had grounded itself for generations. These trends were much broader than the city itself, so they affected the suburban Irish families in the metropolitan area and echoed back from the nationwide arena through the mass media and the critical echelons that had so much influence in New York. A youth revolt in the 1960s, the religious changes affecting Catholicism after Vatican Council II, the continued population changes in the city, and the ethnic succession occurring in neighborhoods, schools, the police force, politics, and labor unions all dismantled Irish hegemonies of local power. In the 1970s New York's congressional delegation still included men named Murphy, Delaney, Rooney, Carey, Buckley, and Ryan, but Carey, Buckley, and Ryan were very different from the old Tammany warhorses. They were from wealthy backgrounds and Buckley was a strident conservative Republican. Robert Kennedy had been U.S. Senator for the state of New York, and his personality—intent, brusque, and oriented toward mainstream national affairs—typified the transition of throngs of educated Irish to national areas of professional and political concern.

The power of the New York Irish in clerical garb was actively employed by Francis Cardinal Spellman, a calculating, assertive, and controversial churchman. His intrusions into public affairs and his behind-the-scenes intrigues to influence high policy were successes of the moment. When political administrations changed and old policies became riddled with failure, Spellman's role, when revealed, redounded to his discredit. His support for the Vietnam War, collaboration with shady American intelligence schemes, opposition to church reforms after the Vatican Council, and other involvements produced strong negative reactions. As the church leader foremost among the Irish-Americans until his death in 1967, his demise and the diminution of the kinds of opinions he stood for were part of the decline of the New York Irish.[46]

The bitter hatreds of Northern Ireland that erupted in violence in 1969 did have an activating effect on the diminished Irish community in the metropolis, especially on those born in Northern Ireland, but the Irish Northern Aid organization that became the chief vehicle for militant support of nationalist dissidents in the north of Ireland was not able to do more than maintain a thin network across the country from its headquarters in the Bronx. It could occasionally break through in the national media, but it was unable to mobilize broad Irish-American or other affiliations for its agitation against British rule in Northern Ireland. Journalists such as Pete Hamill and Jimmy Breslin wrote articles and books about the issue, but most Irish politicians maintained a careful stance supporting vague peaceful intentions for Northern Ireland. Senator Daniel P. Moynihan stated that many Irish-Americans were highly informed about the problem, but there was only a minimal intellectual, organizational, and political response to it over more than a decade of violence and publicity. Irish-American nationalist activity had never involved the larger portion of the Irish in the United States, but the response to the Northern Ireland issue was limited due to the decline of Irish immigrant numbers, the preoccupation of the group with mainstream matters of special American significance (such as the Vietnam War), and the ambiguity of both Irish and American leadership in their statements and actions about the issue.[47]

The analysis of this recession of the New York Irish by Nathan Glazer and Daniel P. Moynihan in the 1960s focused on their loss of political power and the passing of the dominance of the Catholic Church in New York's life, but it also attributes the transfer of power to a fading of Irish nationalism and a lack of Irish cultural influence from abroad. There is a rueful, almost reproachful note in the account, a suggestion of Irish failure, especially in contrast to the city's Jews whose ubiquitous prominence in cultural life and whose ardent support of Israel contrasted so strongly with the general Irish-American preoccupation with other matters and their bemused attitude toward Ireland after the crisis of the Northern Ireland disorders in 1969. The Glazer-Moynihan critique, however, is tendentious. Given the demographic and social changes overtaking New York in the second half of this century, a retention of Irish preeminence would have been very unlikely in the American system of ethnic succession that they themselves had pioneered. The Glazer-Moynihan account does assert that "Irish consciousness would seem to be holding its own in the upper reaches of business as well as the intellectual sphere."[48] This comment points to the very important growth of a new, more perceptive Irish-American perspective related to the literature, development problems, and cultural heritage of Ireland, as well as to a studied concern for resolution of the Northern Ireland problem during the 1970s.

John Higham has written that "all American ethnic groups perpetuate themselves, but none survives intact."[49] For the Irish of New York City to be "intact," some cultural definition of the original or modal character of the group would have to be maintained. But the vast career of the Irish in the metropolis on the Hudson is simply too diverse, too complex to be confined to one period's social and cultural formulation. The historic extent and character of the New York Irish tradition provided evidence that the tradition has taken various forms, and the

changes after the 1960s are simply part of the pattern of ascendency and de-
volution of ethnic change that is inherent in the life of democratic society.

Although the older Irish institutions in the city were fading, the Consulate of
the Irish Republic was still active around the corner from St. Patrick's Cathedral,
and the Bank of Ireland and Allied Irish Banks opened branches in the city. The
Irish-American Historical Society was still ensconced in dignity on Fifth Avenue
across from Central Park, and the Irish airline, *Aer Lingus*, did brisk business
year after year. By 1980 there was a whole new cultural network in place with
an Irish Arts Center, a scattering of Irish bookstores, a booming circuit of folk
musicians giving concerts and recording, and a constant play of literary and
theater commentary and study. It complemented the shrinking but still lively
immigrant circuit. What had emerged was an Irish network focused not on local
politics and immigrant needs, but on the historical and cultural tradition of the
group. It was a weak network, overly associated with academic specialists, but
it was a promising and keenly motivated interaction of interested and even
dedicated people.

The increased ease of travel and communication probably assures that the
Irish will maintain a distinct place in the polyglot life of New York. An artery
of stimulation between Ireland and the city had been kept alive through the entire
history of the country. The Irish had been in daily intercourse with Jews, Germans, Italians, and others in the city in a complex trial of ethnic dealing that
had placed them prominently in the minority spectrum of urban life. As con-
tenders for prestige and power they had entered the democratic gallery of achievers. They had launched a plethora of ambitious careers in finance, cultural
attainment, and public life from New York. The Irish in the city adopted the
dialect, the resilient spirit, and the no-nonsense drive of the place. They were
by the 1980s a confirmed, accomplished, and persistent part of its imagery. And
the imagery included not only the glamour and success of the high achievers,
but the arduous course of the wage-earning Irish still captured in the toils of the
megalopolis with all its trauma and frustration.[50] While some lived in the bright
lights of Broadway, others lived in cavernous shadows of the nation's greatest
city.

For generations New York above all American localities *was* America for the
Irish. Its images of urban romance, success, and brassy vitality seemed to sym-
bolize the excitement of America. Through its economy and educational networks
they could and did rise. As a center of communications it afforded them extraordinary opportunities. As the apex of towering city life it provided its residents
with assurance that they were equal thereafter to any other city and almost any
experience. It was this transforming consciousness that gave the New York Irish
a special edge, a particular cultural thrust that could not be enjoyed by those in
other places. New York was America in roaring exultation, America in super-
charged profusion. For those who succeeded, at least, Manhattan became like
the mythic wonder island of St. Brendan's vision, the Land of Heart's Desire,
where novelty and plenty titillated life.

NOTES

1. Daniel Hosmander, *The New York Conspiracy*, ed. Thomas J. Davis (Boston: Beacon Press, 1971), pp. 415–416; William Harper Bennett, *Catholic Footsteps in Old New York* (New York: United States Catholic Historical Society, 1973), pp. 250–288.

2. Raymond A. Mohl, "Poverty in Colonial New York City," in Raymond A. Mohl and Neil Betten, eds., *Urban America in Historical Perspective* (New York: Weybright and Talley, 1970), pp. 79–90.

3. Robert Ernst, *Immigrant Life in New York City, 1825–1863* (New York: King's Crown Press, 1949), pp. 48–60; Harvey Strum, "Federalist Hibernophobes in New York, 1807," *Eire-Ireland* 16, no. 4 (Winter 1981): 7–13.

4. George F. Scheer and Hugh F. Rankin, *Rebels and Redcoats* (New York: World Publishing Co., 1957), p. 161.

5. William V. Shannon, *The American Irish: A Political and Social Portrait* (New York: The Macmillan Co., 1963), p. 31.

6. Alexander C. Flick, *Loyalism in New York during the American Revolution* (New York: Columbia University Press, 1901), p. 292; Robert McClues Calhoon, *The Loyalists in Revolutionary America, 1760–81* (New York: Harcourt, Brace, Javanovich, 1965), p. 412.

7. David Noel Doyle, *Ireland, Irishmen and Revolutionary America 1760–1820* (Cork, Ireland: The Mercier Press, 1981), p. 132.

8. Howard Zinn, *A People's History of the United States* (New York: Harper and Row, 1980), p. 83.

9. Ibid., p. 98.

10. Ernst, *Immigrant Life in New York City*, pp. 120–24. The poor were chided for "unthriftiness" in not saving in summer for winter firewood in an early *General Meeting to Enable the Poor to Guard against Distress* (n.p., 1831), pamphlet in the collection of the Historical Society of Pennsylvania. New York Pamphlets. John H. Griscom, *The Sanitary Conditions of the Laboring Poor of New York* (New York: J. Griscom, 1865), p. 13.

11. Lee Harvey Benson, *The Concept of Jacksonian Democracy: New York as a Test Case* (Princeton, N.J.: Princeton University Press, 1961), pp. 187–190.

12. Ibid., pp. 317–328. The religious fuel for much of the political controversy of the time is described by Ray Allen Billington, *The Protestant Crusade, 1800–1860* (Chicago: University of Chicago Press, 1964), pp. 93–103.

13. Ira Marshall Leonard, "New York City Politics, 1841–1844: Nativism and Reform" (Ph.D. diss. New York University, 1965), pp. 370–371.

14. The character of this immigration can be reviewed in detail in Ira Glazier, ed., *The Famine Immigrants: Lists of Irish Immigrants Arriving at the Port of New York, 1846–1851*, 6 vols. (Baltimore: Geneological Publishing Co., 1982-); Oliver Mac-Donough, "Irish Famine Emigration to the United States," *Perspectives in American History* 10 (1976): 357–448; Richard Leach, "The Impact of Immigration upon New York, 1840–60," *New York History* 31, no. 1 (January 1950): 15–30.

15. Seymour Mandelbaum, *Boss Tweed's New York* (New York: John Wiley and Sons, 1965), p. 6; Alexander Callow, *The Tweed Ring* (New York: Oxford University Press, 1965), p. 75.

16. Callow, *The Tweed Ring*, pp. 58, 133.

17. George B. McClellan, Jr., *The Gentleman and the Tiger*, ed., Harold C. Syrett (Philadelphia and New York: J. B. Lippincott Co., 1956), pp. 19, 87, 93, 164, 266.

18. David C. Hammack, *Power and Society: Greater New York at the Turn of the Century* (New York: Russell Sage Foundation, 1982), pp. 315 and 352.

19. Ibid., p. 69, Map 3–3, Tables 3–1 and 3–2.

20. *The Irish Nation* (New York) (September 22 to October 22, 1883).

21. Ibid. (September 9, 1883).

22. Bayrd Still, *Mirror for Gotham: New York as Seen by Contemporaries from Dutch Days to the Present* (New York: New York University Press, 1956), pp. 196–197.

23. Ibid., p. 204.

24. John T. Ridge, *The Flatbush Irish* (Brooklyn: Division 35, Ancient Order of Hibernians, 1983), pp. 6–11.

25. Charlotte O'Brien, "The Emigrant in New York," *Nineteenth Century* 16 (1884): 530–549; Still, *Mirror for Gotham*, p. 243; Jacob Riis, *How the Other Half Lives* (New York: Young People's Missionary Society, 1890), pp. 243–254.

26. Jay Dolan, *The Immigrant Church: New York's Irish and German Catholics, 1815–1865* (Baltimore: Johns Hopkins University Press, 1975), pp. 45–67; Thomas F. O'Dea, *Sociology and the Study of Religion* (New York: Basic Books, 1970), pp. 75–76.

27. Archetype of the revolutionary, John Devoy, intrigued in New York from 1866 to 1926. Robert Kee, *The Green Flag*, 3 vols. (London: Quartet Books, 1979), vol. 2, pp. 71–72; William Leonard Joyce, *Editors and Ethnicity: A History of the Irish-American Press, 1848–1883* (New York: Arno Press, 1976), Introduction. Lawyers were a usual part of this cadre. Terence J. McManus, "A Few Outstanding Figures at the Bench and Bar in New York City," *Journal of the American Irish Historical Society* 23 (1924): 101–114.

28. Thomas N. Brown, *Irish-American Nationalism, 1870–1890* (Philadelphia: J. B. Lippincott Co., 1966), pp. 17–42; Florence E. Gibson, *The Attitudes of the New York Irish toward State and National Affairs, 1848–1892* (New York: Columbia University Press, 1981), p. 451.

29. The chief New York Irish newspapers were *The Irish World* (1870-   ) and *The Gaelic American* (1903–57), although *The Nation* (1848–49), *The Citizen* (1854–57), and *The New York Freeman's Journal* (1863–66) were also important.

30. John A. Murphy, "The Influence of America on Irish Nationalism," in David Noel Doyle and Owen Dudley Edwards, eds., *America and Ireland, 1776–1976: The American Identity and the Irish Connection* (Westport, Conn.: Greenwood Press, 1980), pp. 105–116.

31. Philip Foner, "Radicalism in the Gilded Age: The Land League in Irish-America," *Marxist Perspectives* (Summer 1978): 6–55; James F. Donnelly, "Catholic New Yorkers and New York Socialists, 1870–1920" (Ph.D. diss., New York University, 1982), pp. 86, 183–218; John D. Buenker, *Urban Liberalism and Progressive Reform* (New York: Charles Scribner's Sons, 1973), p. 213.

32. Moses Rischin, *The Promised City: New York's Jews, 1870–1914* (New York: Corinth Books, 1962), p. 263; Will Balsamo and George Carpozi, *Always Kill a Brother* (New York: Dell Publishing Co., 1977), pp.9–16; Gilbert Osofsky, *Harlem, The Making of a Ghetto: Negro New York, 1890–1930* (New York: Harper and Row, 1966), pp. 45–46.

33. Oscar Handlin, *The American People in the Twentieth Century* (Boston: Beacon Press, 1954), p. 121; Mandelbaum, *Boss Tweed's New York*, p. 133.

34. John Corry, *Golden Clan: The Murrays, the McDonnells and the Irish-American Aristocracy* (Boston: Houghton Mifflin Co., 1977), pp. 10–11, 48–49, 175–178.

35. Robert Goldston, *New York: Civic Exploitation* (New York: The Macmillan Co., 1970), pp. 115–142.

36. Florence E. Gibson, *The Attitudes of the New York Irish toward State and National Affairs, 1848–1892* (New York: Columbia University Press, 1951), pp. 288–289.

37. William Kennedy, *O Albany: An Urban Tapestry* (New York: Viking Press, 1983), pp. 1–53, 327–356.

38. Clyde and Sally Griffin, *Natives and Newcomers: The Ordering of Opportunity in Mid-Nineteenth Century Poughkeepsie* (Cambridge: Harvard University Press, 1978), pp. 59–70, 258–259; Desmond Greaves, *The Life and Times of James Connolly* (New York: International Publishers, 1961), pp. 168–199; Laurence Glasco, "The Life Cycles and Household Structure of American Ethnic Groups: Irish, Germans and Native-born Whites in Buffalo, New York, 1855," *Journal of Urban History* 1, no. 3 (May 1975): 339–364.

39. Herbert G. Gutman, *Work, Culture and Society in Industrializing America: Essays in American Working Class and Social History* (New York: Random House, 1977), pp. 234–259.

40. Douglas V. Shaw, *The Making of an Immigrant City: Ethnic and Cultural Conflict in Jersey City, New Jersey, 1850–1877* (New York: Arno Press, 1976), pp. 140–185.

41. Susan Hirsch, *Roots of the American Working Class: The Industrialization of Crafts in Newark, 1800–1860* (Philadelphia: University of Pennsylvania Press, 1978), p. 122.

42. Christopher Norwood, *About Paterson: The Making and Unmaking of an American City* (New York: Harper and Row, 1974), p. 256.

43. Thomas Wolfe, *Of Time and the River: A Legend of a Man's Hunger in His Youth* (New York: C. Scribner's, 1935), p. 416. An excellent insight into the hard life of the New York Irish worker is given by Michael Donohue, *An Oral History: Starting Off from Dead End* (New York: Community Documentation Workshop, 1980). Depletion of the older Irish communities is recorded in "Inwood Is Losing Its Brogue . . . ," *New York Times* (August 18, 1984).

44. Frederick Lewis Allen, *Only Yesterday: An Informal History of the 1920s* (New York: Harper and Brothers, 1931), pp. 90, 91. Gene Fowler, *Beau James: The Life and Times of Jimmy Walker* (Clifton, N.J.: Augustus M. Kelley, Publisher, 1973), pp. 126 and 315.

45. Shirley Quill, *Mike Quill Himself: A Memoir* (Greenwich, Conn.: Devin-Adair, Inc., 1985), pp. 66–85; Ronald H. Bayor, *Neighbors in Conflict: The Irish, Germans, Jews and Italians of New York City, 1929–1941* (Baltimore: Johns Hopkins University Press, 1978), pp. 37, 87–126.

46. John Cooney, *The American Pope* (New York: Times Books, 1984), passim.

47. Dennis Clark, *Irish Blood: Northern Ireland and the American Conscience* (Port Washington, N.Y.: Kennikat Press, 1976), pp. 29–40.

48. Nathan Glazer and Daniel P. Moynihan, *Beyond the Melting Pot: The Negroes, Puerto Ricans, Jews, Italians and Irish of New York City* (Cambridge: The MIT Press, 1970), p. 254.

49. John Higham, *Send These to Me: Jews and Other Immigrants in Urban America* (New York: Atheneum, 1975), p. 234.

50. Richard Rogin, "Joe Kelly Has Reached His Boiling Point," *New York Times* (June 28, 1970); Patrick Fenton, "The Brooklyn Irish Quit the Democrats," *New York Times* (October 16, 1984).

6 OFF TO PHILADELPHIA— PENNSYLVANIA

Thin Indian trails were the only human tracings upon the sylvan expanses that clothed the hills, and eons-worn mountains ranged beyond the placid Delaware. This land of glacial plains, rows of blue-green mountain chains, and stream-nourished valleys was the meeting place of the New England cold and the Virginia warmth. William Penn's proprietary lay across a geography full of features that would contradict the Quaker founder's charter. His vision of peace was hemmed in by Iroquois ferocity and French colonial ambition. His seventeenth-century plantation of little regular green plots with a red brick utopian town was a meager intrusion at the edge of wild reaches of wolf-prowled forest and panther-guarded peaks above the turbulent rivers in the interior. Penn, the sedate Londoner, would have to be succeeded by men like Daniel Boone before the traverse of this "sylvania" would be made safe. The orderly Quakers would remain in the pleasant precincts by the Delaware, while other groups homesteaded the wilderness. This was the first circumstance among many that would assure Pennsylvania a pattern of ethnic diversity that would distinctively characterize the state.

Penn's commonwealth held a position from earliest colonial times that made it a fulcrum for American development. Geographically it had Philadelphia as a fine egress to the Atlantic and at its western edge the Ohio River flowed to the heart of the continent. Politically it could balance Yankee acuteness against Southern leadership and add a variegated set of interests—ethnic, religious, and intellectual—that were embodied in the state itself. But almost from the outset its role was compromised by the very variations it contained and by antagonisms it could not reconcile.

Quakers, English and Welsh, had spent time as refugees from royal disfavor and Church of England hostility in Ireland. Penn himself had lived on his father's estates in Cork. For all of the contact he had with the Gaels whose lands he then occupied, he might as well have been resident on the moon. In only two places in his Irish diary does he speak of them, once concerning a former landowner who was uncomfortably nearby and another time to complain of the Irish who stole his wood.[1] He was at pains later to argue strenuously that he was not linked to Catholics, for the venomous religious disputes of the times confused Quakers and others, and radical though Penn could be, he was not so radical as to be thought a Papist.

Philadelphia was Penn's great enterprise and his instructions to those choosing a site for the Jerusalem of the Friends were that it include a deep water port. Like the other great seaboard centers it was to be an English maritime foundation. The plan of the city, so often extolled as a far-sighted design of handsome order and bucolic amplitude, was simply a seventeenth-century colonization town plot without the usual military palisades and blockhouses. The Quaker apostle of peace used the standard military camp plan as old as the Romans. This he obtained from Thomas Holme who had plotted the town site for Waterford in Ireland, for Ireland was the immediate colonial place of experiment from which many American designs were derived.[2]

Penn's religious tolerance laid the groundwork for the immigration policy that would lead to the colony's diversity. German pietists, Sephardic Jews, Lutherans, Baptists, and Scotch-Irish Presbyterians debarked at Philadelphia. James Logan, Penn's agent, himself a North of Ireland man, found his Ulster confreres to be more difficult than all the others, and this confirmed what was to become an enduring factor in public opinion: Irish was Irish and they were to be treated warily, and the group's own distinctions of religion were not broadly germane. They were God-fearing, but they feared little else. With the good land in the rolling country of southeastern Pennsylvania already in Quaker hands, they moved to the frontier in the Tuscarora mountains and beyond. Having lived in hostility with the Irish Catholics whom they had displaced in Ulster, they were inured to vigilance and defensive preparedness. The Irish wars of the 1640s were a living memory. As a result they adapted readily to the atmosphere of isolation and danger palpable on the Indian-menaced frontier. This was the first penetration from Ireland of the green fastness of Pennsylvania, and the Scotch-Irish settlements would have very significant implications for the state and the nation in the future. Their villages of Donegal, Bangor, and Tyrone in the mountains would have a special role as the seedbeds of frontier spirit as more and more people left impoverished Ulster in the eighteenth century.

As these settlements reached out across Pennsylvania, what they created was a trail to the Ohio River, which in turn was the route to the heartland, the Mississippi, and also the immense mountain spine of the eastern half of the country. Because of their early foundations, the Scotch-Irish had access to the mountain frontier, and as an identifiable group they became the prototypes of its settlers. The restless exploration, rustic character, bitter struggles with the Indians, and distrust of authority all came to typify in the American mind the frontier experience, and this group contributed strongly to this imagery. In the French and Indian War, in thousands of lonely skirmishes, and in the war of the Revolution the Scotch-Irish vindicated their fighting qualities. From New

England to Tennessee they created the legend, but Pennsylvania was preeminently the entry place for the frontier career of the group. As agitators for freedom from government constraints and as partisans of westward expansion they would have a strategic effect upon the American revolutionary endeavor. Frontier democrats, they were constantly at odds with the seaboard merchant leaders and the plantation magnates of the older settled areas.[3]

If the Scotch-Irish and Germans moved quickly to occupy the splendid farm land of Lancaster County, the Irish Catholics were rarely so fortunate. They appear intermittently in all kinds of roles. James Fitzpatrick, alias "Sandy Flash," lurked in Castle Rock Cave in Chester County in 1778 where he pursued a career as a highwayman, described by his victims as "tall, broad-shouldered, of enormous strength, yet notedly active and swift of foot, hair bright red." Others were not predatory but vulnerable. An indentured Irish girl was to be sold away to God knows where in this strange country, and Irishmen at the Du Pont powder works near Philadelphia took up a collection to buy her freedom. Bernard McMahon became a gardener and botanist in Philadelphia and made his name a household word by publishing what became the country's most popular gardening manual. John Neagle painted portraits of the well-to-do to be hung in the fine houses on the hills above the Schuylkill River. Although the Irish-born were only five percent of the Pennsylvania population in 1790, they were a larger group if both Irish-born and those of Irish stock are counted because of the cumulative effect of their in-migration, and their influence continued to grow. How many there were who were runaway servants and other marginal inhabitants of the backlands we cannot know.

Those Irish first served by French missionary priests were very scattered. In Philadelphia the first Catholic church was St. Joseph's founded in 1733, built on land purchased by subterfuge to avoid undue attention to the Papist presence. A church at Harris Ferry (Harrisburg) in 1729 drew riverboat men. By 1796 missions existed at McGuire's Station above Altoona and at St. Mary's in Elk County. It was only in 1801 that a Catholic church was set up at Fort Pitt. In 1810 Bishop Michael Egan, an Irish Franciscan resident in Philadelphia, began to administer to this far-flung flock. Pittsburgh did not have its first bishop until 1843 when Rev. Michael O'Connor was called from the Irish College in Rome to shoulder the task.[4]

The American Revolution provided the opportunity for the assertion of Irish influence upon the country's formative years, and in Pennsylvania there were numerous candidates ready to undertake this role. In the upstate wilderness areas there were the restive Presbyterians. In Philadelphia there were merchants, soldier adventurers, and gentleman agitators, most of whom bore a powerful animus toward England as a result of their Irish family histories.[5] The Quaker elite tended to be conservative and propertied. Set against them were the interest groups intent upon revolution. Richard Alan Ryerson has summarized the situation:

Philadelphia before 1765 was a pluralistic community in which political power was concentrated in a few of its many ethnic, religious and economic groups. In the next decade, the city was assaulted by an outside power that its political and mercantile elites neither would nor could check. In the course of building a broadly based political movement that could counter British authority in the early 1770's, Philadelphia radical leaders created the prototype of a modern American urban party.

Immigrants became far more prominent in the city and in Pennsylvania than they had ever been before.[6] The Catholic George Meade, John Mease, Thomas Fitz Simons, John Barry, Stephen Moylan, and Ulysses Lynch, plus a solid phalanx of Scotch-Irish, all members of the Society of the Friendly Sons of St. Patrick founded in 1771, were active politically or militarily in the revolution. In addition, those Irish who came to Philadelphia from other areas of the country, such as Gen. John Sullivan, Washington's aide John Fitzgerald, Charles Carroll, and others, were part of that overseas fraternity that sprang from Ireland.[7] The British attributed their American troubles to Irish disaffection, often overestimating Irish influence, but the Revolution did more than any event of the eighteenth century to heighten respect for the Irish in America.

The Irish in Philadelphia, both Protestant and Catholic, emerged from the Revolution with a keen political orientation. Thomas McKean became governor of the state, and Blair McClenahan, Thomas Fitz Simons, and Sharp Delany became very active in the city's politics. The revolutionary generation basked in the eminence of Philadelphia as the scene of the drama that had created the nation. Theobold Wolfe Tone and Hamilton Rowan journeyed from Dublin to spend time in the city to study the marvels of republican liberty that were forbidden to Ireland. By 1790 there were about 4,000 Irish in the city and each year 3,000 more debarked in Philadelphia, half of all the aliens entering the city. These formed an opportune audience not only for cultivation of an Irish voting bloc in the city, but for the activities of the United Irishmen, the conspiratorial organization of Protestants and Catholics who were bent on acting out the ideals of the French Revolution in Ireland. Their refuges overseas, especially after their failed uprising of 1798, included Philadelphia. A branch of the organization was meeting in Philadelphia in 1797, and disturbed conservatives called them "United Dagger-Men." Two professors at the University of Pennsylvania—publisher and author Mathew Carey, and Dr. James Reynolds—and a network of others were all involved.[8]

When the panicky Federalists passed the Alien and Sedition Acts aimed at cowing immigrant agitators, the United Irishmen circulated petitions in front of churches in the city in 1799 and a riot erupted in front of St. Mary's Church. The Irish, primed by their own backgrounds in Ireland and the hot rhetoric of the United Irishmen, were offended by the Federalists and became ardent advocates of the Jeffersonian Republicans.[9] The tradition of radical politics with which they identified, however, was to become incompatible with the growing wealth, power, and conservative forces that were being consolidated in the city. Of all the states of the original thirteen, Pennsylvania was the one that most reflected the coming industrial age of America, for it was able to overcome its transportation barriers with canals and railroads, and it was a treasure house of forest products, bountiful agriculture, and coal and other minerals. Very early government was placed at the service of the enterprises exploiting this abundance. The restless immigrants and those who took too literally the revolutionary tenets of the eighteenth century had to be controlled, and Philadelphia, a growing and disorderly city, had to exemplify this control.

By the 1820s the Irish numbered heavily among the poor in the city. Priscilla Clement concludes:

The response of Philadelphians . . . was to blame the immorality of the poor and the inefficiency of welfare officials for the rising cost of public relief . . . the object was to make the city's welfare board more efficient and more strict in dealing with the poor . . . repressive measures were taken: cash aid to the indigent was eliminated and all who sought public aid were required to enter the almshouse.[10]

This had been and continued to be the regimen invoked when unemployment and poverty increased in the city.

As industrialization came to the city, such trades as hand loom weaving were slowly and painfully diminished, and the Irish were prominent in this trade. But sailors, coal heavers, and dockers all suffered in the economic downturn of 1837. Those in the sewing and garment trades became part of a low-wage, long-hours occupational treadmill that would use one immigrant group after another in a most oppressive industry. However, the chief problem of the city's Irish in terms of labor was that they were not part of the rapidly developing factory system. They were part of the expendable unskilled work force that was at the disposal of the economy in almost whimsical fashion. After a strike by coal heavers on the docks of the Schuylkill River in 1835 and 1836, the strikers' jobs were given to scabs. Violence ensued and Mayor John Swift leveled fines of $2,500 on the strikers arrested, although the fines were eventually suspended. Four in ten of the Irish were hod carriers, carters, stevedores, draymen, and casual laborers. These were largely shut out of the emerging factory system, and it would be another generation before they got a foothold in the mills and manufacturing plants where the skills of the new machine age were to be learned.[11] This initial handicap was partly attributable, in the view of Bruce Laurie, to the traditionalism of people from a rural background. So was the lack of widespread radical thinking among the new immigrants coming into the city. The Catholic Church was a strong moderating influence in this regard. Having escaped from the horrors of famine Ireland, it is quite possible that the group limited its aspirations and was quite prepared to settle for minimal conditions until the trauma of the famine experience was healed.

Perhaps it was this experience of not sharing in the early phases of industrial work life that gave the Philadelphia Irish a strong sense of separateness. In 1844 riots variously described as anti-Catholic and anti-Irish erupted in the city accompanied by killings, house burning, and the destruction of two Catholic churches.[12] Martial law was declared, and the incidents left the Irish with abiding feelings of victimization. The local Catholics had just recovered from the damages of an acrimonious internal religious schism when the riots and nativist agitation placed them in a beleaguered position, and then the influx of famine refugees began. For a group that had seen itself as heir to a notable record in the American Revolution and that had contributed distinguished intellectual leaders like publisher Mathew Carey and litterateur Robert Walsh to the city, the nativist rebuff cut deep. As in New York the Irish adhered to the Democrats, but with the coming of the Civil War, that party became tainted with the stigma of treason because of its attachment to the South. These factors turned the group in upon itself. The Irish did not become less energetic, for they were the great labor resource of what had grown to be the country's paramount industrial center, but they turned their energies into their own subculture and built a parallel set of Irish Catholic institutions that would eventually embrace a greater proportion of the Irish population than in Boston or New York.[13]

Philadelphia was much larger than Boston, more diverse economically than New York, and less oppressive in its neighborhood life than either. Through their own thrift organizations the Irish abetted the residential expansion of the city and laid upon it a fabric of parish and organizational life that was highly active. As families progressed out of poverty, they did not renounce Irish identity. They cultivated it at different levels. Dale Light's study of the organizational network of the group in the second half of the nineteenth century reveals a burgeoning thicket of Irish associations that ran from the poorest aggregations of mutual benefit organizations to elite clubs for successful business and professional men.[14] In Philadelphia the same kind of social base for ethnic life was created as in other centers, but it was more intent upon its own proximate goals, more devoted to its own identity, and less disposed toward the intermingling characteristic of New York or the combative elan that animated the Boston Irish. The Philadelphia Irish were less direct, more devious, and more calculatedly intent on their own precincts than their counterparts elsewhere.

If there was more housing opportunity and a more diversified economy in the city, the Irish did well to construct a social network of their own, for the dominant elite in the community were hautily separatist, repressive, and eager foes of labor organizations that challenged harsh industrial regimes.[15] The politics of Philadelphia were ardently Republican, initially as a legacy of the victory and prestige of the Republican party after the Civil War. The city's politics for generations really were shaped by the tremendous resources of the Republicans at the state level. Railroads, steel, and commerce in the state had leadership proud of its Ulster Presbyterian background, and this included the vastly wealthy Mellon family in Pittsburgh and Franklin B. Gowen, president of the Philadelphia and Reading Railroad, as well as such artful schemers as Simon Cameron. These men regarded the Philadelphia wards as plantations where the people could be directed at will to vote as they were told. As a result, Philadelphia's politics were left in the hands of a continuously corrupt clique of obedient manipulators, beginning with Scotch-Irish Jimmy McManes in the 1870s.[16]

There did arise, however, a prototypical urban boss whose career would embrace half of the century. William McMullen held public offices from 1856 until his death in 1901. He was the arch-populist Democrat, durable leader of the turbulent Irish wards of the city. Carpenter, street fighter, printer, and saloon keeper, he led fire companies and election day brawls for decades. His service in the Mexican War gave him his first celebrity which led to his election as alderman. Through two generations of political combat he led his South Philadelphia Irish adherents in thousands of schemes and stratagems to force their way into a city government that did its best to exclude them.[17]

Irish Catholics could rise in this situation only so far, so that a succession of them within the Republican ranks accepted second-rate status in return for circumscribed local power. Lewis Cassidy, E. Tracy Tobin, Michael J. O'Callaghan, and others were tame performers. It was not until construction contractor James "Sunny Jim" McNichol arose in the late 1890s that any serious Irish Catholic challenge appeared for leadership in the Republican party, and McNichol never won the field.[18]

Philadelphia was a worrisome concern for Abraham Lincoln early in the Civil War. Many of its socialite leaders had family and business ties to the South. The 100,000 Irish-born and the great majority of other Irish in the city were not happy with the prospect of slave emancipation which would mean more competition for unskilled employment. The idea of being drafted into a Union army that seemed to be losing most of its battles was not inspiring, in spite of the enlistment bonuses that lured young men into uniform. Irish Democrats were not too quick to make common cause with Republicans who were led by stridently anti-Catholic New England abolitionists. Philadelphia was the industrial arsenal for the Union, a key port and rail center, and the great marshaling center behind the Union lines. Baltimore mobs had stoned Union troops, so the stability of Philadelphia was crucial.

Conferences with Union supporters in the city led to a mass meeting at the Academy of Music addressed by lawyer Daniel Dougherty, a Democrat and one of the founders of the Union league. Dougherty gave a magnificent oratorical performance to the heavily Irish audience and brought it to its feet with ringing cheers for the Union cause.[19] Thereafter, enlistments rose and the Irish became committed to the Union, so much so that the 116th Pennsylvania Regiment was one of the hardest-fighting units Lincoln had. It was the Irish in this unit who held the bloody angle in the climax of battle at Gettysburg when Robert E. Lee sought to cut through to strategic Philadelphia in a last bid for victory. The Irish sacrifices at Antietam, Fredericksburg, and Gettysburg should have stilled nativist fears about the loyalty of the group, but they did not. The military deeds did create for the Irish a fervent patriotic heritage that was extolled endlessly for the rest of the nineteenth century.[20]

Enmeshed in the war were thousands of young Irishmen who became the objects of a recruitment effort by the Fenian Brotherhood. The revolutionary group was headed in the city by printer James Gibbons, and it was defended against the censure of Archbishop James Wood by Rev. P. J. Moriarty, a fiery Augustinian priest. Gibbons and his cohorts were in touch with the branches of the organization in the Union army and in New York and other cities. Volunteers were drilled, arms were purchased, and schemes to foment an uprising in Ireland were devised that sent former Union officers from the city to Ireland, but the plan failed. Still, the underground effort stimulated the nationalist circles in Philadelphia. They had been active since before the Rising of 1798 and had aided Daniel O'Connell's campaigns in the 1830s and 1840s. The secret Fenian Brotherhood brought new hope after the disaster of the Great Famine. The successor group to the Fenians, the *Clan-na-Gael* (Children of the Gael), would be even more active in the city and would launch several spectacular revolutionary forays.[21]

Two men who were young in the Civil War period came to be ardent Irish nationalists for sixty years afterward. One was Dr. William Carroll who had been a medical corps major in the conflict. Born in Donegal, he was a keen champion of the Irish language. He was a Fenian and later known to the British secret service as "the most dangerous man in America." He was a Presbyterian and became the confidant of Charles Stewart Parnell. As one of the three-man directorate of the *Clan-na-Gael* in the 1880s he commanded hundreds of dedicated Irish nationalists who were prepared to intrigue, organize, propagandize, bomb, and kill for their cause.[22] One of the men who would be directed by Carroll and old John Devoy of New York was Luke Dillon, son of emigrant parents, army veteran, and dynamite handler. Dillon would carry out dynamite missions to England in the 1880s and would spend his entire life, of which fourteen years would be suffered in prisons of the Crown, as a revolutionary agent of the *Clan-na-Gael*.[23]

These men formed a tradition in and of themselves. In the 1890s they would influence a young man from County Tyrone who came to Philadelphia to try his luck. He was very lucky, and with hard work amassed a fortune that he openhandedly devoted to Irish revolutionary activities. His name was Joseph McGarrity, and he became the most important single Irish-American of his generation. He financed the conspiratorial travels of Roger Casement, executed by the British in 1916, and also aided the original gunrunning of the militants who would lead the Rising of 1916 in Dublin that would announce the birth of a new independent Irish state, an ideal that had been pursued since the days when America first won its freedom.[24] Carroll, Dillon, and McGarrity were political radicals in their day, but they were complemented by moderate Irish nationalists like Martin I. J. Griffin, top organizer for Parnell's American Land League, and Michael J. Ryan, head of the powerful Irish National League that financed nationalist parliamentary campaigns in Ireland for several decades. This combination of radical and moderate effort was almost a model of Irish nationalist tradition.[25] It existed in dozens of large centers in the United States. It was not as sharply attuned to American or Irish events as the nationalist cadre in New York, but it was populist, persistent, and exceptionally well led. In Philadelphia the Irish nationalist activists functioned with less publicity than in New York, but they were very much alive to the pulse of the overseas Irish aspiration for political and religious liberty.

Philadelphia's upper class was subject to the same kind of inflated vanity that affected the Boston Brahmins, but it was not nearly so productive of intellectuals. It was really a diverse agglomeration of Episcopalians, Quakers turned Episcopalians, Presbyterians, Methodists, and even some converted Jewish families. But the lifestyle it adored was that of the English gentry, and this was enacted by naming estates after English models, affecting Anglo behavior, and patronizing Irish servants. Anti-Irish sentiment was part of the essential outlook of the doyens and dowagers of the socialite Main Line where the entrenched wealth that overbore Philadelphia society was ensconced amid cricket clubs, great estates, and fox-hunting fields. Noblesse oblige was professed by this elite as long as vital interests were not touched. Any real challenge to industrial control, social governance, or Anglo conceit, however, was met with forceful refutation. Thus, the city was renowned for its anti-labor militancy. The corruption of its municipal government, condoned by the ruling elite, slums, red light districts, and an active underworld became notorious throughout the nation, and it was in these areas that the Irish were dominant for over a century.

Although an Irish Catholic middle class grew up in the city, replete with Victorian homes, huge Gothic churches, and an array of convent and prep schools, most of the city's Irish attended the strongly supported parish school system and a network of secondary schools in the working-class areas. Congressman Charles McAleer, banker William F. Harrity, and steel manufacturer Jeremiah Sullivan were members of a self-conscious Irish elite that had developed its own educational and literary coteries, but they were not part of the exclusivist social set that viewed itself as Philadelphia's leadership. This continued separateness, lasting halfway through the twentieth century, along with the peculiarly impregnable Republican machine, gave the Philadelphia Irish their own mentality of exclusiveness. The city was large enough that they could construct an entirely self-sufficient institutional world for themselves with its own hierarchy of values, prestige, and annual calendar of events. Having done so, however, the successful families adopted a socially conservative, smug, and pretensious attitude that was quite different from the more raucous Boston Irish style or the energetically resilient New York manner.

In such a powerfully based industrial city the greater proportion of the residents remained close to the mills, foundries, and wharves where productivity thrived. And in these places social prestige was not an issue. There was none. Job security and earning enough to support one's family were the issues that counted. In grimy alley houses such as those on Kater Street, the family battle for subsistence was unremitting. From that street came William Z. Foster, son of a County Carlow dock worker. Converted to socialism by soup kitchens and beatings by police strikebreakers, he eventually became head of the Communist party in the United States. On the docks the labor wars were endemic. In 1913 John J. Walsh and others from the Industrial Workers of the World organized a strike of long-shoremen. They won their strike goals, but increased the enmity of the shipping companies. When the United States entered World War I, the shippers induced the federal government to jail Walsh and his IWW agitators, who had won the allegiance of not only the Irish dockers but of Blacks as well. Not only were Walsh and several other IWW men imprisoned for the duration of the war, but some were still behind bars in 1923, so vindictive was the anti-labor combine in the city.[26]

Irishwomen dominated the work force in the city's huge carpet mills. Families of skilled operatives filled the ranks of the twenty major carpet producers that manufactured half the nation's carpeting. In a great strike in 1878 the women workers shut down the mills for six months to fight a ten percent wage cut. The strike was bitter, well-organized, and well-supported, but it failed. That failure sent women into the Knights of Labor. Mary Hanifin, a Philadelphia union delegate to the Knights of Labor General Assembly in 1886, said, "We think we should be accorded the privilege of forming an association inside the Knights of Labor" for women "to investigate the abuses to which our sex is subjected by unscrupulous employers, to agitate the principles which our Order teaches of equal pay for equal work and the abolition of child labor."[27] A brave and far-sighted agenda, indeed.

Even within the framework of constructive humanitarian pursuits there was unending struggle. Mary A. O'Reilly had been a burler in textile mills. She became active with the Knights of Labor in the 1880s and then became a factory inspector dealing especially with child labor exploitation. She found children under twelve years of age working for two cents an hour in the Kensington mills and in shirtmaking sweatshops throughout the city, and she campaigned fervently for reforms to bar such abuses through the Civic Club of Philadelphia. O'Reilly and her male colleagues, all Irish, were at grips with the grim realities of work life in the city, and the opposition they faced was formidable.[28] When labor unions came to the textile industry after World War I, the industry gradually abandoned the city and moved to nonunion Southern states.

Eventually the Republican political machine of the city eroded amid the waves of its own corruption. The invasion of the city by national influences added to the process of its slow demise. The 1928 presidential election bid by Al Smith stirred the demoralized Irish Democrats in the city in spite of themselves. Then the New Deal brought Democrats federal patronage, and in 1936 John B. Kelly, an Olympic oarsman and brick contractor, ran for mayor. He lost in a close race, but he put heart into his party. Mathew McCloskey, Congressman Michael Bradley, and others raised money and fielded real Democratic candidates willing to fight. After World War II a combination of liberal reformers and Democratic professional politicians at last put together a coalition that toppled the century-old Republican monolith. The figureheads of this reform coalition were Joseph

S. Clark and Richardson Dilworth, two socialite lawyers, but the muscle belonged to Congressman William J. Green and a very unusual and gifted returned army veteran, Col. Jim Finnegan, who was the brain and the finesse of the political reform endeavor. In 1963 the city got its first Irish Catholic mayor, James H. J. Tate, two generations after most other major cities had Irish mayors. The retardation and repression of Philadelphia had made it very different from other cities in its unwillingness to accept immigrant mobility and to entrust power to ethnic leaders. As a result the self-conscious ethnic identity of the Irish in the city, in an oddly adept and independent form, lasted longer than elsewhere.

As lifestyles changed dramatically in the 1960s the Philadelphia Irish community remained active and reflected an interesting complexity. On one level symbolic traditional events drew faithful homage. Movie star Princess Grace Kelly, daughter of the man who had run for mayor against the country's most powerful Republican machine, could draw crowds wherever she appeared. The Friendly Sons of St. Patrick, founded in 1771, continued to meet as a charitable organization, and Mayor William Green, son of the old congressman, led the revitalized St. Patrick's Day parade. On another level a whole spectrum of musical and cultural groups gathered young people to enjoy Irish dancing, folklore events, lectures, and exhibits. Ethnic identification had become popularized even among the Irish in the suburbs and those with no recent ties to Ireland. Another whole circuit existed among the diminished Irish-born community, and this remained focused on family networks, surviving county societies, and clubs that were more reminiscent of nineteenth- than twentieth-century connections. Part of this strata was the Irish Northern Aid chapter that persevered in trying to influence American opinion about the violent and protracted conflict in Northern Ireland. The city's Irish were a revelation of the diversity of the group's ethnic affairs, and *The Irish Edition*, the local Irish monthly newspaper edited by Tony Byrne, former Marine Corps pilot, and Jane Duffin, feminist sociologist, provided an extensive record of the vitality of its organizational and cultural life.

In the suburban areas around the city there had long been smaller Irish contingents. Bucks County, Montgomery County, and industrial areas along the Delaware had their own Irish societies. Southern New Jersey had had its own official port of entry in the 1800s at Gloucester, and Irish railroad workers had settled across the state and formed a lively community in Atlantic City where they ran boardinghouses for the large seaside tourist trade. As the suburbs and satellite cities of the entire Philadelphia area and its adjacent districts changed from its base of nineteenth-century heavy manufacturing and diversified fabrication, the Irish moved out of the steelworkers' and longshore unions, the construction trades, and railroad work into service jobs, white collar enterprises, the professions, and the world of computer management. The transition in the Delaware Valley was difficult, but the higher education system built largely by their forebears through Catholic religious orders was a most important resource. For most the ties to Ireland were attentuated, but family memory and cultural traits were persistent.[29]

Outside of the Philadelphia metropolitan area the commonwealth was a panorama of scenic and ethnic variety. North and west of Philadelphia the rolling hills of the countryside extended to the mountain chain that stretches diagonally from northeast to southwest through the state. In the plain before those mountains the "Pennsylvania Dutch," actually German pietist, farmers occupied the rich farmland. To the northeast in the "hard coal" region a strong Irish heritage mixed with Slavic elements. The mountain highlands partook of the Appalachian culture as well as Pennsylvania ways. The southwestern corner of the state historically combined mining and heavy industry. This geographical and regional difference produced a state with marked discontinuities and divisions that permitted the railroad and mining interests to long dominate it.

Melvin Dubovsky refers to the years 1865 to 1897 in American industry as "the Time of Chaos." For the Irish in the Pennsylvania coal regions the chaos began much earlier. Schuylkill, Lehigh, Wyoming, and Lackawanna counties were a wilderness in 1825, but by the Civil War they had been overrun by industry. Mine shafts, tipples, and collieries laced the landscape. Carbondale had fifty people in 1828, and five years later it had 2,500. Pottsville was similarly disordered by boomtown expansion. The disconnected mine towns became unified by half a dozen railroad combines. Depressions, such as those in 1850 and 1873, caused a turbulent uprooting of miners and others, who moved on to Illinois, Wisconsin, Colorado, and California. Community ties, never very strong, were easily disrupted. Mine owners tended to be English or Scotch-Irish, mine bosses Welsh, and miners and colliery and railroad laborers Irish. The bonds of loyalty were to the ethnic group. As late as the 1880s there were few marriages across ethnic lines. Divisions in this crude and troubled environment were severe. Bishop Francis Patrick Kenrick journeyed arduously through the area by stagecoach, canal barge, steam car, wagon, horse, and foot, struggling to bring some order and education to mine and railroad camps and towns.[30]

After the Civil War John Siney organized the Workingmen's Benevolent Association (WBA), the first extensive attempt at labor organization in the region. Overinvestment in mines, glutted coal markets, strikes, and wage cutting made the miners' lives miserable. Child labor, wretched housing, exploitative company stores, and payment in company scrip gave rise to a storm of grievances. Interethnic violence, Irish against Welsh, and Irish against English and native-born Americans, was an accepted feature of coal region life. The response of the coal and railroad operators to the WBA was one of intense vigilence and repression. William W. Scranton, son of a founder of the Lackawanna Coal and Iron Company, personally led the posse that fired on unarmed marching strikers in 1877. Men like Terence V. Powderly, born in the town named for the Scranton family, would never forget such repression and would spend a lifetime fighting the economic interests that victimized working people.[31]

Even more militant than Scranton was Franklin B. Gowen, son of a Northern Ireland Orangeman and a clever advocate of industrial triumphalism. Under the guise of campaigning for law and order, he created a web of provocation, frame-up, and judicial corruption to execute the leaders of the secret society of the Irish miners, the Mollie Maguires, that had served as a conspiracy to oppose abuses against labor and to contend with the Welsh and English mine masters and supervisors. At a cost of $150,000 Gowen hung twenty Irishmen, but the price in money was cheap for there were millions involved in keeping labor organizations from disrupting the unfettered sway of the rail and mining companies. Gowen used the Molly Maguires as scapegoats to achieve full sovereignty over the region, a dominance that would last till the 1890s when John Mitchell's United Mine Workers would at length achieve some semblance of justice for the men who toiled in the black, dangerous pits of the coal fields.[32] Gowen's name would be cursed in the mining towns for a century, and after a hundred years a governor of Pennsylvania would exonerate, long after his judicial murder, John Kehoe, the leader of the Mollies, in response to a petition from his descendants and those of other Irish in the Pottsville area.

The personality and novels of John O'Hara are threaded with this history of injury and ethnic antipathy that loomed so large in the social environment of the area. O'Hara never recovered from the fact that he did not gain entry to Yale University, a bastion of Anglo privilege. Nor did he ever free himself or his fictional personae from the social discrimination and striving of Pottsville, the "Gibbsville" of his novels. Well-to-do families setting themselves above the Irish in the narrow world of upstate Pennsylvania towns are the stuff of much of his work, creations that reveal vividly the angular and cutting animosities of the areas's life.[33]

In the second half of the twentieth century the coal industry declined in northeastern Pennsylvania. Increased use of oil and other energy sources closed dozens of mines. The beautiful green countryside was still marred by ugly slag heaps, polluted waters, and old mine debris after more than a hundred years of hectic digging. Colorful local characters like Congressman Daniel Flood did what they could to bring government aid to the area, but a hurricane in 1972 tore through the coal regions and flooded miles of mine tunnels forever. As in previous generations, people moved out of the coal field towns with names like Dunmore and Avoca. The speech of the area still had strong traces of Irish brogue, one of the few places in the United States where this was true. Some Irish organizations continued to function in the cities of Scranton and Pottsville, and John McKeown of Wilkes-Barre organized local people to host visiting Irish teachers each summer. The memory of the hard life in the mines remained one of the most outstanding cultural features of the district.

Southwest of the hard coal region in western Pennsylvania there had been little early influence to temper the raw frontier spirit. James Croghan came there from County Sligo in 1742, then brought out his brothers and friend Daniel Clark. At first he settled at Harrisburg, but after learning several Indian languages he became an indispensible figure in the wilderness. Tough, shrewd, and daring, he dealt with the dangerous Indian tribes as the Revolution began to make the frontier even more fitful and perilous.[34]

By the 1760s there were numerous Irish in the Fort Pitt area. Patrick Archbold had a settlement near Ligonier, and Tim Murphy had become widely known as a woodsman and Indian fighter. Hugh Brady and his sons of Shippensburg were all in the Revolutionary army, and as peace was restored the eager search of the Allegheny Mountains for minerals and forest products expanded. The problem of shipping the crops and products of the area was intimidating. Distilled spirits were far cheaper to ship than grain, so whiskey making was a profitable trade. The ''Whiskey Rebellion'' was about the government's control of this whiskey trade, and the farmers and still tenders of the area were ready to challenge any authority that fettered their distilled commerce.[35]

James O'Hara, born in County Mayo, precociously contrived a shipping route that would become the historic highway of mid-America, but he did so with a boldness that was remarkable. He was a glass manufacturer and had various enterprises in the Pittsburgh area. O'Hara constructed a ship on the Ohio River and sailed it to the Mississippi and then south to New Orleans, where it continued off and away across the ocean to Liverpool in 1805. O'Hara was an extraordinary man who built a Moravian church for German glass blowers. He also attended the Presbyterian Church while maintaining a Catholic priest at home.[36]

The Irish Presbyterians set a definitive mark on the area by their early leadership. Rev. John McMillan, who in 1791 founded the Canonsburg Academy, stands for all the teachers and ministers who labored in the rude settlements. In later generations the saying that Pittsburgh was three things—the Mellon Bank, the Presbyterian Church, and steelworkers—was largely true in terms of major forces in the city. It was 1843 before Pittsburgh had its own Catholic bishop, but an active Catholic business class did arise. James D. Callery headed the city's railways, as did John Murphy. John Farrell became a millionaire, as did Thomas Lynch, who was head of the Frick Coke Company. Henry Oliver led an iron and steel company. Early mayors were William Collum and Bernard McKenna, followed later by William A. Magee, Cornelius Scully, and Peter Flaherty. Along with business support the Pittsburgh Irish had pockets of Irish residence as political resources. In hilly Allegheny County their neighborhoods were segregated quite markedly in the nineteenth century by affiliations based on Irish attachments. Galway people were nestled downtown at the Point where the city's two rivers met. Waterford and Tipperary people were in Irishtown along Penn Avenue, Corkonians in Hazelwood, and Dubliners in the Southside.[37] The attitudes toward Irish nationalism varied from one area to another.

The great railroad strike of 1877, the Homestead steel strike begun by Hugh O'Donnell in June 1892, and other steel, mine, and railroad strikes were part of the labor wars of the area. By the 1890s the Irish were on both sides of these battles. In 1893 they were among the crowds fired on by Pinkerton detectives. The sheriff was William McCleary and he called for troops. Thomas Lynch and Henry Oliver as business heads were certainly not pro-labor. The working-class population included growing numbers of Slavs who began to take the worst jobs as the Irish moved up the occupational ladder. Work in the steel mills was especially dangerous. The heat, molten metal, noise, dirt, and exhausting labor produced a steady accident toll. The poisoned atmosphere of the mills gradually became the atmosphere of all of Pittsburgh, and there are classic photographs of the city in the 1930s with grimy frame houses ranked below vast palls of toxic fumes from the steel and coke plants. Industry had created a city where the primary human function of breathing was a constant peril.

Thus, the major Irish settlements in the state of Pennsylvania in the districts ranged around Philadelphia, Scranton–Wilkes–Barre, and Pittsburgh were all areas of historic efforts by the group to contend against antisocial forces produced by the extraction and processing of the state's rich resources. This magnificent commonwealth with its splendid scenery, glorious natural endowment of colorfully changing seasons, and delightful topography had a disappointing record in its human ecology. After bitter frontier bloodshed, the extractive industries and disorderly urban growth had denied to generations of working families the ''domestic tranquility'' the lofty Constitution framed in Philadelphia had promised. Only the Pennsylvania Dutch by denying themselves technology and ''progress'' had built a secure and rooted cultural heartland for themselves in the farms of Lancaster and Berks counties.

Robert D. Cross maintains that the evolution of Irish-American leadership represents a movement from dependence to psychological autonomy, and the Philadelphia example illustrates such an evolution. From clerical and distinctively ''in-group'' leaders such as Rev. P. J. Moriarty and Dr. William Carroll, the community moved to men who could be pluralist leaders like Jim Finnegan and Mayor William Green. From minority protest leaders to accommodationist arrangers, from face-to-face folk figures to public organizers, the path was traced, paralleled by a weakening of explicit ties to the old country. The capacity of the group to produce new kinds of leadership through an extraordinary series of transformations one generation after another was a long testimony to its vigor and effectiveness as an ethnic subculture.[38]

The Irish accommodation had been built on a Catholic school and church system that eventually embraced more Catholics proportionately than that in any other area of the country. In the 1960s Pittsburgh's Catholic schools drew more than ninety percent of the area's Catholic children, and Philadelphia's parish schools and high schools were a massive investment. But uneasy ethnic rivalries laced the church in upstate areas, and there the stability of Irish associations was at hazard in the rapidly changing industrial and mobile occupational environment. Intermittent political power was no substitute for a stable way of life. In the large cities social problems were all too evident, but even in outlying areas the collapsed mining towns, cut over and devastated lumber districts, and the old mill towns along the rivers were aged monuments to the uncertainty of an economic and social life developed in headlong cycles of furious enterprise.[39]

Rapid Irish organizational decline and diminished identity occurred in most areas despite the growth of a scholarly and then popular interest in ethnic studies that aroused a nostalgic and retrospective indulgence in the history of Irish-

American communities throughout the state in the 1970s. The increased popularity of Appalachian music, for instance, although it related to the Irish folk music revival in some ways, represented a stronger identification with indigenous themes in upstate areas. In the larger cities the commercialized entertainment and mainstream mores of mass culture overbore the Irish-American distinctiveness more and more. A sharp decrease in immigration after 1965 due to revised immigration legislation cut to a trickle direct Irish infusions even in the cities of Philadelphia and Pittsburgh. While the Catholic institutional establishment remained large and influential, it was transformed and had fewer Irish traits than ever before since it now served great numbers of Blacks, Hispanics, and a fully Americanized clientele. Political tributes to the group no longer signified a great deal, since the Irish no longer voted as a bloc, but were diffused throughout the political spectrum.

Still, Pennsylvania bore the imprint of the Irish influence on its life to a greater extent than archives or historical sites of names on the land could testify. The entire industrial and transportation fabric of the state had been erected with their labor, and at times with their leadership. They had contributed to the political spirit of the state, both in their timely support for their religious and civil rights and in their political ability to manage public affairs amid the acute ethnic rivalries in its communities. Their mark upon its educational tradition was powerful through Presbyterian, Catholic, and general endowments. They had manifested what were perhaps the most notable characteristics of the state, a steady persistence and a pride in their heritage. Through them the workings of democracy proceeded.

NOTES

1. William Penn, *My Irish Journal: 1669–1670* (New York: Longmans, Green and Co., 1952), pp. 40, 42–47, 57.

2. John W. Reps, *Town Planning in Frontier America* (Princeton, N.J.: Princeton University Press, 1969), pp. 22–23. Gary Nash attributes Quaker wealth to the siting of their city on a harbor. Gary B. Nash, *Class and Society in Early America* (Englewood Cliffs, N.J.: Prentice-Hall Co., 1970), p. 186; Gary Nash, *Quaker Politics in Pennsylvania, 1681–1726* (Princeton, N.J.: Princeton University Press, 1968), pp. 321–342.

3. George Chambers, *Tribute to the Principles, Virtues, Habits and Public Usefulness of the Irish and Scotch Early Settlers of Pennsylvania* (Chambersburg, Penn.: M. A. Foltz, 1871), p. 15. The conflict between the Quaker rulers and the Scotch-Irish is explained in Herman Wellenreuther, "The Quest for Harmony in a Turbulent World: The Principle of 'Love and Unity' in Pennsylvania Politics," *Pennsylvania Magazine of History and Biography* 107, no. 4 (October 1983): 537–576. Wayland F. Dunaway, *The Scotch-Irish of Colonial Pennsylvania* (Chapel Hill: University of North Carolina Press, 1944), p. 40, details heavy emigration from Ulster. Raymond Martin Bell, *Heads of Families in Mifflin County, Pennsylvania, 1790* (Lewistown, Penn.: Mifflin County Historical Society, 1958) and *Heads of Families at the First Census of the United States*

Taken in the Year 1790, Pennsylvania (Washington: U.S. Government Printing Office, 1908), pp. 245–257, shows the strong Scotch-Irish presence in upstate areas.

4. Dennis Clark, *The Irish in Philadelphia: Ten Generations of Urban Experience* (Philadelphia: Temple University Press, 1973), p. 15; Arthur J. Ennis, "The New Diocese of Philadelphia," in James F. Connelly, ed., *The History of the Archdiocese of Philadelphia* (Philadelphia: The Archdiocese of Philadelphia, 1976), pp. 63–113.

5. John M. Campbell, *History of the Society of the Friendly Sons of St. Patrick and the Hibernian Society* (Philadelphia: The Hibernian Society, 1892), pp. 1–60.

6. Richard Alan Ryerson, *The Revolution Is Now Begun: The Radical Committees of Philadelphia, 1765–1776* (Philadelphia: University of Pennsylvania Press, 1978), pp. 73–74, 250.

7. Owen B. Hunt, *The Irish and the American Revolution: Three Essays* (Philadelphia: Owen B. Hunt, 1976), pp. 45–101; David Noel Doyle, *Ireland, Irishmen and Revolutionary America, 1760–1820* (Cork, Ireland: The Mercier Press, 1981), pp. 109–120, 137–151, 188.

8. Ibid., pp. 152–165.

9. Harry M. Tinkcom, *Republicans and Federalists in Pennsylvania, 1790–1801* (Harrisburg: Pennsylvania Historical and Museum Commission, 1950), pp. 231–246.

10. Priscilla Ferguson Clement, "The Philadelphia Welfare Crisis of the 1820s," *Pennsylvania Magazine of History and Biography* 105, no. 2 (April 1981): 164.

11. Sam Bass Warner, *The Private City: Philadelphia in Three Periods of Its Growth* (Philadelphia: University of Pennsylvania Press, 1968), pp. 74–75; Bruce Laurie, *Working People of Philadelphia, 1800–1850* (Philadelphia: Temple University Press, 1980), pp. 29, 158–159.

12. Michael Feldberg, *The Philadelphia Riots of 1844: A Study of Ethnic Conflict* (Westport, Conn.: Greenwood Press, 1975), pp. 99–161.

13. Robert Edward Quigley, "Catholic Beginnings in the Delaware Valley," and Sister Mary Consuela, "The Church in Philadelphia: 1884–1918," in Connelly, ed., *The History of the Archdiocese of Philadelphia*, pp. 1–62 and 271–338.

14. Dale B. Light, "Class, Ethnicity and the Urban Ecology in a Nineteenth Century City: Philadelphia's Irish, 1840–1890" (Ph.D. diss., University of Pennsylvania, 1979), pp. 111–150.

15. E. Digby Baltzell, *The Philadelphia Gentlemen: The Making of a National Upper Class* (Glencoe, Ill.: The Free Press, 1958), pp. 181–185, shows the character of the elite caste. By 1860 the wealthiest ten percent of the population in Philadelphia owned fifty percent of the wealth, and the lower eighty percent owned only three percent. Edward Pessen, *Riches, Class and Power before the Civil War* (Lexington, Mass.: D. C. Heath and Co., 1973), p. 40. John N. Ingham, "Rags to Riches Re-Visited, The Effect of City Size and Related Factors on the Recruitment of Business Leaders," *Journal of American History* 63, no. 3 (December 1976): 615–637, shows the old family dominance in the city. Daniel Dougherty protested their corruption in 1878: Daniel Dougherty, *The Cameron Dynasty: Earnest Protest against Its Continuance* (Lancaster: Daniel Dougherty, 1878), Historical Society of Pennsylvania pamphlet, Vb. 9193.

16. Dorothy Gandos Beers, "The Centennial City, 1865–76," in Russell F. Weigley, ed., *Philadelphia: A 300 Year History* (New York: W. W. Norton, 1982), pp. 417–470; Erwin Stanley Bradley, *The Triumph of Militant Republicanism, 1860–72* (Philadelphia: University of Pennsylvania Press, 1964), pp. 222–325.

17. Harry Silcox, "Politics, Survival and Adaptability: The Life of Nineteenth Century

Philadelphia Democrat William McMullen, 1824–1901'' (Unpublished paper shared with the author).

18. Dennis Clark, *The Irish Relations: Trials of an Immigrant Tradition* (Rutherford, N.J.: Fairleigh Dickinson University Press, 1982), pp. 91–92.

19. Dennis Clark, *The Irish in Philadelphia: Ten Generations of Urban Experience* (Philadelphia: Temple University Press, 1973), pp. 121 and 135.

20. Campbell, *History of the Society of the Friendly Sons of St. Patrick and the Hibernian Society*, pp. 290–313.

21. Clark, *The Irish Relations*, pp. 103–113.

22. Thomas N. Brown, *Irish-American Nationalism, 1870–1890* (Philadelphia: J. B. Lippincott Co., 1966), pp. 65–83.

23. Clark, *The Irish Relations*, pp. 114–125; Joseph George, ''Philadelphia's Catholic Herald: The Civil War Years,'' *Pennsylvania Magazine of History and Biography* 103, no. 2 (April 1979); 196–221.

24. Sean Cronin, *The McGarrity Papers* (Tralee, Ireland: Anvil Press, 1972), pp. 50–81.

25. Clark, *The Irish Relations*, pp. 114–119.

26. William Seraile, ''Ben Fletcher: I.W.W. Organizer,'' *Pennsylvania History Magazine* 46, no. 3 (July 1979): 213–232.

27. Susan Levine, *Labor's True Woman: Carpet Weavers, Industrialization, and Labor Reform in the Gilded Age* (Philadelphia: Temple University Press, 1984), pp. 104–105.

28. *The Public Ledger* (Philadelphia) (January 14, 1893); *Annual Report of the Factory Inspectors* (November 29, 1894), Official Document No. 22, Commonwealth of Pennsylvania. Irish labor leadership in the area continued into the 1980s: Jack McKinney column, ''God Bless 'Em Every One,'' *The Philadelphia Daily News* (December 23, 1981).

29. Joseph John Kelly, *The Irish in Camden County* (Camden, N.J.: Camden County Historical Society, 1984), pp. 14–24.

30. Joseph J. Kelley, Jr., *Pennsylvania: The Colonial Years, 1681–1776* (Garden City, N.Y.: Doubleday and Co., 1980), pp. 175–176; William A. Gudelmas and William G. Shade, *Before the Molly Maguires: The Emergence of the Ethno-Religious Factor in the Politics of the Lower Anthracite Region, 1844–1872* (New York: Arno Press, 1976), p. 125; Rowland Berthoff, ''The Social Order of the Anthracite Region, 1825–1902,'' *Pennsylvania Magazine of History and Biography* 89, no. 4 (December 1965): 261–291; Hugh J. Nolan, *The Most Reverend Francis Patrick Kenrick: Third Bishop of Philadelphia, 1830–1851* (Philadelphia: American Catholic Historical Society, 1948), pp. viii, 293, 307, 417.

31. Berthoff, ''The Social Order of the Anthracite Region, 1825–1902,'' p. 68.

32. Melvyn Dubofsky, *Industrialism and the American Worker, 1865–1920* (New York: Thomas Y. Crowell Co., 1975), pp. 33–40.

33. Margaret E. Maloney, *Fág An Bealach: The Irish Contribution to America* (Pittsburgh: United Irish Societies of Pittsburgh, 1977), p. 47.

34. Nicholas B. Wainwright, ''George Croghan's Journal, 1759–63,'' *Pennsylvania Magazine of History and Biography* 71, no. 4 (October 1947): 320–342.

35. Samuel Eliot Morison, *The Oxford History of the American People* (New York: Oxford University Press, 1965), pp. 340–341; Leland D. Baldwin, *Whisky Rebels: The Story of a Frontier Uprising* (Pittsburgh: University of Pittsburgh Press, 1939), pp. 20–22.

36. Wainwright, "George Croghan's Journal, 1759–63," pp. 305–444; Margaret E. Maloney, *Fág An Bealach*, p. 47.

37. Ibid., pp. 77, 94, 107.

38. Robert D. Cross, "The Irish," in John Higham, ed., *Ethnic Leadership in America* (Baltimore: The Johns Hopkins University Press, 1978), pp. 193–195.

39. Thomas Taber, Walter Casler, and Benjamin F. G. Kline, *The Logging Railroad Era of Lumbering in Pennsylvania*, 3 vols. (Williamsport, Penn.: Published by the authors, 1920), vol. 2, p. 441; vol. 3, p. 106. As late as 1905 the Gaffney brothers were still building the Potato Creels Railroad into the declining lumber area. Michael Weber, *Social Change in an Industrial Town* (University Park: Pennsylvania State University Press, 1976), passim, shows slow Irish progress in Warren, Pennsylvania.

7 DEEP IN DIXIE— THE SOUTH

The social experience of the Irish in southern states affords a far-reaching opportunity to examine the regional differences that have resulted in broad variations in the history of ethnic groups in American society.[1] The potency of regional cultures, the adaptability of ethnic minorities, and the capacity of ethnic consciousness to persist amid isolation and hostility all command attention. An examination of both Irish occupational and Irish religious standings in the South should aid this process.

By far the most geographically extensive and, indeed, geographically varied region of the country, the cultural region of the South extends from the Chesapeake Bay to west Texas with an irregular northern border that crosses the nation from northern Virginia to Kansas, then across Oklahoma to the Panhandle area and down to the Mexican border. Within this vast expanse are a lowland arc reaching back from the Atlantic and Gulf coasts, a mountain belt from Virginia's Blue Ridge to the Ozarks, and a western component including Texas and most of Oklahoma. It embraces the states of the old Confederacy, the lower Mississippi basin, and several distinct variations of the Southern regional tradition. The eastern lowlands contain the colonial heritage of the South. The mountain chains were its frontier lands. The western section is, especially in the twentieth century, part of the New South of oil, cotton, cattle, and light industry.

In this region the agricultural experience of early America persisted longer than elsewhere, and there spread a regional culture with a public-spirited elite, a slave society that would profoundly condition the area, and a white, largely poor population that was both traditionalist and individualist. Traditionalism and individualism contended in the hearts of Southerners and generated a tension that produced not only a vivid and romantic heritage, but a splendid regional literature glorifying the South and its folkways.[2]

This tremendous arc of geography that came to be the Southland sent at first only tobacco from the Chesapeake, a mere weed on which fortunes were made. Cotton cultivation, then rice and a catalog of foodstuffs, developed as eighteenth-century farming improved. Cotton and sugar shaped the Gulf plains. But to plant meant war.[3] The struggle with the Indians was again enacted, a genocidal fury that was to deeply condition Southern life and help shape its disposition toward violence and denial of equality to men of color. The displacement of the Indians was partly motivated by the unsettled nature of the South's borders around which France, Spain, and Britain intrigued. The Southern Indian wars were as much a source of American nationalism as the New England concepts of citizen liberty. The relentless invasion of the areas beyond the coastal lowlands is termed a process of "primitive accumulation and paternal authority" by Michael Paul Rogin.[4] It was a disorganized, brutal, passionate process of daring, gambling, and vanity. For the Irish who joined it, the movement of settlement suited both the needs of the educated adventurer, such as the grandson of Rory O'Mara who became a Carolina governor in 1700, and the outcasts with all to gain and little to lose, such as the immigrants brought from Kinsale in 1669, one of the earliest records of Irish embarkation to the Carolinas.[5]

In the South the fighting of the Revolution was more of a civil war than anywhere else in the country. Loyalist Banastre Tarleton and his Tory raiders left bloody wounds across the countryside. He slaughtered Continental troops at Camden, South Carolina, and at Waxhaws Irish women cared for 150 maimed survivors.[6] At King's Mountain the loss at Camden was avenged, and James Collins, a private on the American side in company with his father, wrote of how the animals rooted hastily buried Tory bodies from the ground after the battle in 1780.[7] By October 1781 the Battle of Yorktown, in which units of the Irish Brigade in the French forces sent to aid Washington took part, sealed the destiny of the South in American victory. Thomas and Aedanna Burke, both friends of Washington, mustered out in South Carolina and returned to the pursuit of wealth in a newly independent nation. Land grants in Georgia and the Carolinas reflect the Irish reaching for the rich soil, while near Washington's home at Mt. Vernon a number of Irish families could now seek property without any favor of the king.[8] The Carrolls of Maryland not only had one of their number as a signer of the Declaration of Independence, but they would strengthen their position as the country's leading Catholic family. The dedication of Irishmen who shared the ideals of the Revolution is a vivid feature of the generation of the founding fathers. John Daly Burke, a Virginian by adoption, "touched America's nationalist and revolutionary core" when he penned such lines as: "When dark tyranny rears its fell head, Strike a blow that shall sound from the earth to the skies."[9]

There is ample evidence of the presence of the Irish in the South during the earliest periods of exploration and settlement. Under both Spanish and English auspices, Irishmen found themselves in pioneer settings as adventurers and entrepreneurs. Often the adventurers were serving as military explorers or in garrisons in ill-defined colonial enterprises. As trappers, traders, scouts, or simply wandering renegades, the Irish crop up in the vast Southeastern region. Irish priests in Florida's Spanish missions, Irish officials for the Spanish crown in Louisiana and Texas, Irish convicts in Georgia, Irish settlers in the Carolinas, and Irish traders among the Indians appear in the records of the seventeenth and eighteenth centuries.[10] These appearances in the landscape of a barely explored continent were part of the habit and legacy of exile that were one of the abiding traits of Ireland's progeny.

The Scotch-Irish communities thrust into the Southern mountains both by migration from the coastal plain and by overland settlement starting from New York, Pennsylvania, and Virginia were the most strenuous examples of frontier penetration. Clannish family groups moved into the Carolina backlands and into Kentucky in a determined pattern of log-fort villages. The conflict with the Indians was murderous. The Irish and Scotch-Irish largely remained an outgroup in much of Southern life, especially in relation to the Anglophile Whigs in the mountain areas. Despite this political isolation, they had a notable impact on the folklore, behavior patterns, and history of the region.[11]

The early Scotch-Irish outposts were almost all eighteenth-century phenomena. It is the opinion of James G. Leyburn that by the end of the eighteenth century the role of this group had been all but fulfilled, but this seems too severe a judgment.[12] The eastern frontier was tamed. Emigration of Presbyterian Irish decreased in the nineteenth century as industrialization absorbed Ulster's poor into factories. Thus, the original settlements did not draw replenishment as did the larger Irish Catholic urban enclaves. The very mountain terrain isolated the group, and as the South became a distinctive region, impoverished after the Civil War, the mountain people were largely excluded from the mainstream. Lumber, railroad, and mining interests exploited them and drove them further into seclusion. As a result their tradition did not have the amplitude required to fully sustain itself. The more successful examples so often cited—the wealthy magnates of Pennsylvania and families such as those of Presidents Buchanan, McKinley, and Wilson—do not contradict this general condition. The attempts to maintain Scotch-Irish identity included a long and at times acrimonious dissent from association with the Irish Catholic tradition, but eventually the group had to be content with a sharply circumscribed identity, and in the Southern mountains this was subsumed within the broader Appalachian mountain culture.

It is notable that the Scotch-Irish as a group achieved so vivid a record in the early South, and then became adumbrated within the region's life, but poverty, isolation, and subverted ambitions were thematic for much of the South as a whole as well. Still, the frontier vitality symbolized by Andrew Jackson was a powerful influence up through the nineteenth century. John Fitzgerald of Pensacola was typical of the wildly nationalist editors who supported Jackson in the South. George McDuffie, governor of South Carolina, in 1835 pronounced the sectional credo in his "fire-eater" speech before his legislature. Were slaves worse off than Irish peasants trapped in Northern factories? he asked. His rhetoric was soon taken up and given theoretical power by John C. Calhoun.[13] These men were nineteenth-century exponents of the earlier Scotch-Irish vigor, but the individualism they represented further diminished the tradition from which they sprang.[14]

The Appalachian Mountains—that immense spine that imposed the principal geographic barrier to the physical unity of the South—were influenced by the Irish in an oblique but definite way. For generations, indentured servants formed a significant and regular component of the American laboring population. Indentured workers with terms ranging from seven to twenty-one years came to America as immigrants, and their importation was a common colonization procedure. The Irish made up the most numerous group among this indentured class. In early America orphans, prisoners, runaways, delinquents, debtors, and vagrants were frequently seized by local authorities and indentured, with officials making tidy profits from the traffic, and with the labor for the least desirable domestic and unskilled jobs benefiting tradesmen and householders while legal enforcement of the work contract was presided over by sympathetic courts. Slavery, of course, decreased the use of indentures in the South, but still they were not uncommon. From the eastern settlements in both North and South indentured servants escaped to the refuge of the mountain wilderness. Eighteenth-century provincial papers steadily carried advertisements with rewards for such runaways, and the Irish had the reputation for being the servants most likely to flee.[15]

Hence it was not only Ulster Irish Protestants such as those who moved south through the Appalachians as pioneers who peopled the deep mountains. Irish Catholic fugitives—whose attachment to what was basically an obligation under Anglo-Saxon law was bound to be slight considering their ancestral problems with that law—also made the mountains their own. This fugitive population gained security in the impenetrable mountains. They played a role in creating the mountaineer's distrust of strangers, authority, and inquisitive influences. As fugitives, such people were loath to tolerate governmental intrusions. Their hardy individualistic lifestyle, their racy Irish music, and their suspicious secretiveness were already a tradition in the Southern mountains from the Smokies of Virginia to the Ozarks before the Civil War.

The emergence of large concentrations of Irish in the South had to await the development of more major centers and the need for the kind of labor that characterized Irish employment in the period when Irish immigration swelled after 1820. As in other regions, the need for "internal improvements" from the time of Andrew Jackson onward created a strong market for menial construction labor. The canal and railroad construction that advanced across the terrain brought Irish digging crews into one territory after another, and afterward left them clustered along these lines of communication. As well, the need for longshore labor rose as the ports grew along the Atlantic and Gulf coasts.

Riverboat and barge men were also part of the Irish diffusion along major lines of travel. This channeling of Irish labor was the chief medium for the settlement of the Irish in Southern ports, river and rail centers, and inland cities.

Whether persistent communities of Irish Catholics resulted from these population clusters depended upon such factors as the size of the Irish enclaves, the existence of further economic opportunities, and the prospects for the maintenance of religious and social facilities. In New Orleans, Charleston, and a few other cities where Irish communities had formed in the eighteenth century, strong merchant families had ties to their Irish counterparts in Northern cities, the Caribbean, and England. They maintained an interest in Irish writing, politics, and culture through their Hibernian societies, but these port city communities were exceptional in the South.[16]

During the 1850s, after the calamity of the potato famine had sent a vast tide of hungry refugees to American shores, the Irish were engaged in the urban labor that was part of the expansion of Southern cities in these years. They also continued their work as contract laborers for excavation, repair of levees, and lumber clearing, and were active in riverboat and railroad labor. In some respects they were more reliable and valued than slaves, especially if only recently arrived in the country. But in other respects they were expendable. Frederick Law Olmsted notes that in ports they were employed in dangerous loading because they had no monetary value as slaves did. They were, too, more intractable than black labor and would strike for better wages and working conditions, as they did in New Orleans in 1853, tying up the entire steamboat traffic.[17]

The identification of the Irish with labor in opening the nation's transportation routes is no less significant for the South than for other areas of the nation. Their employment in canal building in the 1820s took them hundreds of miles from the Eastern cities, as Mathew Carey noted. The cholera, yellow fever, typhus, dysentery, malaria, and other epidemic diseases, in addition to the brutal nature of the excavation work, exacted a fearsome toll wherever the Irish work gangs labored. So grim was the toll that some planters expressed reluctance to use valuable slaves for it; also, most slaves were trained for agricultural work, not the body-breaking labor of the hard-driven digging crews. Strikes and violence marked canal construction in Virginia as routes to the tidewater were dug by the Chesapeake and Ohio Company and the 184-mile canal to Cumberland, fifty to eighty feet wide, progressed. Company bankruptcies, broken wage agreements, fury at the abusive gang bosses, and terrible working conditions caused repeated outbreaks. In one famous case, Simon Cameron shipped Irishmen from Philadelphia to work on the drainage and canal projects near New Orleans, and the result was a disaster of disease and exploitation. Whatever the human cost, much of the 500 miles of canal works built in the South prior to 1860 was the work of Irish labor.[18]

One episode reveals that colonization projects did on occasion accompany railroad development. In Georgia the building of the Ocmulgee and Flint Railroad was conceived as a combined commercial, colonization, and missionary venture. Abbott Brisbane, who had served with Irish-American soldiers against the Seminole Indians, became a Roman Catholic. He was an engineer and planned a wooden track railway from Mobley's Bluff to the Flint River near Albany,

Georgia. With the aid of a Catholic priest, he recruited Irishmen from Charleston and New York in 1842 and began construction. Workers expected to receive settlement land near the railroad right-of-way to form a Catholic colony, the Mission of St. Ignatius, in the heart of Georgia. Immigrants were sought from Ireland. The scheme failed when the business structure for the road collapsed, the Irish workers stormed Brisbane's headquarters, and the priest involved died. Some of the Irish stayed in the area and settled land on an individual basis.[19]

Whether clearing right-of-way for the Natchez Trace, building wharves in the river cities and ocean ports, or heaving and hauling freight in the "J. Murphy" wagons of St.Louis (the competitors of the Conestoga wagons), the Irish threaded through the land on its travel routes. This usually meant that their presence was transitory and what residence they made was temporary at the beginning. For this reason, their first major treks through the South in significant numbers are largely without community record. The shelter for the male labor gangs simply consisted of shanties, lean-tos, and canvas stretched from wagons. Sanitation was primitive and food of the rudest kind. Poverty bound them to the work and moved them on to the next work site. The touring actor Tyrone Power encountered them repeatedly—clannish, strangers to the local population, sharing their own speech and secret morale. Their itinerant work on flatboats, railroads, and drainage gangs made them peripheral to the religious and social communities they touched.[20]

When priests did reach the transient Irish Catholics working on levees or building railroads, it was partly to beg money from them. "Working the Irish" for collections became a common practice on the Mississippi River in the 1850s, but it did not bring the workers into organized Catholic life. Nature and the lack of missionary priests made such visits brief and irregular. Work and contractual arrangements also interfered with religious observances. The sixty Irish Catholics repairing levees near Vicksburg, Mississippi, in 1853, for example, were denied fast-day food by labor contractors unwilling to purchase the more expensive fare.[21]

Gradually, enough immigrant Irish workers clustered in cities to establish distinct community groups. Richard Wade has pointed out the decline of Black population in Southern cities in the antebellum decade, even though commercial and manufacturing activity in most of these cities increased. The work force for their urban economic base was partially augmented by Irish increments.

Good examples of the Irish as urban workers existed in Savannah, Georgia, and Charleston, South Carolina. Conditions in Savannah were so chaotic and destructive of decency for the Irish that they gained reputations as "the grand movers in all disturbances." Larceny, malicious mischief, buying and receiving stolen goods, fraud, illegal voting, assault and battery, and murder were common offenses for which they were brought to court. Drunkenness and gambling were vices that, when spread among slaves by Irish grogshop owners, caused deep local concern. Also, on the Savannah waterfront shipping agents named Kelly,

Dunn, and Hussey became notorious for their victimization of sailors in the 1850s.[22]

In an excellent analysis of Irish workers in Charleston in the years 1840–66, Christopher Silver has presented the best material on this immigrant group, outside of Earl Niehaus's study of New Orleans. Silver's investigation reveals the same pattern of Irish alternation of the population balance toward a predominantly white pattern that is noted by Wade and Niehaus. The pressure on Black urban workers by Irish newcomers altered the occupational structure of the city. This was especially true in the heavy work of carting and drayage. Free Blacks in trades such as blacksmith, carpenter, millwright, and tailor resisted the Irish penetration in a way slaves were unable to do, so the Irish intrusion did not sweep them from the occupational structure. Because of this accession to semi-skilled and skilled work, many of the Irish were able to purchase property and move toward respectability. But the climate of Charleston, the diseases endemic to it, and the inability to displace Blacks sufficiently led to a high rate of transiency for the Irish in the city. The Irish who came to Charleston were largely recruited from New York on a seasonal basis, and finding inferior conditions and a labor situation replete with Black resistance, the immigrants soon concluded it was best to move on. Thus in the winter months packets arrived with immigrants, and in the summer months they departed with Irish passengers, sometimes causing a net annual loss for the port. Although Charleston's Irish maintained their religious institutions and identity, the city itself became increasingly "nativist" and reflective of rural Southern attitudes.[23]

By 1860 there were 84,000 Irish-born people in the Southern states, a total smaller than the numbers of Irish in individual cities in the North. Only Louisiana, Tennessee, Missouri, and Virginia had more than one percent of their population made up of Irish-born. Cities such as Richmond, Savannah, and Memphis had more than 3,000 Irish-born, but outside of these centers there were few identifiable concentrations.[24] Whole states were thus barely acquainted with an ethnic group that was in the mid-nineteenth century having a far-reaching effect on politics, religion, and social development not only in the North but in the Old Northwest and Far West.

The religious organization of this widely scattered Irish population evolved slowly and unevenly. The primary problem was simply the difficulty of providing priests and even rudimentary ecclesiastical administration for a region of such great distances and varying conditions. In states such as Maryland, Virginia, and Missouri, the Irish were able to build church facilities, and because of geographic location and communications, could maintain liaison with the major Catholic dioceses of the Northeast. In 1801 Irish, English, and French Catholics subscribed for their first church in the nation's capital, and in Louisiana the French-speaking Catholics made provisions for their Irish co-religionists. In Savannah, Mobile, and Natchez stable religious administration was possible, as it was in Charleston, but it was often a hard struggle. Priests declined to work in the South because of the poverty of the Catholics there, the circuit riding required to visit remote missions, and the heat and sickness that were part of the subtropical environment. Prior to 1850 there were never more than six priests in the Natchez diocese, and only twenty in the Mobile diocese, both of which lay close to the chief Catholic center of the South, the diocese of New Orleans, which by 1850 had a Catholic population of 170,000.[25]

It is clear from the sources used by John Gilmary Shea in his review of Southern dioceses that institutional development was very uneven. In 1850 in Savannah, two bishops died from fever, leaving the thin Catholic network of twelve chapels without episcopal leadership. The Charleston diocese reached into three states, and the bishop reported "poor and struggling congregations" in such places as Raleigh and Fayetteville. Bishop Ignatius Whelan of Charleston journeyed all the way to Paris to seek aid for his flock. Bishop Andrew Byrne reported that "within the whole diocese of Little Rock there exists no means to erect a single altar." During this period of seminal labor even the largest concentrations of Catholics such as New Orleans, Charleston, Louisville, and Galveston remained heavily dependent upon the Society for the Propagation of the Faith in Rome for annual subsidies. And although the Irish imparted some militancy to Catholicism in the South in the 1840s and 1850s, such militancy was a defensive response to the intimidation emanating from a strident evangelical Protestantism rather than an expression of institutional assurance and power.[26]

Early Catholic prelates such as Bishop John Carroll and Bishop John Hughes had acceded to a scheme of parish administration that vested property control and administration decisions in the hands of laymen. The lay role was qualified and in missionary conditions entirely warranted. As time passed, however, disputes inevitably arose among trustees and clergy. The feeble Catholic dioceses of the South were weakened in the 1820s by such trustee disputes in St. Augustine, Florida, Charleston, and St. Louis. Even New Orleans was not exempt, but in that city the disputes initially emerged within the French-speaking community, and the Irish strongly supported the bishop, who was French.[27]

From the outset of missionary activity in the region, Catholics had to face the hostility of the overwhelmingly predominant Protestants in most of the South. Even the long-established Irish in Charleston had to refute charges that they were political foils of Rome. In 1824 such a refutation was circulated from "A Catholic Clergyman, A Native of Ireland." Nativist and Know-Nothing prejudice against the Irish flared repeatedly in the 1840s, and Louisville, Savannah, St. Louis, and New Orleans all had incidents of violence or fierce controversy.[28] Such hostility was not merely part of the national effusion of Protestant militant sentiment in the 1840s and 1850s. In the South it was part of a regional tradition of religious homogeneity of a Protestant character and an antagonism against immigrants in a setting where vigilance with respect to maintenance of the existing social order was believed to be imperative because of the potential for disruption inherent in a slaveholding society.

In addition to religious hostility, new Irish Catholics faced Southern upper-class prejudice. The baronial lifestyle of England's upper class had an attraction for the Southern plantation elite, particularly in Georgia, the Carolinas, and Virginia where both genealogy and education emphasized the cultural connection to England. From England the stereotypes, prejudices, and anti-Irish attitudes deriving from the ancient English-Irish conflict passed to much of the Southern leadership.[29] The presumption of Irish inferiority repeatedly led English travelers in the South to compare the Irish with the slave populations, often to the detriment of the former. Fanny Kemble's view of the Irish was not unusual among celebrated English visitors to the great plantation houses, for she saw them as "savage, brutish, filthy, idle and incorrigibly and hopelessly helpless."[30] The fact that there were wealthy merchant cliques, successful plantation magnates, philanthropists, and distinguished leaders among the Southern Irish-Americans was irrelevant to Anglophile ignorance.

Under such conditions the Irish communities of the South evolved in a slower and more deliberate way than the larger Irish concentrations in northern and western regions. It was 1833, a full century after prominent Irish leaders had emerged in New Orleans, before the Irish had a church of their own. The vitality of the Charleston community declined as that port's fortune receded. In 1860, only eight of the more than 1,800 churches in Georgia were Roman Catholic. Outside of Louisiana and larger urban areas, the religious organization of the scattered Catholics was tenuous at best. An occasional Catholic plantation owner would maintain a tiny religious enclave but the record was very uneven.[31]

Although social handicaps and lack of resources retarded religious development, Southern Catholics did have an episcopal leadership that was educated and committed to an orderly ecclesiastical growth. The folk Catholicism of Ireland was being transformed in both the old country and the United States by increasing regulation and administrative directives. At diocesan synods the bishops of Charleston and Galveston shared a concern for promoting the use of financial accounts, discipline in liturgy and the contracting of marriages, stricter regulation of the clergy, and the encouragement of special devotions. The organizational elaboration of Catholic life was proceeding in spite of the handicaps, and this was a reassuring influence for the scattered Southern Catholics.

Probably the most outstanding Roman Catholic leader in the antebellum South was Bishop John England. Born in County Cork in 1786, he became bishop of Charleston in 1820. He was well-read in Irish history and deeply committed to the advancement of the Irish people. His addresses and writings on Irish subjects revealed not only a rich knowledge and acute judgment about Irish affairs, but a resolution to refute prejudicial opinions and submit the premises of his people's advancement to reasoned and democratic discussion. Bishop England's travels throughout the South made him widely known and respected. In cities like Savannah he even celebrated St. Patrick's Day with religious leaders from the major Protestant denominations. He wrote regularly for his own diocesan newspaper and contributed to others. Whether seeking support for Catholic emancipation in Ireland, seeking aid for his seminary from the church officials in

Havana, begging charity for the families of fever victims, or recruiting nuns from France for his early schools, Bishop England worked arduously and intelligently. He was able to administer his diocese with great skill, astutely balancing the English and French priests with the growing number of Irish priests. His qualities of missionary zeal, administrative flexibility, and democratic outlook prefigured Irish-American clerical traits that were to become commonplace in American Catholicism.[32]

New Orleans offers another perspective on the impact of Irish Catholics in a Southern city. In New Orleans the Irish came into a Latin Catholic community already established. As the Irish had in France and Spain for generations before 1800, they adapted readily. A merchant class of Irishmen flourished in the polyglot Gulf metropolis. When the great Irish influx to America swelled in the 1830s, the newer, poorer Irish actually changed the demographic composition of the city. From being predominantly Black, it became predominantly foreign-born with the Irish forming more than half the immigrant population. By the eve of the Civil War, out of a population of 168,000, which was eighty percent white, the Irish formed a component of at least one-fourth. Politically and economically this Irish augmentation was very important, but religiously it was decisive, since it challenged the Latin Catholicism that had set the historic social and communal character of the city. In both numbers and ecclesiastical ambitions, the Irish altered the city's Latin heritage and imparted a new kind of Catholicism to it.

The religious energy of the Irish immigrants was not immediately evident because of the poverty and affliction of the group. In their emergence from a rural folk Catholicism to an urban modernized church system, the Irish in New Orleans—and in other cities—were setting a pattern that would have broad effects on American Catholic life. This is one pattern for which documentation exists in numerous places. The more flexible Latin Catholicism, steeped in ties to aristocratic ideas and patronage and rich with Latin cultural effusion, was displaced by a driving and rigorous religious movement that represented an Irish immigrant vision of free development after centuries of persecution. It was a novel Catholicism for the Irish and for those who beheld it, for it was popularly supported financially and popularly recruited in its leadership and ethnic vitality. It was, for all the European usages with which the Church was structured, distinctly un-European, for it simply lacked a European context. Its context was immigrant, Irish, and American. It was, because of Irish demographic weight and Irish religious and social affinity, a major force in American Catholic history. In New Orleans before the Civil War this process had been begun. Prior to 1860 the three Irish parishes' growing charitable and social groups, schools, and other institutions formed the matrix of the post-Latin Catholic establishment that would dominate the religious life of the city in the future.[33]

The result of this demographic and cultural minority position in an inhospitable region was that Irish Catholics came to be affected in a thoroughgoing way by the local mores. Although they succeeded, where sufficiently numerous, in establishing their own schools, orphanages, hospitals, and auxiliary groups for religious service, they were rarely in a position outside of Louisiana to exercise cultural leadership themselves. In the border states this was not true, for in Maryland and Missouri there were vigorous Irish Catholic components.[34]

Texas also represented a special case. Texas shared only part of the cultural orientation of the South. Its frontier atmosphere, the vast prairies, and the connection with Hispanic culture made it a distinct extension to the South proper. The Irish Texans forged several frontier colonies for themselves prior to the Lone Star revolt against Mexico in the 1830s. The San Patricio colony to the north of San Antonio drew Irish immigrants and petitioned for English-speaking priests. The Refugio colony near Corpus Christi, founded by James Power in the 1830s, sought immigrants from Ireland in famine times in the 1840s, but hundreds of those recruited in Ireland died in sea disasters and of disease on the journey to Texas. In these Irish-settled areas, and in the Beaumont-Liberty district, several Catholic chapels served the settlers. Some of these chapels were in ranch houses, and both Hispanic and Irish Catholics worshiped there. Religious practices brought from Ireland persisted in these colonies, such as the strict "Black fast" from all food in Lent, the family rosary at evening, and the presence of statues of Irish saints in the chapels. The Irish Catholics in Texas suffered greatly during the turbulence of the territory, but they maintained a strong identity with active traditions of social service and charity, as exemplified especially in the career of Margaret Mary Healy-Murphy, foundress of the Holy Ghost Sisters. Irish Catholicism in Texas was more robust than that in many areas of the Old South.[35]

For most of the South, however, the Irish had to be content with a circumspect role. They maintained their identity where education and group ties were possible, but there was no parallel to the political, religious, and social impact they made in other regions.

The Irish figured in the factious politics of the antebellum South in a marginal way. Sectionalism and the eccentricities of local pressures effectively baffled Irish combination in the Democratic party, and Whig particularism had the same effect in the strongholds of the Whigs in Kentucky, Tennessee, Georgia, and western Virginia. In urban areas the group did coalesce on occasion but rarely sent its members to the level of state office. The minority position of the Irish in such cities as Memphis, for instance, generated resentment among them that proved significant for political activity in the post–Civil War years.[36] The keys to the weak Irish regional political profile were the lack of numerical strength almost everywhere outside of urban areas and the inability of the group to advance its specific needs in the Southern regional context.

If the Irish were not capable of challenging the existing political alignments, they were on the whole less disposed to challenge slavery. While there were some antislavery Irish in the North, the dean of American Catholic historians says that "wherever they were the Irish adopted the local point of view regarding slavery."[37] Typical of Irish sentiment, Bishop John Quinlan of Mobile declared in 1861, "We must cut adrift from the North in many things of intimate social conditions—we of the South have been too long on leading strings."[38] This statement well illustrates the sectional mentality the Irish as a whole adopted.

Still, some Irish dissented from the proslavery outlook of their countrymen in the South. Irish landholders in the South did not usually hold slaves themselves. Thus fifty families from Tipperary in Taliaferro County, Georgia, worked their own land successfully without slaves. While there were few such as Michael Healy, father of a Catholic bishop of mixed blood, who married Blacks, there was a stubborn representation of Irish, Catholic and Protestant, who were at least pro-Union, and in a few cases sympathetic to moderate antislavery arguments. Much of what is known of Irish views in the South derives from travelers and commentators with little regard for the Irish or the contradictions of their local situations. The presence of some dissenters suggests that where the Irish had the benefit of education, the hostility to Blacks attributed to them was not at all automatic.[39]

Even as they blended into the regional consensus, however, the Irish retained their identity. By 1860, they had established their basic Catholic institutional network, thin though it was regionally. There were many examples of individual success, and group ties were nurtured. Southern Irish-Americans followed closely the activities of Daniel O'Connell's Repeal Associations, welcomed exiled nationalist leaders such as John Mitchel, and kept nationalistic aspirations alive in the years prior to the time when the Fenian Brotherhood would coordinate nationalist undertakings. The preexistence or swift creation of special Irish units for service with the Confederacy revealed the persistent group identity among the Irish and the group's need to manifest its loyalty to the region. Not only did Mobile's bishop bless the banners of the Emerald Guards, but Irish units fought bravely in the Civil War.

W. J. Cash chooses an Irishman as the exemplar of hard-scrabble enterprise in the rough agricultural country of the South in his classic study, *The Mind of the South*. Starting with a log house and one slave, the Irishman by midlife had a "big house," rude but serviceable. He would educate his sons and make his daughters polite. After serving in the state legislature, the man would die leaving 2,000 acres, 114 slaves, and four cotton gins. The point that Cash makes with this brief biography is that the South was not by any realistic examination led by aristocrats, but by self-made men or their sons, and Irishmen among them.[40] The sentimental infatuation with aristocratic pretensions became part of the sectional cult of nostalgia that compensated the South for its own poverty and slower development. Theodore O'Hara's poem, "The Bivouac of the Dead," typified the cult that had been begun as early as 1832 with John P. Kennedy's bucolic novel of Virginia country life, *The Swallow Barn*.[41]

The reality of the South on the eve of the Civil War, as Cash notes, was that most of the South was still in the frontier stage of development. The poor whites were, in economic terms, not a great deal better off than the freed Blacks or, in some cases, the slaves. "Northern and English travellers to the South repeatedly compared the slaves to the Irish, often to the detriment of the latter, and hardly a racial stereotype poured forth without its being a modest modification of familiar descriptions of the Irish.''[42] The fear of social disturbance applied to immigrant Irish and Blacks alike. Striking Irish railroad laborers in South Carolina were reviled by a judge for their inclination to "make war on the Negroes." Governor William McCarty of Florida, like many others, cautioned his officials about the possibility of slave revolts, but white labor disruptions were feared as well.[43] In the irascible Southern expansionist climate of land greed and "get rich quick" schemes, social order was ever vulnerable. The greatest sectional crisis of American history grew in large part out of this vulnerability and the temperamental volatility of the South.

The American Civil War was calamitous, not only in that it tore the nation in two, but in that it ushered in the era of the mass army to the United States. Casualties were appalling because medical and sanitation services were primitive, and also because the numbers of combatants were unprecedented. Ella Lonn estimates the figure of Irish-born in Confederate armies alone at about 30,000. As a very large and poor minority and therefore composed of those most likely to be recruited, the Irish caught up in the conflict paid a shocking price for their involvement. At Fredericksburg the Irish Brigade on the Union side lost two-thirds of its complement and Confederate losses were at times as high.[44]

In the South, Irish units were raised in eight of the Confederate states. Five of the Confederate generals were Irish-born: Cleburne, Finnegan, Hagan, Lane, and Moore. Most of the Irish, though, served in units that mingled men from many backgrounds. It was as difficult for the Confederate Irish to understand why Yankees fought states seeking "independence"—a long-cherished goal of Ireland—as it was for the North's Irish to see why the South should split from a country that provided immigrants freedoms unattainable in Ireland. Both were subject to the jingo emotionalism that reached ungovernable levels and helped bring on the war. Both were bled unmercifully by the military romanticism that heightened the tragedies and blunders of the fighting. Resolute, daring, badly led youths were roundly slaughtered by the new technology of killing that industrial production made possible after the political leaders had haggled endlessly and failed in all their bitter perversity.

The fortunes of the South's Irish, whether well-to-do or laboring people, sank with the Confederate defeat. The great proportion of Irish faced the thing they had feared most—direct competition from Blacks for low-skill jobs. The resulting rancor was a further inflammation of what had become a traditional conflict. Such reactionary spokesmen as John Mitchel, himself a former felon and a man who had been imprisoned and exiled from Ireland by England, strongly supported proslavery principles, and in doing so lent credence to the racist prejudices that were accepted by whites and at times were even more enthusiastically embraced by immigrants seeking to elevate their own status.

The Civil War was more disorienting for the South's Irish than for others, it could be argued, for they were mostly placed at the edge of Southern society and less wedded to its institutions. Nevertheless, they were to pay the price of combat from Fort Pulaski in Georgia, where Lieutenant Christopher Hussey rescued the Confederate colors amid defeat, to Kenesaw Mountain where they died with the Tennessee Regiments. Some Irish served with the "Orphan Brigade," a Kentucky unit of Confederates disowned by that state when Kentucky joined the Union cause. As in the North, the Irish as unskilled and young immigrants were more likely to be involved in military service in cities like Richmond, Charleston, Mobile, and Nashville where they constituted a large part of the white work force. But in Charleston, as the Yankees marched in to victory, they were able to form an Irish Union unit on the spot. As Commodore W. F. Lynch said of one of his naval battles with the Federals, the war for the Irish was "about as confused an engagement as can be imagined."[45]

The legacy of disillusionment, poverty, and alienation in the South after the Civil War is a sharp contrast to the euphoric, warlike "Celtic" spirit strangely attributed to the region in a fantasy of hyperbole by Grady McWhiney and Perry D. Jamieson in their book on the Civil War and the South's heritage. The imputation of some wild élan to the South, linked by the most illusory supposition to the Celts of pre-Roman Europe, is a historical confection surpassing that of the magnolia-drenched plantation fantasies of cheap Southern novels. The postwar South is to be found with far more authenticity in the historical consciousness of limitations described by C. Vann Woodward in *The Burden of Southern History*.[46]

Despite attempts to encourage foreign immigration, the percentage of foreign-born in Southern cities declined notably between 1860 and 1900. In Richmond the percentage dropped from 13.0 to 3.4 percent, in Savannah from 21.0 to 6.3 percent, and in New Orleans from 8 to 1 percent. This modified but did not erase their identity. Hence, the Irish communities in such cities which had expanded before the Civil War were not replenished with immigrants. It did mean that in many places the Irish, though retaining a family recollection of their identity, participated in civic life as individuals rather than as a group. In larger cities such as Memphis, Richmond, and New Orleans they did, however, maintain their own ties for political purposes.[47]

In Memphis the epidemics in the raw river city were a threat to the very survival of the group in the 1870s, for 2,000 Irish, thirteen priests, and thirty nuns perished of yellow fever in that decade. The early success of the Irish in that city was no assurance of continuity.[48] In Washington the capital city had several thousand Irish by the 1870s. Patrick T. Moran, a banker and a political orator, was one of the first of a long line of resident Washington figures mingling with the changing tide of elected representatives from throughout the country. Cities like St. Louis, where the Irish numbered 29,000 in 1860, had steady traditions of Irish prominence. Bryan Mullanphy had been mayor in 1847, and William Carr Lane had preceded him. The city's first newspaper was founded by Joseph Charles, and James Rankin was its first sheriff. The Irish Catholics of Louisville and Nashville maintained strong family traditions of political and religious activity through the Stritch, Malley, Farrelly, and Morris families.[48] It is notable that the urban presence of the Irish was strongest in the second half of the nineteenth century in those cities around the edges of the Old South and in border regions. Thus, the condition that prevailed from the earliest days, that the Irish as a group were not centrally determinant and seldom locally dominant, was continued in Southern life.

Whatever the actualities of demography, the Irish did figure symbolically in the plantation mythology of the South. There was a substantial basis, of course, for their inclusion, for as early settlers some had become part of the planter class, especially in the Carolinas and in Louisiana. The accomplished and diverse careers of men like John McDonogh of New Orleans and John H. Reagan, a cabinet member of the Confederate government, were the basis in reality for the sentimentalized novels like the *Foxes of Harrow*, and the apotheosis of all such depictions, Margaret Mitchell's *Gone with the Wind*.[49] Margaret Mitchell's own family background with a Tipperary grandfather who was a plantation owner served as the model for her fictional creation of Tara, the family home of tempestuous Scarlett O'Hara.

The record of Irish nationalist activity in the South is impressive and compares favorably with similar exertions elsewhere in the country where the group was thinly settled. A continuous organizational effort in behalf of Irish independence existed in New Orleans from the days after the failed Rising of 1798. Campaigns in support of Daniel O'Connell and the agitators of 1848 were conducted in New Orleans and Mobile. A liaison among *Clan-na-Gael* supporters in the 1880s was led by Timothy Maroney from New Orleans, and Mississippi Valley cities had a continuing nationalist representation through the nineteenth century. In the conflict prompted by the Sinn Fein movement after World War I, several Southerners played important roles in mobilizing American opinion to support the Irish independence drive.[50] Thus, the Irish in the South maintained long-term connections with the nationalist organizations that were threaded through the rest of the country and which produced materials and events to promote their cause.

The exposition of ideas of commercial and industrial development that became a program for what was known as the ''New South'' was led by Georgian Henry Grady in the 1880s. Editor and orator, Grady promoted the use of local resources, diversification of crops, and relatively benign race relations practices within the framework of segregation as a platform for regeneration of the South. This movement sought to overcome the stagnation that had followed the Civil War and Reconstruction periods. Cities like Charleston had remained practically stationary in population from the Civil War until 1910. John P. Grace displaced the immobilized upper-class faction in that city in 1911 and became mayor. Opposed to the ''bourbons,'' Grace made city government work for municipal benefits for the first time in two generations. A similar achievement occurred with the election of Andrew J. McShane as mayor of New Orleans, where his competitive spirit summoned a challenge from Arthur O'Keefe, who followed him and expanded city cooperation with business in the busy port.[51]

The expression of Populism in the South brought an articulation of those grievances of the lower-class whites, and to a lesser extent Blacks, against those who considered themselves the elite of the region. The powerful grip of bankers and business leaders on the political representation of the South evoked the protest and agitation that matched the outcry of the Midwestern farmers in the 1890s. In the South, as Richard Hofstadter has noted, reformers often lapsed into a reactionary posture when their frustrations and yearning for a paternalist past overcame their sense of current needs.[52] Native radicals added anger to the movement, and the Irish-Americans were part of the protest. Dan Hogan, a lawyer, publisher, and socialist, ran for governor of Arkansas in 1894 and was a fiery example of such radicalism.[53] Such radicals were the rare exception, however, thrown up by transient waves of discontent. Far more typical of the region was the political corruption of such cities as Atlanta and Memphis maintained by the apathy of the putative leadership class and the general public. The Pendergast machine in Kansas City became a byword for thieving municipal government, and Southern cities showed they could be as lax as those in the North.[54]

In the bitter campaign of 1928 Al Smith was denied the votes of the Southern Democrats because of the still-virulent anti-Catholic prejudice that infected the region's life. The resurgence of the Ku Klux Klan in the 1920s fed anti-Catholic sentiment, but this was nothing new for the religious minority that had built an educational and community tradition in the Southern cities. Militant Protestantism, always at the heart of the South, and the harsh attitudes toward Catholics, Blacks, foreigners, and mill workers all betrayed the truculent and insecure phobias alive in the mind of a region that had tasted defeat in rebellion and long-term poverty.[55]

The brutal poverty of Lyndon Johnson's boyhood in Texas was part of the underdevelopment that afflicted so much of the rural South. It deeply marked the political life of his generation. Radio evangelist Lee "Pappy" O'Daniel played on its frustrations to be elected Texas governor. George Mahon of the Texas Panhandle and Dan Quill of San Antonio dealt with it daily. The careers of Senators Tom Connally and John B. Connally rose above it, but it was still a major fact of Texas life that marked that state's partly Southern orientation.[56]

Even where industry had come to the South, Bourbon rule repressed any semblance of labor organization. Edgar Gardner Murphy described the condition in the early period of textile growth that would continue for two generations: "I have known mills in which for ten or twelve days at a time the factory hands—children and all—were called to work before sunrise and dismissed from work only after sunset."[57] The great migration of Blacks out of the South during the two world wars somewhat relieved their condition as the largest impoverished group, but as industrialization increased in the 1960s, influxes of Spanish-speaking immigrants in the "Sun Belt" reenacted the exploitative cycle.

Farsighted men such as crusading Atlanta editor Ralph McGill saw that the future of the South depended on a broad renovation of race relations, class attitudes, and economic development. As the greatest city of the Old South, New Orleans provided an example of urban reform under DeLessups Morrison. In the 1940s he took advantage of wartime changes to increase port business, design a new city charter, and fight the arrogantly inept Governor Earl Long. The man behind the Morrison drive was David R. McGuire, Jr., a shrewd and energetic journalist who was Morrison's chief resource for policy and guidance.[58] In the years that followed, Atlanta, Charleston, and Nashville all undertook civic reforms stimulated by new commercial activity, tourism, and the influence of national companies reaching into the region.

The Irish Catholic ties and institutions developed in the South during the post–Civil War decades were the nuclei through which the group's identity would be maintained. That religious heritage in Southern urban centers appeared to be secure in the second half of the twentieth century. Churches and schools had moved to racially integrate their facilities without jeopardizing their stability, sometimes in advance of the general community as was the case in New Orleans. In rural areas, however, the missionary character of Catholicism declined though the work of missionary orders like the Holy Ghost Fathers, the Josephites, and the Sisters of the Blessed Sacrament among Blacks was part of an evangelizing tradition that had been subsidized in the region for generations and that had been directed at whites as well as Blacks. The long dispute within Catholic circles about the proportion of people who had abandoned Catholicism in the South diminished, since there was little clarity about the issue, adequate statistics never having been assembled. In an interesting fashion Catholicism did fit into the South. It reenforced conservative attitudes about individual ethical responsibility and honor. It represented a long tradition and was part of the region's antebellum recollections and did not contradict the basic elements of ''Southernness'' and the ''Southern tradition'' that were so actively cultivated in the region.

The differences of physical environment, economics, and social organization that produced a strong regional culture in the South affected Irish-Americans more thoroughly than other regional variations in the United States.[59] The fact that immigration of foreign-born whites declined markedly after the colonial period was a fundamental factor that limited the group's influence. The rural character of the South, shaped by isolation, poverty, and individualist fundamentalist Protestantism, originally bore marks of Scotch-Irish infusions. The Protestantism of the South, however, was too diverse, too personalized, and too fractious to form a civic constitution like that of New England. As a result the Scotch-Irish rural presence became diffuse.

The Irish Catholics for their part were either a thin minority in small towns or countryside or were more numerous in the larger cities, but they were culturally constrained in both situations. Their influence on population patterns was decisive in the larger cities, and they tenaciously affirmed their creed and identity against the prejudices of those hostile to them. In doing so they contributed toward that conservative set of values that is part of the Southern tradition. In Southern regional literature one of the major themes is the conflict between those of no ethical code and those who uphold revered values. Vivid novels and plays express this concern repeatedly, and Frank Marion O'Donnell was one of the first literary critics to show how William Faulkner's works revolve around it. Flannery O'Connor, indelibly Irish in family background, fully expressed this preoccupation of Southern thought, and even John Kennedy Toole's anti-novel, *A Confederacy of Dunces*, traces the tension between New Orleans Catholic values and disordering influences.[60]

The interaction of Blacks and Irish, never a sympathetic association in any of the country's regions, was further irritated in the South by the mutual vulnerability of both groups. Catholic missionary endeavors were not capable of redressing this blighted relationship. The Irish in the ports, on the railroads, in the mills, and in the farmlands of the South were in direct competition with both slave and free Blacks. The notorious poverty of port slums, shantytowns, and mountain hollows embraced them both, and only fleetingly did they ever make common cause. The defeat of the Confederacy, with its popular tableau of the fall of the great plantation house, would be better symbolized by the three-generation predicament of such poor Blacks and whites amid sharecropping, shacks, and unemployment. The Irish, who had earlier displaced free Blacks in various trades, found they had succeeded only to places sorely beset by class prejudice and privation.[61]

While the Irish were never numerous enough or distinctive enough to shape the South's institutions in the way that they affected labor, religion, politics, and urban growth in other regions, they were still able to define an identity for themselves within the context of Southern life. In a traditionalist culture where family history and shared regional pride were intently regarded, the long Irish presence could not be disregarded. It has continued in localized but notable ways. The historic Irish communities of Charleston and Savannah celebrate St. Patrick's Day, and the newer city of Miami has joined them. In New Orleans civic pride insisted that the Irish Channel area be preserved, and with it the memory of Irish diggers who died to drain its land.

Because of their long experience with minority status in the South, the Irish-Americans of that region may have much to teach their ethnic compatriots elsewhere, since the decline of Irish immigration in the twentieth century makes the conditions of marginality and subordinate status once again a probability for the group as a whole in the United States. It is the record of conscious regional identification and discrete familial and ethnic memory that has sustained Dixie's Irish-Americans. The South's inheritance of a quasi-mythical planter class and the saga of Blacks who have dreamed of freedom must also include the inheritance of the Irish who coursed its rivers, laid its rails, and served its broken Confederacy.

NOTES

1. See, for example, Carl Wittke, *The Irish in America* (Baton Rouge: Louisiana State University Press, 1956); William V. Shannon, *The American Irish: A Political and*

Social Portrait (New York: The Macmillan Co., 1963); Lawrence M. McCaffrey, *The Irish Diaspora in America* (Bloomington: Indiana University Press, 1976). All try to give a perspective on Irish-American dispersion but do not examine the South. Parts of this chapter appeared as an essay, "The South's Irish Catholics: A Case of Cultural Confinement," in Randall M. Miller and Jon L. Wakelyn, eds., *Catholics in the Old South* (Macon, Ga.: Mercer University Press, 1983), pp. 195–208.

2. Gastil, *Cultural Regions in the United States* (Seattle: University of Washington Press, 1975), p. 174; Ralph McGill, *The South and the Southerner* (Boston: Little, Brown and Co., 1959), p. 1.

3. Frederick Mark, *A History of the Westward Movement* (New York: Alfred A. Knopf, 1978), pp. 20–21.

4. Michael Paul Rogin, *Fathers and Children: Andrew Jackson and the Subjugation of the American Indian* (New York: Random House, 1976), pp. 165–205.

5. Margaret E. Maloney, *Fág An Bealach: The Irish Contribution to America* (Pittsburgh: United Irish Societies of Pittsburgh, 1977), p. 28.

6. George F. Scheer and Hugh F. Rankin, *Rebels and Redcoats* (New York: World Publishing Co., 1957), p. 463.

7. Ibid., p. 485.

8. Maloney, *Fág An Bealach*, p. 28.

9. Joseph I. Shulim, *John Daly Burk: Irish Revolutionary and American Patriot* (Philadelphia: The American Philosophical Society, 1964), p. 49.

10. See, for example, W. S. Murphy, "The Irish Brigade at the Capture of Pensacola, 1781," *Florida Historical Quarterly* 45 (January 1966): 215–225; John G. Coyle, "Cornelius Harnett of Wilmington, North Carolina," *Journal of the American Irish Historical Society* 29 (1930–1931): 148–156; A. S. Salley, ed., *Warrants for Lands in South Carolina, 1672–1711* (Columbia: University of South Carolina Press, 1973); Clarence L. Ver Steeg, *Origins of a Southern Mosaic* (Athens: University of Georgia Press, 1975), p. 83; Margaret Seton Fleming Biddle, *Hibernia: The Unreturning Tide* (New York: Vantage Press, 1974), pp. 20–28; Harnett T. Kane, *Natchez on the Mississippi* (New York: William Morrow and Co., 1947), p. 90.

11. Harriette Simpson Arnow, *Seedtime on the Cumberland* (New York: The Macmillan Co., 1960), pp. 23–24, 156, 292–93; Harriette Simpson Arnow, *The Flowering of the Cumberland* (New York: The Macmillan Co., 1963), pp. 1–29; Robert Kelley, *The Cultural Pattern in American Politics* (New York: Alfred A. Knopf, 1979), pp. 172–175.

12. James G. Leyburn, *The Scotch-Irish: A Social History* (Chapel Hill: University of North Carolina Press, 1962), p. 317.

13. Herschel Gower, "John Fitzgerald: Presidential Image-Maker for Andrew Jackson," *Tennessee Historical Quarterly* 42, no. 2 (Summer 1983): 138–150; John A. Scott, ed., *Living Documents in American History* (New York: Washington Square Press, 1963), p. 323–336, 411.

14. James G. Leyburn, *The Scotch-Irish: A Social History*, p. 317. On the "Scotch-Irish" versus Irish Catholic views, see R. J. Dickson, *Ulster Emigration to Colonial America, 1718–1775* (London: Routledge and Kegan Paul, 1966), pp. 65–67; Edward F. Roberts, *Ireland in America* (New York: G. P. Putnam's Sons, 1931), p. viii, presents the opinion of historian Claude Bowers, who saw the term *Scotch-Irish* as an "amusing device" and "an absurd manifestation of intolerance." Graham Kinlock finds the Irish Protestants competitive yet intensely committed to the status quo, and exclusive, elitist,

but lacking in self-discipline. This is a distinctly unusual analysis: Graham Kinlock, "Irish-American Politics: Protestant and Catholic," in Joseph Roucek and Bernard Eisenberg, eds., *America's Ethnic Politics* (Westport, Conn.: Greenwood Press, 1982), pp. 172–197.

15. Abbott Emerson Smith, *Colonists in Bondage: White Servitude and Convict Labor in America, 1607–1776* (New York: W. W. Norton Co., 1971), pp. 167, 212, 267.

16. Richard Niehaus, *The Irish in New Orleans, 1800–1860* (Baton Rouge: Louisiana State University Press, 1965), pp. 4–5; John I. Cosgrave, "The Hibernian Society of Charleston, South Carolina," *Journal of the American Irish Historical Society* 25 (1926): 150–158.

17. Ella Lonn, *Foreigners in the Confederacy* (Chapel Hill: University of North Carolina Press, 1967), p. 28; David R. Goldfield, "Cities of the Old South," in Blaine Brownell and David R. Goldfield, eds., *The City in Southern History: The Growth of Urban Civilization in the South* (Port Washington, N.Y.: Kennikat Press, 1977), p. 64; Frederick Law Olmstead, *The Cotton Kingdom*, 2 vols. (New York: Mason Publishers, 1861), vol. 1, p. 276.

18. Niehaus, *The Irish in New Orleans*, pp. 33, 44–45.

19. Fussell Chalker, "Irish Catholics and the Building of the Ocmulgee and Flint Railroad," *Georgia Historical Quarterly* 54 (1970): 507–516.

20. George Rogers Taylor, *The Transportation Revolution, 1815–1860* (New York: Harper and Row, 1951), pp. 42, 75–84, 290. The unenviable position of Irish immigrants in relation to slaves posed a further cultural problem for them. In many work situations the two groups competed. Olmstead observed that some Virginia farmers preferred the Irish field hands to Blacks. The defensive reaction of the Irish workers to the manifest cruelties of slavery led them to insistently distinguish themselves from Black slaves and workers. Although sharing many of the same social and economic disabilities with Blacks, the Irish strove to confirm their own independence and identity, and this imparted a special individualism to Irish behavior in the South. See Eugene Genovese, *Roll, Jordan, Roll: The World the Slaves Made* (New York: Random House, 1974), p. 229; Frederick Law Olmstead, *The Cotton Kingdom*, 2 vols. (New York: Mason Publishers, 1861), vol. 1, p. 276. New England's Edward Everett Hale in 1852 wrote of the Irish immigrants:

They are fugitives from defeat, or without a metaphor, from slavery. . . . Here in Massachusetts we writhe and struggle, really with one heart, lest we return one fugitive who can possibly be saved to Southern slavery; but when there come these fugitives from "Irish bastilles" as they call them, we tax them first and neglect them afterwards.

Edward Everett Hale, *Letters on Irish Immigration* (Boston: Phillips and Samson, 1852), p. 8.

21. On soliciting money from and serving the Irish workers, see, for examples, Fr. F.R. Pont to Antoine Blanc, 25 November 1856, and Fr. Peter McLaughlin to Blanc, 29 January 1859, New Orleans Papers, Library of University of Notre Dame. On the denial of fast-day food, see Fr. John Fierbras to Blanc, 3 February 1853, ibid. I thank Randall M. Miller for these and other references.

22. Richard Haunton, "Law and Order in Savannah, 1850–1860," *Georgia Historical Quarterly* 56 (1972): 10–11.

23. Christopher Silver, "A New Look at Old South Urbanization: The Irish Worker in Charleston, South Carolina, 1840–1860," in Samuel M. Hines and George W. Hopkins,

eds., *South Atlantic Urban Studies* (Columbia, S.C.: University of South Carolina Press, 1979), vol. 3, pp. 141–171.

24. Lonn, *Foreigners in the Confederacy*, p. 31.

25. N.T. Maguire, "Catholicity in Washington, Georgia," *American Catholic Historical Researches* 11 (January 1894): 17–28; Bishop John England, "Memoirs of the Roman Catholic Church in America: North Carolina," Ibid. (July 1894): 119; Donald A. Debats, "Elites and Masses: Political Structure, Communication and Behavior in Antebellum Georgia" (Ph.D. diss., University of Wisconsin, 1970), p. 436.

26. John Gilmary Shea, *History of the Catholic Church in the United States*, 4 vols, (New York: The American Press, 1892), vol. 3, pp. 93 and 295.

27. James J. Pillar, "Catholicism in the Lower South," in Lucius F. Ellsworth, ed., *The Americanization of the Gulf Coast, 1803–1850* (Pensacola, Fla.: Historic Pensacola Preservation Board, 1972, pp. 34–43.

28. Ray Allen Billington, *The Protestant Crusade, 1800–1860* (Chicago: University of Chicago Press, 1964), pp. 132, 168, 256; *American Catholic Historical Researches* 9 (January 1892): 43. The Irish in the North read of these hostile anti-Irish incidents. *The Evening Bulletin* (Philadelphia), (September 13 and 18, 1856).

29. Kelley, *The Cultural Pattern in American Politics*, pp. 172–175.

30. Frances Anne Kemble, *Journal of a Residence on a Georgia Plantation in 1838–1839* (New York: Harper and Row, 1961), p. 129.

31. Niehaus, *The Irish in New Orleans*, p. 28; Debats, "Elites and Masses," p. 429; John Tracy Ellis, *American Catholicism* (Chicago: University of Chicago Press, 1956), pp. 75–89; Randall Miller, "The Failed Mission: The Catholic Church and Black Catholics in the Old South," in Edward Magdol and Jon L. Waklyn, eds., *The Southern Common People: Studies in Nineteenth Century Social History* (Westport, Conn.: Greenwood Press, 1980), pp. 37–54.

32. Peter Guilday, *The Life and Times of John England, First Bishop of Charleston, 1786–1840*, 2 vols. (New York: America Press, 1927), vol. 1, p. 5454, vol. 2, pp. 18, 163.

33. Niehaus, *The Irish in New Orleans*, pp. 98–111; John Gilmary Shea, *History of the Catholic Church in the United States*, 4 vols. (New York: The American Press, 1892), vol. 3, pp. 269–291. For Irish religious development see Emmet Larkin, "The Devotional Revolution in Ireland, 1850–1875," *American Historical Review* 77 (June 1972): 625–652, and Jay Dolan, *The Immigrant Church: New York's Irish and German Catholics, 1815–1865* (Baltimore: Johns Hopkins University Press, 1975), pp. 159–169.

34. Ellen Meara Dolan, *Old St. Patrick's Church* (St. Louis: Old St. Patrick's Church, 1967); R. Emmet Curran, "Mission to Province: 1805–1813," *The Maryland Jesuits: 1634–1833* (Baltimore: Loyola University Press, 1961), pp. 47–68; James Crotty, "Baltimore Immigration" (Master's thesis, Catholic University of America, 1951), pp. 20–21.

35. John Brendan Flannery, *The Irish Texans* (San Antonio: Institute for Texas Cultures of the University of Texas, 1980), pp. 91–96, 103–108, 129–132.

36. Ralph Wooster, *Politicians, Planters and Plain Folks: Courthouse and Statehouse in the Upper South, 1850–1860* (Knoxville: University of Tennessee Press, 1975), p. 32; Kelley, *The Cultural Pattern in American Politics*, p. 175; Debats, "Elites and Masses," p. 436; Joseph P. O'Grady, "Immigrants and the Politics of Reconstruction in Richmond, Virginia," *Records of the American Catholic Historical Society* 83 (1972): 87–101.

37. Ellis, *American Catholicism*, p. 89; Robert A. Sigafoos, *Cotton Row to Beale*

Street: A Business History of Memphis (Memphis: University of Tennessee Press, 1979), pp. 39–40.

38. Quinlan to Bishop Patrick Lynch, May 19, 1861, Lynch Papers, Archives of the Diocese of Charleston, South Carolina.

39. Clement Eaton, *The Freedom-of-Thought Struggle in the Old South* (New York: Harper and Row, 1964), pp. 249, 385–391.

40. W.J. Cash, *The Mind of the South* (New York: Vintage Books, 1960), pp. 16–17.

41. Charles Sydnor, *The Development of Southern Sectionalism: From Nationalism to Sectionalism, 1819–48* (Baton Rouge: Louisiana State University Press, 1968), p. 308.

42. Genovese, *Roll, Jordan Roll*, p. 298. Blacks had their own mockery of the Irish: Herbert G. Gutman, *The Black Family in Slavery and Freedom, 1750–1925* (New York: Pantheon Books, 1976), pp. 298–301.

43. Richard B. Morris, "The Measure of Bondage in Slave States," *Mississippi Valley Historical Review* 41, no. 3 (1954): 229; Malcolm J. Rohrbough, *The Trans-Appalachian Frontier: People, Societies and Institutions, 1775–1850* (New York: Oxford University Press, 1978), p. 257.

44. Thomas J. Mullen, "The Irish Brigades in the Union Army," *The Irish Sword* 9, no. 34 (Summer 1969): 50–58.

45. Lonn, *Foreigners in the Confederacy*, p. 31; Cosgrave, "The Hibernian Society of Charleston," pp. 150–158; Howell and Eliabeth Purdue, *Patrick Cleburne: Confederate General* (Hillsboro, Tex.: Hill Junior College Press, 1973), pp. 1–41; I.W. Avery, *The History of the State of Georgia: 1850–1881* (New York: Brown and Derby, 1881), p. 230; "The Battle of Kenesaw Mountain," *Annals of the Army of Tennessee* 1, no. 3 (June 1878): 114; Ira Berlin and Herbert G. Gutman, "Natives and Immigrants, Free Men and Slaves: Urban Workingmen in the Antebellum American South," *American Historical Review* 88, no. 5 (December 1983): 1181–1187; William C. Davis, *The Orphan Brigade: The Kentucky Confederates Who Couldn't Go Home* (Baton Rouge: Louisiana State University Press, 1980), pp. 47, 125, 139, 152, 185; John G. Barrett, *The Civil War in North Carolina* (Chapel Hill: North Carolina Press, 1963), p. 50.

46. Grady McWhiney and Perry D. Jamieson, *Attack and Die: Civil War Military Tactics and the Southern Heritage* (Birmingham: University of Alabama Press, 1982), pp. 170–179; C. Vann Woodward, *The Burden of Southern History* (New York: Mentor Books, 1968), p. 35.

47. Blaine Brownell and David Goldfield, eds., *The City in Southern History: The Growth of Urban Civilization in the South* (Port Washington, N.Y.: Kennikat Press, 1977), p. 116; James J. Flanagan, "The Irish Element in Nashville, 1816–1890" (Master's thesis, Vanderbilt University, 1951).

48. George Capers, "The Yellow Fever in Memphis in the 1870's," *Mississippi Valley Historical Review* 24, no. 4 (March 1938): 483–502; James A. Davis, *The History of the City of Memphis* (Memphis: Hite, Crumpton and Kelly, 1873), pp. 1–18; Ellen Meara Dolan, *Old St. Patrick's Church*, pp. 1–14; Thomas J. Stritch, "Three Catholic Bishops from Tennessee," *Tennessee Historical Quarterly* 37, no. 1 (Spring 1978): 3–35.

49. Carl Degler, *The Other South: Southern Dissenters in the Nineteenth Century* (New York: Harper and Row, 1974), p. 41; John H. Reagan, *Memoirs* (New York: The Pemberton Press, 1968), passim; Ann Edwards, *Road to Tara: The Life of Margaret Mitchell* (New Haven: Ticknor and Fields, 1983), pp. 15–16.

50. Michael F. Funchion, ed., *Irish-American Voluntary Organizations* (Westport, Conn.: Greenwood Press, 1983), pp. 117, 132, 173, 237, 242–243.

51. Blaine Brownell, *The Urban Ethos in the South, 1920–1930* (Baton Rouge: Louisiana State University Press, 1975), pp. 24–31.

52. Woodward, *The Burden of Southern History*, pp. 118–119.

53. W.B. Heartsill, "The Arkansas Knights of Labor," *Arkansas Historical Quarterly* 42, no. 2 (Summer 1983): 127.

54. Lincoln Steffens and Claude H. Wetmore, "Tweed Days in St. Louis," *McClure's Magazine* (October 1902).

55. Cash, *The Mind of the South*, p. 343. Gerald Shaughnessy, *Has the Immigrant Kept the Faith?* (New York: The Macmillan Co., 1925), p. 254.

56. Robert A. Caro, *The Years of Lyndon Johnson: The Path to Power* (New York: Alfred A. Knopf, 1982), pp. 267, 495, 532, 695–98.

57. Cash, *The Mind of the South*, p. 204.

58. Brownell and Goldfield, *The City in Southern History*, pp. 164–165.

59. John Shelton Reed, *One South: An Ethnic Approach to Regional Culture* (Baton Rouge: Louisiana State University Press, 1982), pp. 11–32.

60. Sally Fitzgerald, "Root and Branch: O'Connor of Georgia," *Georgia Historical Quarterly* 64, no. 4 (Winter 1980): 377–387.

61. Randall M. Miller, "The Enemy Within: Some Effects of Foreign Immigrants on Ante-Bellum Southern Cities," *Southern Studies* 24, no. 1 (Spring 1985): 30–53. A notorious case of class and race violence had Irish-American leaders involved. H. Leon Prather, Sr., *We Have Taken a City: Wilmington Racial Massacre and Coup of 1898* (Cranbury, N.J.: Associated University Presses, 1984), pp. 21, 96–97.

8 PRAIRIE PADDIES— THE MIDWEST

Beyond the shining waters of the Ohio River the prairies lay across the heart of the North American continent for a thousand miles, an irresistible lure to settlement. It was as if a divine hand had set a vast geographic table upon which Americans could feast. The first uncomprehending belief that the Midwest led into an endless desert was formed as if the people of the republic simply could not believe the opportunities that the prairie world promised. In the wavering struggles with France, the English in the Indiana Territory encountered M. de MacCarty MacTigue sent from New Orleans to Kaskaskia to defend the empire of the fleur-de-lis in the wilderness. Far to the north John MacNamara led the militia that Indian traders had formed near Mackinac. To these men the prairies were very real, indeed—full of Indian dangers and bizarre climatic contrasts. Still, settlement could not be held back, and among the dots of humanity in the land-sea of prairie was the O'Hara community near St. Louis on the Illinois side of the Mississippi which was set up in the 1790s.[1]

The early penetration of the area by trappers and hunters was followed by the official expedition of Lewis and Clark. They gazed upon timbered land up to the 98° parallel, but in Illinois and Iowa and on into the plains the winds blew through the high buffalo grass. A free-ranging Indian way of life faced expanding white challenge. Indian agent John O'Fallon foretold to the Sauk tribes how the white man would come irresistibly to their hunting lands: "As you have seen the whirlwind break and scatter the trees of your woods, so will your warriors bend before them on horseback."[2] As the tide of Yankees and Southerners swept into the prairies his prophecy was borne out, and with the Anglo-American settlers and drovers there came Irish men and women, some fresh from Ireland, now transported to this terrain of limitless flatlands and vastness of sky. Other Irish people, migrating again after unsatisfactory trials in Eastern states, made their way by river routes into the territories where the world's richest agriculture would be cultivated.

That agriculture had to wait upon a great regional struggle with the Indians, however, and all the tragic misperception and fury of the conflicts of the East and South had to be enacted again. Thomas L. McKenney of the Bureau of Indian Affairs in the 1820s acquiesced to Indian removal on philanthropic grounds to save tribes from physical decay and extinction, but the white man's assaults were unrelenting.[3] Battles obscure and renowned swelled the morbid legacy. In 1812 the half-Indian sons of one Judge Riley of Schenectady—John, James, and Peter—were all killed in the massacre at Fort Dearborn in Michigan Territory. Duncan MacCarty and John Dougherty had to fight for their lives at the Chicago flats, and Captain Hugh McGary killed an Indian chief with safe conduct papers in Ohio in a fury over a previous massacre. All across the Midwest, the "Gateway to Empire," the whites and Indians clashed. Indian agent Thomas P. Moore traced the conflict to the "wanton destruction of game, the firing of the prairie," and other white man's transgressions. Tecumseh, the chief who had fought at Tippecanoe in 1811, put it succinctly from his point of view: The white race was a monster and what it ate was land.

Good men tried to stem the hostility, but their names are rarely recalled. John Dougherty was one. As government agent at Leavenworth, Kansas, he was interpreter and counselor there from 1819 to 1832. Buffalo hunter Tom Fitzpatrick urged agreement with the Indians before migration across their lands. John Conner, interpreter among the Delawares in Indiana, sought mutual understanding. Mother O'Connor of the Sisters of the Sacred Heart opened a school at Sugar Creek, Kansas, in 1841 to help Indian girls deal with the white world's inrush.[4] They did not prevail.

In 1810 a farmer in Pittsburgh counted 236 wagons on the way to Ohio. Another in upstate New York saw 260 wagons pass in nine days moving west. Between 1810 and 1820 the population of Ohio doubled and that of Indiana quadrupled. The area between the Ohio River, the Great Lakes, and the Mississippi was a region by 1810 drawing migrants from the whole Eastern seaboard.[5] Prior to the financial crash of 1837 millions of acres of public lands were sold to settlers and speculators in Illinois and Missouri. Between 1820 and 1842 more than 30 million acres of such land were bought in Ohio, Illinois, and Indiana.[6] As river transport became more available the flow of settlers grew even greater. James Lannon wrote in 1841 that "steam navigation colonized the West."[7] Rivers, canals, and railroad lines were the lines of settlement. In 1823 the Irish were at work in the lead mines in Illinois. On the rivers they were helping to move the growing traffic in pork, corn, lumber, and coal generally southward through the Mississippi corridor. Reaching back from the rivers were the six-mile-square townships; the mile-square, 640-acre "sections;" and the 160-acre "quarter sections" by which the lands were platted and sold. Where the land was wooded the trees would defy clearance for decades. As one Ohio settler's descendant recalled, "half the land was in the shadow of these mighty poplars and hickories, elms and chestnuts, ashes and hemlocks; and the meadows that pastured the red cattle were dotted with stumps as thick as harvest stubble."[8]

By 1836 there was a good representation of Irish in the Dubuque area of Iowa.

The water routes across the Great Lakes led them to the railroad and lumber camps in Wisconsin. The financial panic in 1837 led many Irish to abandon mill work in New England and move to Milwaukee. At the southern end of the region they were prominent in St. Louis, with the notable Mullanphy family at the head of a strong Irish community. On the plains of Kansas in Arapaho County they wintered hard and toiled in the baked summer fields. Life was very hard in that flat, windswept state and tales of family breakdown were part of the regional lore for generations.[9]

The flow of population into the territory beyond the Allegheny plateau resulted at first in a primarily agricultural society, but shipping and commerce were part of that society, and the Irish were engaged early in the economy. Alfred Kelley journeyed tirelessly through Ohio as canal commissioner, crossing forests and swamps, suffering fevers, to seek the best routes. He was adroitly involved in businesses and later in the first railroads in Ohio, an example of the vibrant business activity of his times.[10] The prairie farming that rapidly developed based on cereal crops was radically different from that known in Ireland. Climate, scale, soil, seed, and markets were all different. For the Irish who came to the Ohio or Illinois country the learning process had to be complete. Stock raising also required new knowledge, but it was rewarding. By 1850 Ohio had almost 2 million hogs. The Civil War period brought a sudden rise in demand and exports while land cost remained fairly stable, so that in these years a whole new wave of farm growth ensued. The institutions of this new farming society grew rapidly, and they were plastic, subject to adaptation, but a staunch Protestantism and the natural conservatism of men who could own land placed limits on the flexibility of local life.[11]

Not only were the river cities and lakefront cities that became the major market and rail centers transport and soon manufacturing areas, but they thrived on the basis of migration itself. Cleveland, Cincinnati, St. Louis, and Kansas City as older cities drew their Irish early from river, canal, and railroad workers. In Cleveland they settled in Farley Flats.[12] By 1850 the Irish-born were 12 percent of the St. Louis population, 12 percent in Cincinnati, and 15 percent in Detroit, and it was estimated that by that date there were 150,000 Irish in the Midwest.[13] Such estimates, based on Irish-born only, usually underestimate the Irish-American presence. Scattered across the prairies were places like O'Harasburg in Randolph County, Illinois, dating from 1820; Galena, Illinois, with Irish settlers from 1828; and a variety of Irish enclaves visited by Father James O'Meara in the 1830s such as Irish Grove, New Dublin, and St. Patrick's in Peoria County.[14] Often fluid communities, many would lose their Irish character quickly as the population changed and original inhabitants moved on.

There was also a conscious planting of Irish colonies across the Midwestern lands for both benevolent and exploitative purposes. In Missouri's Ozark Mountains Father John Hogan sought to establish an Irish colony for immigrants in what became known as the Irish Wilderness. Outlaws drove the settlers from the area during the turbulent Civil War years. The St. Patrick's colony set up by Father Jeremiah Trecy in Dakota County, Nebraska, was led by Captain Cornelius O'Connor, a Corkman, and was more successful and persisted in the 1850s. Daniel Duggan, who had failed to make a decent livelihood in Boston, led two dozen families to an area near Dubuque.[15] The Irish Aid Society of Boston was formed in 1855 to transport Irish to the West, and Archbishop John Hughes favored similar projects. Kerry-born engineer John Gregory as agent for the Irish National Emigration Society attempted a number of colonizations.[16] Ignatius Donnelly, transplanted from Philadelphia to Minnesota, promoted various colonization schemes.

The common belief that rural life was superior to city life, that a moral community could best be maintained in a rural setting, and the desire to do something to ease the plight of the famine refugees led to such communitarian schemes from Virginia to Texas and from Ohio to the Dakotas. Charles Collins, editor of the *Sioux City Times*, planned an Irish colony in the Dakota Territory, not from religious motives but from political ones. Collins was a Fenian and saw his colony as a base from which to attack British Canada in the late 1860s. He believed also that Irish miners finding gold in the Black Hills would provide the financing for Irish revolutionary activities.[17]

These colonization efforts have been believed to be hair-brained schemes, but this is too harsh a judgment. The authentic colonization plans were a desperate effort to relieve a stricken people. Many were successful in that they created stable settlements such as those at O'Fallon, Missouri, and Garryowen, Iowa. They could not realistically have diverted the mass of famine refugees to rural settings. As Father Stephen Byrne pointed out in 1878 in his advice to immigrants, the Eastern lands were too expensive, but the Midwestern lands were thousands of miles from the ports of entry, so the immigrants of the 1840s usually chose to stay in cities.[18] The transition from Ireland was so marked, so radical, so unpredictable that contemporaries could hardly realistically be faulted for not being able to direct the tremendous influx socially and demographically.

The skepticism of the great majority of the Irish about colonization schemes, whether blessed by bishops or not, was more than warranted by the promotional frauds that bedevilled settlements in the Midwest. A hero of the Mexican War, James Shields, attracted Irish settlers to his town of Shieldsville, Minnesota, and still others to the shaky townships of Erin, Kilkenny, Montgomery, and Fairbault in southern Minnesota in the 1850s, but they were ghost towns and Shields was accused of fraud. Thousands of fake towns and settlement frauds promoted by railroads and speculators dotted the maps of the region. As early as 1836 nine towns were advertised in Eastern papers on the Des Plaines River in Illinois, none of which ever existed. It was part of the greatest land game in history, and it was boosted when canal companies paid diggers in land scrip, as on the Illinois and Michigan Canal. Illustrations of quaint Irish villages magically planted on the prairies went along with coaxing verses like:

The Irish homes of Illinois,
The happy homes of Illinois,
No landlord there
Can cause despair
Nor blight the fields in Illinois.[19]

Irish settlers, though, tended to shrewdly avoid such blandishments and work out their settlement on an individual basis of firsthand experience in what had become the normal American pattern of pragmatic placement on the lands. This was fortunate because often the mere rumor of an Irish Catholic settlement would generate Protestant hostility.

Some Irish could evade the constraints of small-town life by taking to the steamboat routes, and a whole fellowship of them thrived as Mississippi riverboat gamblers. Men like Mike Carroll, William McGawley, and Dad Ryan used aliases and disguises repeatedly to work the steamboats as card sharks and confidence men, a clever fraternity of rascality, by turns rich and poor, as they fleeced the wealthy cotton planters and cattle kings on their river journeys.[20]

The town of Jacksonville, Illinois, could stand as the archetype for Irish Catholic experience in the prairie Midwest from the 1830s to 1870 outside of the larger cities. Irish railroad and roadwork gangs found cheap housing in the town and were at the bottom of its social order. They later gathered their families in an area called "The Patch." The middle-class Protestant leaders of the town found the consumption of alcohol to be a scandal among these people. The local newspaper decried their saloons. The Irish were unregenerate Democrats, while the town's elite and non-Irish residents were almost all Republicans. The Irish built the Church of Our Savior. More families were formed and a Hibernian Temperance and Benevolent Society was founded in 1860, and a library and charitable service group later. St. Patrick's Day was celebrated with a temperance parade led by the Catholic Men's Association. Thus, the influence of prohibitionist Protestant community pressure shaped the group's main annual social festivity. A new and larger church was erected in 1865, with some donations coming from the non-Catholic community. The nationalist Fenian Brotherhood in the same period served as a vehicle for the local political assertion of the Irish community, and they were able to elect a town alderman in 1867. Protestant hostility, however, was never far below the surface of community life, and it would be generations before Catholics would be seen as other than lackeys of a conspiring Pope and the Irish as other than a disorderly and unrespectable element in the community.[21]

Irish Protestants played a vigorous part in the evangelization of the Midwest. Setting out from cities like Pittsburgh and Cincinnati, they established churches in town after town. They carried a distinct resentment against New England Protestantism because of its pretentious self-regard. Presbyterians were especially active in the wave of religious root setting prior to 1850. The Presbyterians had 282 churches in Indiana alone by mid-century, and wherever they went they were zealous for education. Circuit-riding Methodists also organized Protestants of Irish background into faithful congregations. There were doctrinal disputes, competition from revivalist "jack ministers," and the occasional village atheist, but the Midwestern "Bible Belt" took shape early and prayed for sobriety and salvation.[22]

In some towns there were often not enough Irish to have any real impact on the general community. South Bend, Indiana, was an example. Growing up after 1850, it drew an Irish cohort of railroad workers that remained less than three percent of the population. They formed a small and rather exclusive enclave. Although their incomes rose over the next two decades, they remained below those of the native-born and English and German immigrants. Instead of forming their own fraternal groups they joined the Masons or Odd Fellows. Thus, the same kind of social pressures exerted in Jacksonville, Illinois, were present in this manufacturing city, and they resulted in Irish families' being culturally submerged in the period before 1880. South Bend became singular, however, in that the University of Notre Dame grew up there, and this drew Irish-Americans to the faculty and later made the institution one of the chief symbols of Irish presence in the country.[23]

The "Heartland" of the Midwest—Ohio, Illinois, and Indiana—consisting of 500 miles of rich farmland from the Ohio River to the Mississippi, would not have been productive without a drainage system. As one Indiana historian observed, "The Irishman with his shovel was a necessity . . . an angel of mercy."[24] After the Civil War tile drains began to be built across hundreds of thousands of acres below the wheat, oats, and barley. Log fences, then lines of trees at the edges of fields, and finally barbed wire enclosed the croplands.

As the Irish in this tableland of growing abundance maneuvered among their suspicious neighbors as farmers or townspeople, a few of their number became spectacularly successful. James Shields, while not particularly successful financially, still was elected a senator from three states and at length governor of the Oregon Territory. William Scully bought up land scrip from soldiers after the Mexican War and eventually owned 200,000 acres, most of the holdings located in Illinois. Scully's agents brought scores of Irish families to America to work on these immense tracts. Scully himself had little taste for the Midwest and lived lavishly in London, an Irishman who aped the ways of English landlords.[25]

In the larger cities the pattern of Irish concentration, institutional formation, ethnic organization, and political activity developed as it had in the Eastern centers as industrialization invaded the Midwest. The coming of the railroads stimulated tremendous outlays of capital for furnaces, rolling and rail mills, foundries, and locomotive works.[26] Human capital was part of the investment as well, and the Irish were a large component of that capital. Small industrial cities with specialized products of glass, motors, electrical equipment, brick, tile, steel plows, and oil substances flourished as industrialization spread in the second half of the nineteenth century. Lancaster and Mansfield, Ohio; Springfield, Illinois; and Terre Haute, Indiana, were part of this belt along the fortieth parallel. The northern tier of the region shone with the red glow of steel mills from Youngstown, Canton, Cleveland, Lorain, Gary, and South Chicago, and this massive industrial sequence was continued westward into Michigan.[27] Into these centers streamed the Irish labor supply that would play a role similar to that in the seaboard cities. By the 1880s over one-third of the immigrants from Ireland listed by one Irish newspaper as arriving in New York were headed for destinations in Ohio, Illinois, Wisconsin, Minnesota, and other states following what had become familiar migration routes for their group.[28]

Even while this great regional industrial strength was evolving in the settled areas around the Great Lakes, migrations wee continuing into the still-open areas of the Upper Midwest of Michigan, Wisconsin, Minnesota, and North and South Dakota. From Kanesville, Iowa, and O'Neill, Kansas, both outfitting centers for the trek west, wagon trains were constantly setting out across the prairies. By 1860 there were 28,000 Irish in Iowa and many were primed to move further west. Land records show the Irish as almost invariably among the first home-steaders in North Dakota. Many later sold their land, perhaps not because they abandoned the tough Dakota farming but because more money could be made running shops, hotels, and saloons. Irish farmer enclaves persisted, however, in St. Thomas, North Dakota, near Crystal City, and in Turtle River Township. In the Dakotas the Irish were among early petitioners for county government to stem disorder. Some had married Indians. One account recalled that Gaelic could be heard along with French, English, and Indian tongues there.[29]

It should be noted that the style of violence that we identify with the Far West really began in the Midwest. Wherever there were adventurous young men, the danger of violence was present. There was no law to hold them and horrifying incidents occurred constantly. Patrick O'Connor killed George O'Keefe in 1860 in Iowa and the right or wrong of it was never determined, for O'Connor was lynched immediately.[30] Red Dan and Black Dan McDonald and Jim Powers, all experienced frontiersmen, were working small claims in the Black Hills of South Dakota when John Kane and others found gold at Spruce Gulch in 1875, and then the rush was on. All kinds of footloose characters poured into the area. Lame Johnny Donahue was caught after stealing horses and robbing stage coaches in the territory. He was summarily hung, but Jack Furey memorialized the overly talkative robber with this verse on his grave marker:

> Stranger, pass gently o'er this sod,
> If he opens his mouth, you're gone, by God.[31]

White violence against the Indians was the usual cause of conflicts between the two groups. William Kelly thought the Indians craftier traders than the English merchants he had known in Ireland, and disputes over trading were a frequent source of fights with Indians.

As the frontier moved west the small-town life of the Middle West settled into itself to become the archetypal lifestyle that would be cited with extollation by writers, politicians, and eulogists well into the twentieth century. The proportion of Irish-born in states like Indiana declined as the population became more Americanized. In towns like New Burlington, Ohio, made into an emblematic Midwest community by John Baskin's study, or in Muncie, Indiana, where Robert and Helen Lynd produced their classic analysis of middle America, the Irish were a tiny minority. Mary Deasy's novels provide a picture of the Irish families adjusting to this situation, but also moving out beyond the Middle Border to the new cosmopolitan life of the cities made accessible by better transportation and new kinds of employment.[32]

This peaceful consolidation did not occur, however, without first being preceded by a momentous spasm called Populism. It was the greatest uprising of political dissent since the Civil War, and from its prairie fires of protest in the Midwest it burst through to the South and East. Ignatius Donnelly's wife summed up the basis of the rural protest well when she wrote: "When I think of farming I get almost sick. Think how hard they work, and they invariably come out in debt, and then more borrowing, and then misery. Life is scarcely worth such struggle." Donnelly himself wrote a fiery program for the Populist party in 1887 and campaigned hard against the fierce exploitation of farmers and small towns by the gigantic powers of the railroads and banks, against the land sharks, lobbyists, and loan sharks who served them. When Mary Elizabeth Lease toured Kansas shouting for farmers to "raise less corn and more hell," she bespoke the frustration of hundreds of thousands of mud-booted prairie farmers who not only had to cope with hostile climates and crop plagues, but were squeezed by an oppressive mortgage and marketing system beyond their control. One of Lease's repeated arguments was against British investment in the Midwest, which she claimed would reproduce the tyranny fixed on Ireland by the English investor and landlord class.

William Jennings Bryan became the symbol and hope of this protest that stormed out of rural isolation and agricultural depression. In states like Nebraska the Irish farmers joined their German neighbors politically for the first time to vote for Bryan and against the business combines that made life a dreary hell for them. For those Populists who were Irish, the arguments of Henry George for justice in taxation were much like the arguments of Michael Davitt for land reform in Ireland. Populism and Progressivism were both complex and emotional movements, but they represented the democratic imperative for reform that could be freely found in the United States, but which could barely function in Ireland.[33]

In the new cities of the Upper Midwest such as Detroit and Milwaukee the Irish, although still overrepresented in unskilled work in the 1880s, made good progress if they were able to move into the skilled occupations. They had been fixtures on the railroads for a generation in these new areas, and some families stayed in the railroad work literally for generations. The coming of heavy immigration from Eastern Europe and from the South, however, was a threat to hard-pressed Irish, so that the Irish reacted to this economic competition with violence.[34] Employers often played new immigrants off against the old beginning in the 1880s, and this continued into the twentieth century.

Chicago is the mega-city of mid-America and it shares with New York the characteristics of massive size, domination by technology, and magnetic regional power. But while New York is a true national focus of communications, talent, and interests, Chicago is more of a regional focus, the urban summation of Midwestern power. It is the business and agribusiness epicenter of a continental basin formed by the Great Lakes and the prairies. Yet it is more of a neighborhood city than New York and, anomalously, more a city of pluralist interaction than New York, where ties to Europe are more pronounced and where group exchanges tend to be less necessary than in the Midwestern milieu.

The building of the Illinois and Michigan Canal in 1836 brought the first substantial numbers of Irish to the lakefront log town that would be Chicago. A halt in canal work resulted in laborers' being paid in land scrip, which most sold, and settled in Bridgeport, the eastern terminus of the canal. A ramshackle settlement was also formed at Kilgubbin, a Northside slum full of lawlessness and raw mud alleys. Germans, Swedes, and others moved into these areas in the 1850s and the Irish began to filter into other localities.[35] Thus, from the start the Irish were less concentrated than other groups that tended to be more cohesive for language reasons.

In 1844 Bishop William Quarter, the city's first Irish-born bishop, broke the tradition of French domination of Catholic life in Illinois when he came to Chicago, and he began the long struggle to obtain priests, pay for churches, and deal with a growing restless and largely unchurched Irish population. James A. Mulligan rallied the Irish into the Shield's Guards in behalf of the Union in 1861 and the regiment fought for over two years as the Civil War swirled through the battlefields in Virginia. The Fenian Brotherhood was strongly organized in the city in the 1860s. A Hibernian Benevolent Emigrant Society tried in a limited way to assist the influx of famine refugees, but it was not until after the Civil War that organizational development of the Chicago Irish increased.[36]

The great fire that devastated the city in 1871 really prepared the way for the construction of modern Chicago, and the Irish were in a more advantageous position to take part in the enterprise than in any other urban situation in the nineteenth century. They were available in large numbers for the required labor force to undertake the rebuilding task. They had previously formed an extensive network of leadership and political activity. They had increasing control of the police force and had overcome Nativist sentiment in the city. Although the fire destroyed a million dollars in Catholic property, the Irish still controlled fifteen of the city's twenty-three parishes.[37] In 1870 there were about 40,000 Irish-born in the city. Seventeen of the forty members of the City Council were Irish-born in 1874, and they had reliable support in their widely distributed wards. Limerick-born Michael Bailey as superintendent of buildings for the city erected many of its new government structures, and in his long career presided over a huge building effort.[38] If Chicago had to be rebuilt from the ground up, the Irish were in position to do it and they did it.

The familiar individualist pattern of economic success was repeated for a small minority of Irish in Chicago in the Gilded Age. This is most familiarly illustrated by citing Kilkenny-born Michael and John Cudahy, meatpacking millionaires; Patrick Touhy, real estate magnate; Daniel Corkery, coal merchant; and others. But in the 1880s only a handful of the Irish were among the city's hundreds of lawyers, physicians, bankers, and leading businessmen.[39] Where the Irish were heavily represented was in the unskilled working population and in the industrial work force, and their experience there rivalled that of the other urban areas where labor was used without humane considerations or government protection. The Back of the Yards district, a warren of tenements and hovels behind the fetid enormity of the stockyards, became a synonym for all that was unholy in the brutalization of workers. It was here that the flamboyant Father Maurice Dorney crusaded for his worker flock in St. Gabriel's parish, making himself their spokesman from 1880 to 1914. The Irish had long preceded the Slavs and Italians in the meatpacking work force when *The Jungle*, published by Upton Sinclair in 1906, revolted the nation with its portrayal of the filth and degradation of the industry.

Similarly, the steel industry was a panorama of accidents and exploitation. William Hard, another muckraker like Sinclair, described the steel plants at the turn of the century as operating in a "cave of smoke" on the north bank of the Calumet River. In one year forty-six men died and 368 were permanently injured in the roaring, perilous mills and foundries.[40] These conditions, however, had actually improved over previous years before literate America dared examine them, and those were the years when the Irish were the primary victims of the reckless enterprises serving the railroad and banking empires of the "Robber Barons."

After twenty years of punishing abuse, workers at last, in the 1890s, began to effectively organize defenses against corporate power. Mike Donnelly, muscle to every bone of him, organized twenty-seven union locals in the stockyards in the 1890s, a heroic achievement. Mary Kenny O'Sullivan was one of the organizers of the Women's Trade Union League and collaborated with reformer Jane Addams to fight for decent working conditions. John P. Fitzpatrick, a former blacksmith, became head of a Chicago Federation of Labor after organizing steel and butcher workers. And from the sweatshops of Chicago emerged a leader of iron purpose and rousing oratorical gifts. A widow with children to support, Cork-born Mary Harris knew the realities of labor abuse firsthand, and she became a national legend as the "Miners' Angel" in the coalfields that ran from Pennsylvania through West Virginia to Kentucky and southern Illinois. She traveled relentlessly to mining camps in Colorado to shame the miners into organizing to help themselves, and would be beloved of impoverished families into her nineties as "Mother Jones," the tireless advocate of those who suffered in the industrial wars.[41] These leaders testify to the fact that the reformers of the Progressive period were not all middle-class do-gooders, and much of the motive force for the drive to tame social abuses came from those who knew in their own lives the ravages of the brutal industrial system that had grown up in the country.

In Irish nationalist activities Chicago followed the pattern of most major American cities in forming groups in response to events in Ireland, but it also had a distinctive temper and solidarity about it. It was less subject to the leadership of New York–based exiles than other cities. It showed the familiar cycle of organizational effort, beginning with an association supporting Daniel O'Connell in the 1840s, then the Fenian Brotherhood in the 1860s, and the *Clan-na-Gael* and various constitutionalist groups in the 1880s and 1890s. But, as historian Michael Funchion has shown, the Chicago Irish did not have to contend with bishops who militantly campaigned against the revolutionary organizations as was the case in New York and Philadelphia. Archbishop Patrick Feehan was close to *Clan-na-Gael* leaders and did not sermonize against them. The revolutionary republican tradition suited Chicagoans better than the constitutional agitation that was more congenial to middle-class Irish in other places. As a heavily working-class population the Chicago Irish were not too impressed with the protracted dickering with English politics that parliamentary nationalism represented. They preferred the direct, full-franchise American republic as the model for Ireland's future.[42]

The period of greatest power for the city's Irish nationalists was during the 1880s when Alexander Sullivan, a lawyer of doubtful probity, led the *Clan-na-Gael* in splitting his Midwestern faction away from the control of John Devoy's directorate located in New York. Wealthy men such as John M. Smyth and Daniel Corkery contributed to the *Clan*, and congressmen and John P. Hopkins, the first Irish Catholic mayor of the city, were members. Sullivan was discredited when some of his lackeys murdered Dr. Patrick Cronin, a man who opposed Sullivan's mishandling of *Clan* funds, a horrible crime that once again revived the stereotypes of the Irish as a violent, conspiratorial, and dangerous alien group. Even after the *Clan* directorate declared Sullivan anathema, he was hard to dislodge, for in Chicago the nationalist secret society was deeply enmeshed in local politics where it participated in deals to advance its members and promote its interests.[43]

The course of Chicago's Catholic Church was influenced by the Irish somewhat differently than in the Eastern seaboard cities. First French and later German populations played major roles in Catholic development, the first group because of the early formative years before the 1840s, the second because of their large numbers after the Civil War. Still, the imprint on the Church in Chicago was notable in all the years after 1840. By 1900 Poles, Bohemians, Belgians, and others were present in sufficient numbers to create a truly multi-ethnic Chicago Catholicism that limited Irish control. In a statesmanlike action, the Irish did set a policy of accommodation by establishing under their Irish bishops an array of sixty-three churches for various ethnic groups in the diocese along with the forty-

seven territorial parishes founded by 1902. Irish ethnic solidarity was reinforced
by their own parishes, but their sense of being part of a broader multi-ethnic
religious aggregation was stronger than elsewhere, and this became even more
true in the mid-twentieth century when social reform ideas growing out of German
Midwestern Catholicism and out of progressive forces in Chicago Catholicism
itself led by Monsignor John Egan and Father Dennis Geaney interacted positively
with social-action networks across the country in the fields of race relations and
urban renewal. Loyalty to Catholic schools was strong until after 1920 when the
Irish immigrants moved up economically.[44]

The church and nationalist networks underlay the increasing power of the Irish
in Chicago politics. A succession of leaders consolidated Irish dominance over
the city's other ethnic groups between 1880 and 1890. Big Jim O'Leary, Bath-
house John Coughlin, and Hinky Dink Kenna were the practitioners of that
raucous and primitive politics that was barely distinguishable from extortion,
slum thuggery, and grand larceny while it flourished in the raw and growing
city. Part of the appeal of such characters was their antic novelty and their
colorful resilience. Mike McDonald, a ward boss, had a wife who ran off with
a minstrel man, returned, and then ran away with a priest. Such a fate garnered
to him the sympathy of observers. Coughlin and Kenna presided over the "Levee,"
a roaring gambling and prostitution district where the violent, the bizarre, and
the madly comical were never lacking.[45] To the Irish, the zany and humorous
clowning of such figures counted for much more than their political probity,
especially when the depradations of the lionized business elite of Chicago were
hardly less scandalous.

It could be argued that the pluralism of Chicago made the Irish there more
skillful politicians as time went on. Judging by the Kelly-Nash machine of the
New Deal era a great deal of evolution had taken place. There was less violence
than there had been in the 1920s when Dion O'Bannion and Bugsy Moran traded
in murder. Mayor Ed Kelly's use of New Deal programs saved the city from
anarchy in the Depression years, and his endorsement of Black political participation and advancement was an unusual political strategy for the times and this
Black alliance with the Chicago machine would have portentous effects on
Chicago. Kelly, amid all the corruption of Chicago, was a remarkably astute
leader. However, the racial portion of the pluralist pattern would be continuously
troubling to the coalition-forming Irish. Blacks moving into the city from as far
away as Louisiana produced intense hostility among prejudiced whites. The
terrible race riot of 1919 was but the largest of a long series of clashes, many
at the edges of Irish neighborhoods.[46] Thus, it was not unexpected that Mayor
Richard Daley would leave a legacy of racial estrangement in the city when
power passed to others after his death. Daley came to typify the tough Irish
political potentate of urban America as he disdained the reformers of the 1960s,
presided over violent repressions of Blacks and antiwar protesters, and attempted
to do business as usual while television and journalism indicted his boss rule.
There was a life of Daley published in Gaelic in Ireland, and films about him

were made by Irish television. The fascination with his power and his ability to turn away challenges was shared from Chicago to County Mayo, from which his ancestors had set out. Whether or not he was "just another political boss" as political writer Bill Gleason states, he was the ultimate Irish-American urban power broker and perhaps the most powerful of them all until his death in 1976.[47]

Daley was succeeded by Jane Burke Byrne, the first woman to become mayor of an American metropolis. Solemn-faced, combative, and articulate, she was a product of the Chicago Catholic bourgeoisie of the North Side. Her network of Irish professionals, executives, wealthy brokers, bankers, and public figures along with parts of Daley's old machine brought her to victory in a hard-fought election in which, at the outset, few gave her a chance. The Irish she knew and typified had few contemporary ties with Ireland, were less vocal about their identity, and lacked the clannishness of the Irish in the south and west sides of the city. In addition to representing the new widespread affluence of the Irish in the 1970s, Byrne represented the dramatic change in the public role of women that accompanied the renewal of militant feminism.[48]

It is appropriate given the middle-American orientation of Chicago, its giant scale, and its combative Irish tradition that the works of James T. Farrell should so effectively and accurately portray its Irish-American distress. Beginning with *Studs Lonigan* in 1935 and moving through a whole cycle of novels about the O'Neill and O'Flaherty families, Farrell portrayed with unsparing realism the grimness and deranging social predicaments of nineteenth-century laboring immigrants and their twentieth-century progeny who became executives, artists, and intellectuals. Acutely honest and unsentimental, Farrell's works reveal the dissatisfaction and lack of fulfillment of the urban Irish, alienated from the elaborate rituals and folklore of Catholicism, twisted by the daily competitiveness of America, yet yearning for some touch of goodness and loveliness in the metropolis of the stockyards. Marcus Klein detects in Farrell's work a mood that is "yearningly conservative," heavily freighted with nostalgia, "implying the heart's ultimate need for some status quo ante when the tribal institutions were harmonious with life."[49] Perhaps only the rudely punishing environment of Chicago could have produced this great literary panorama of urban disillusion.

The city of Detroit constitutes in its history a sequence of Irish involvement that could be judged to characterize conditions in Midwestern urban areas outside of Chicago. Such industrialized areas as northern Ohio and Indiana were "heartland" in outlook but polyglot labor areas as well. By 1880 the major Midwestern cities outside of Chicago generally had less than eight percent of their populations composed of Irish-born inhabitants. Though the Irish established early footholds in Detroit and other cities, they were not so large a proportion as to generate community hostility as had been the case in Eastern cities. The Irish in Detroit remained in Detroit to a greater extent than the transient workers in various Eastern centers. The economic opportunities permitted more family stability, personal status, and civic participation than elsewhere.[50] Detroit had its Corktown on the West Side, and the Irish were a sufficient stimulus in the community in the nineteenth century that their presence was termed "the Irish Aphrodisiac" by one historian. Thomas Mayberry from County Cork conducted a business that was one of the early motor enterprises which would be taken over by Ford, the automotive giant that would make Detroit the world capital of auto production.[51]

Detroit had a colorful Populist and Progressive political leadership and one of those Progressive reformers, Frank Murphy, was mayor of the city during the Great Depression of the 1930s. Murphy had all he could do to hold back the violence generated by militant workers, the unemployed, and hostile corporations. The anxieties of the times also promoted the career of Father Charles Coughlin, the "radio priest" from Royal Oak, Michigan, whose addresses hearkened back to the small-town Midwestern values that were such a nostalgic social recollection for those caught in economic collapse in the big cities. Coughlin set out a cast of villains to explain the Depression, bankers, plutocrats, and government bureaucrats. He offered a vague scheme for reform based on decentralized economic power and government prevention of abuses. Coughlin also excoriated English influence in America, a line of argument congenial to the Irish as well as the Midwest's Germans. His rhetoric was really a delayed exposition of themes long familiar to the Midwest as echoes of the Populist gospel of the 1890s. Coughlin could not have made his national rhetorical crusade had he not been fully supported in his views, including his anti-Semitism, by Bishop Michael Gallagher of Detroit. It is notable also that the Irish in Detroit as elsewhere were deeply split in their views about Coughlin and his agitated sermonizing, for many detested his clerical intrusion into politics.[52]

While Coughlin was orating, others were fighting—often literally fighting—to build industrial unionism. Pat Quin, a former member of the Irish Republican Army, was made first president of Dodge Local No. 3 as the rush to unionize the auto industry burst forth amid strikes and wholesale layoffs. Pat Rice, Jack Thompson, and Mike Magee, a veteran of James Larkin's famous 1913 Dublin lockout struggle, played similar roles in their plants.[53]

The massive growth of the automobile industry into a national and then international complex of enormous power was paced by the General Motors Corporation. And at the top of that industrial colossus would preside James Roche and the man he would choose as his corporate collaborator, Thomas Murphy. They represented the first wave of executive bureaucracy to be derived from business areas that had little to do with actual manufacturing experience. Murphy, the patient accountant, confessed he knew little of actual plant management, but he ran the corporation despite that.[54]

By the 1940s there were Irish-American business figures who represented a whole new class of Midwestern entrepreneurs. Father John O'Hara was head of the University of Notre Dame School of Business, and he knew dozens of them. Bill O'Neil from an Akron, Ohio, merchant family had gotten into the tire business in Kansas City in 1912. He and his sons built the General Tire and Rubber Company, which became an international conglomerate of chemical, communications, and electronics manufacturing. Many of its dozens of plants and holdings in nineteen countries were administered by graduates of Holy Cross College where all the O'Neils went to school. Like hundreds of others the O'Neil enterprises moved from regional to national to international status in the mid-twentieth century.[55]

The fortunes of the Irish in the Central Midwest, that is, Ohio, Indiana, Illinois and Iowa, and Kansas and Nebraska, are different from those of the group in the Upper Midwest of Michigan, Wisconsin, Minnesota, and the Dakotas. After World War II Thomas A. Burke could be elected progressive mayor of Cleveland, but in the heartland the Irish in a city like Omaha became more and more like their neighbors, having long since abandoned their Democratic politics for Republican allegiance and moved from sociocultural assimilation to psychological assimilation. About half of those surveyed in a study by Frederick Luebke have made such a transition. The period of their original arrival, socioeconomic status, social relations, and group size have all determined such assimilation differences.[56] Although the Central Midwest could send a liberal like Illinois Congressman Barrett O'Hara to Congress for years, its conservative grain cannot be denied, and this delimited perspective in politics is part of the "cult of the average" in the prairie states that distrusts activism and cosmopolitan pretensions.

In the 1920s the Ku Klux Klan was a widespread and malign force in the heartland as well as in the South. Dennis John O'Neill, a Notre Dame graduate, went to work for the *Indianapolis Times* in 1926 and became involved in covering state politics in Indiana as a newsman. He and editor Boyd Gurley began an investigation of the Klan's grip on the state's politics, and an exposé resulted which broke the power of the Klan and won the Pulitzer Prize in 1928 for their newspaper. Such work made being anti-Catholic and anti-Semitic less respectable, but improvements in race relations had to wait another generation.[57]

In the Upper Midwest the tradition of Irish religious and political leadership has been more vigorous and continuous. In Wisconsin the Irish have been deemed to have persisted clearly in social, benevolent, religious, and cultural affairs. The Irish in the Progressive political tradition of the region, such as legislative wizard Charles McCarthy and Governor Frank McGovern of Wisconsin, took up where the Populists left off. Mayor Frank Murphy of Detroit made a distinguished career in surmounting the terrible years of the 1930s, vowing that no person would starve in his city. Only Mayor Jerome Cavanaugh faced similar civil disorder in that city in the 1960s.[58]

Eugene McCarthy from Minnesota is the true product of the northern Midwest, heir to the reforming ethos and liberal to the point of ardent provocation. The great aberration in the northern Midwest was, of course, Senator Joseph McCarthy, the anti-Communist Robespierre of the 1950s. He spoke to Midwestern conservatism above all with his barbed assaults on "Eastern establishment eggheads" and hence his popularity in Wisconsin. The Farmer-Labor party, the Populists, and the Progressives never won all the hearts of Wisconsin or Minnesota, and McCarthy appealed to those who remained suspicious of all government. He capitalized on the same kind of Irish Catholic audience that was swayed by Father Charles Coughlin. This audience was distrustful of Ivy League State Department officials who spoke and acted like Englishmen. These Irish Catholics had been treated to decades of anti-Communist tirades in their churches and accounts of antichurch outrages in Mexico, Spain, and Russia. They were a ripe audience for Joseph McCarthy, and the shock in many circles at the extent of the following McCarthy could gather was testimony to how little intellectuals, editors, and officials knew of sentiments within the country's complex Irish population. But, as with Father Coughlin, Joseph McCarthy faced tough Irish critics as well as supporters, as when Bishop Bernard Sheil of Chicago took the senator's measure before many others dared to criticize him.[59]

In the Midwest as elsewhere the "politics of displacement" have taken their toll. In Chicago the end of Mayor Daley's regime sharply reduced Irish confidence in that city. The Northern Ireland issue is largely uncomprehended in the land-locked Midwest. Perhaps one of the most notable achievements of the period since the decline of Irish immigration due to the restrictive legislation of the 1960s has been the development of the Irish-American Cultural Institute by Dr. Eoin McKiernan based in St. Paul, Minnesota. Largely on the strength of personal commitment, but with aid from the Butler Foundation and the O'Shaughnessy Foundation, McKiernan has been able to organize an entire national cultural network that is served by books, films, publications, lectures, and the best of touring Irish talent appearing before chapters of the group in every section of the country.[60]

If the Irish in the Midwest were less clannish politically outside of the big cities, they were also more closely attached to their communities, to their neighbors, and to local concerns. Their especially Americanized Catholicism was in many ways more creative than that of the big Eastern dioceses. They were religious with a solidity like that of their German and Scandinavian neighbors. And they mixed their religion with a plain faith in American values, so that John O'Hara, born of immigrants in Ann Arbor, Michigan, became successively priest, head of the University of Notre Dame Business School, head of the military chaplains service, and finally a cardinal.

What did this far-ranging filtering through the tableland in midcontinent signify for the Irish-Americans? It was a primal experience of America. If Louis Hartz finds a special significance for democracy in the absence of aristocrats and potentates in America, then the Midwest was the egalitarian ethos of America brought to full life. In its rural dominated landscape, American fraternity had a fundamental meaning. No Virginia grandee and no Yankee blueblood set the pattern here. The only snobberies were popular prejudices of the common man. Into this agrarian world of the plowed prairies the Irish of the nineteenth century sank their roots.

The strains of farm failure and industrial exploitation, however, also produced a Midwestern turbulence that could arise like a swift tornado, and cohorts of Irish political and protest leaders would express this reforming energy. If the big cities around the Great Lakes and along the great rivers had cynical Irish bosses, there were priests and lawyers and leaders who fought furiously against their corruption. The golden dome of the University of Notre Dame reflected this Irish idealism playing across the land, a light in the heart of the heartland.

The Irish in the heartland of the Midwest would face hard times again in the 1970s as the basic industries of the area moved south and overseas. Irish labor union leadership watched its constituency dwindle. The urban politics of the old bosses were changed by television campaigning and the increasing power of black political cadres. The Catholic Church, which had been strongly influenced by German social justice ideas in St. Louis and by active reformers in Chicago, was in rapid transition. These changes meant that the profile of the Irish in the region declined as assimilation eroded an identity that had been supported by nineteenth-century codes of religious practice and political interest. The fortunes of the group, however, were permanently conditioned by the adjustments that had been made in the prairie states in both urban centers and small towns. The Irish had fitted themselves into that Midwestern society that was so character-istically American that it could be easily mistaken for an archetype of the whole, except that the diversity and change of the whole would not permit that to be. In the middle of the continent the Irish had journeyed into a landscape that was like an ocean of prairie, and there they had found a changing harbor. Having entered the great land-ocean as refugees, wayfarers, railroad hands, and stock drovers, they became part of the region's deep-moving human current.

NOTES

1. John D. Burkhart and Dorothy R. Kare, *Indiana to 1816* (Indianapolis: Indiana Historical Society, 1971), pp. 109–110; Reuben Gold Thwaites, *Early Western Travels, 1748–1846*, 32 vols. (New York: AMS Press, 1966), vol. 2, p. 185; Mark Wyman, *Immigrants in the Valley: Irish, Germans and Americans in the Upper Mississippi Country* (Chicago: Nelson-Hall Publishers, 1984), p. 10.

2. Walter Prescott Webb, *The Great Plains* (New York: Grosset and Dunlap, 1931), p. 47.

3. Lawrence J. Friedman, *Inventors of the Promised Land* (New York: Alfred A. Knopf, 1975), p. 199.

4. Allan W. Eckert, *Gateway to Empire* (Boston: Little, Brown and Co., 1983), pp. 318 and 559; Louise Barry, *The Beginnings of the West: Annals of the Kansas Gateway to the American West, 1540–1854* (Topeka: Kansas State Historical Society, 1972), entries for 1819 and 1841; Burkhart and Kare, *Indiana to 1816*, p. 375.

5. Russell Blaine Nye, *The Cultural Life of the New Nation: 1776–1830* (New York: Harper & Row, Publishers, 1960), p. 118.

6. Benjamin Horace Hibbard, *A History of the Public Lands Policies* (Madison: University of Wisconsin Press, 1965), p. 102.

7. Eric Haites et al., *Western River Transportation: The Era of Early Internal De-velopment, 1810–60* (Baltimore: Johns Hopkins University Press, 1975), p. 75.

8. J.C. Furnas, *The Americans: A Social History of the United States, 1586–1914* (New York: G.P. Putnam's Sons, 1969), p. 261.

9. Ronald V. Jackson, Gary R. Teeples, David Schaeffermeyer, *Iowa Territorial*

Census of 1836 (Bountiful, Utah: Accelerated Data Systems, 1976), see alphabetical entries under Dubuque; Sister M. Justille McDonald, "The History of the Irish in Wisconsin in the Nineteenth Century" (Ph.D. diss., Catholic University of America, 1954), pp. 9–13; Ronald V. Jackson and Gary Teeples, *Kansas Territorial Census Index, 1860* (Bountiful, Utah: Accelerated Data Systems, 1978), p. 87; Percy G. Ebbutt, *Emigrant Life in Kansas* (New York: Arno Press, 1975), pp. 146–147.

10. Harry N. Scheiber, "Alfred Kelley and the Ohio Business Elite, 1822–59," *Ohio History* 87, no. 4 (Autumn 1978): 365–392.

11. Arthur E. Bestor, "Patent Office Models of the Good Society," *American Historical Review* 58, no. 3 (April 1953): 505–526.

12. Michael Pap, ed., *Ethnic Communities of Cleveland* (Cleveland: John Carroll University, 1973), pp. 181–185.

13. Jo Ellen Vinyard, *The Irish on the Urban Frontier: Nineteenth Century Detroit, 1850–1880* (New York: Arno Press, 1976), Table IX–6, p. 330; Frederick Mark, *A History of the Westward Movement* (New York: Alfred A. Knopf, 1978), p. 168; Robert Savage, "Irish Colonists on the Plains," in Kevin M. Cahill, ed., *The American Irish Revival: A Decade of the Recorder, 1974–1983* (Port Washington, N.Y.: Associated Faculty Press, 1984), p. 371.

14. "A Chronology of Missions and Churches in Illinois—1675 to 1844," *Illinois Catholic Historical Review* 1, no. 4 (April 1919): 103–107; the State Historical Society of Iowa, *The Annals of Iowa* (Iowa City: State Historical Society of Iowa, reprint of 1863 volume), entries for 1836–1846; James P. Shannon, *Catholic Colonization on the Western Frontier* (New Haven, Conn.: Yale University Press, 1957), pp. 90–91.

15. Thomas A. Kuhlman, "The Captain Cornelius O'Connor House in Homer: A Symbol of the Dakota County Irish," *Nebraska History* 63, no. 1 (Spring 1982): 16–32. An account of early farm struggle in Kansas by Mary O'Loughlin is given in Joanna Stratton, *Pioneer Women: Voices from the Kansas Frontier* (New York: Simon and Schuster, 1981), p. 59.

16. Kuhlman, "The Captain Cornelius O'Connor House in Homer," pp. 30–32; Shannon, *Catholic Colonization on the Western Frontier*, pp. 90–91, 267.

17. Watson Parker, *Gold in the Black Hills* (Norman: University of Oklahoma Press, 1966), p. 22.

18. Stephen Byrne, *Irish Emigration to the United States* (New York: Catholic Colonization Society, 1874), p. 78.

19. Walter Havighurst, *The Heartland: Ohio, Indiana, Illinois* (New York: Harper and Row, 1974), pp. 146, 168–175; A.R. Fulton, *Iowa: The Home for Immigrants, Being a Treatise on the Resources of Iowa* (Des Moines, Iowa: Mills and Co., 1870), p. iii; Wyman, *Immigrants in the Valley*, p. 101.

20. George H. Devol, *Forty Years a Gambler on the Mississippi* (New York: Johnson Reprint Co., 1968, originally published by the author in 1892), pp. 74, 94–95, 128.

21. Kuhlman, "The Captain Cornelius O'Connor House in Homer," p. 32; Don Harrison Doyle, *The Social Order of a Frontier Community: Jacksonville, Illinois, 1825–70* (Urbana: University of Illinois Press, 1978), pp. 127, 140–145.

22. William Warren Sweet, *Circuit Rider Days along the Ohio* (New York: The Methodist Book Concern, 1923), pp. 135–138; *One Hundred and Fifty Years of Presbyterianism in the Ohio Valley* (Cincinnati: Commission on History, Assembly of the Presbyterian Church in the United States, 1941), pp. 1–80; L.C. Randolph, *Hoosier Zion* (New Haven, Conn.: Yale University Press, 1963), pp. 73–74, 157–188, 191.

23. Dean R. Esslinger, *Immigrants and the City: Ethnicity and Mobility in a Nineteenth Century Midwestern Community* (Port Washington, N.Y.: Kennikat Press, 1975), pp. 58, 94, 112–113.

24. Havighurst, *The Heartland*, p. 145.

25. Ibid., p. 171.

26. Albert Fishlow, *American Railroads and the Transformation of the Ante-Bellum Economy* (Cambridge: Harvard University Press, 1965), pp. 118–119.

27. Havighurst, *The Heartland*, pp. 6 and 7.

28. *The Irish Nation*, September 9, 16, and 23, 1883, lists Irish immigrants as do other Irish newspapers of the time.

29. John D. Unruh, *The Plains Across: The Overland Emigrants and the Trans-Mississippi West, 1840–1860* (Urbana: University of Illinois Press, 1979), p. 162. Conflicts with Blacks were also part of the frontier violence as well as those with Indians. Robert Conot, *American Odyssey: Detroit* (New York: William Morrow and Co., 1974), p. 72; A.G. Burr, "The Organization of Bottineau County," *North Dakota Historical Quarterly* 9, no. 1 (October 1941): 3–20; Sister Ursula Dunleavy, "Canadian Halfbreed Rebellions, 1870–85," *North Dakota Historical Quarterly* 9, no. 2 (December 1941): 104.

30. Unruh, *The Plains Across*, p. 68; Parker, *Gold in the Black Hills*, pp. 30–31; Leland Sage, *A History of Iowa* (Ames: Iowa State University Press, 1974), pp. 52, 94, 157.

31. Cited in Parker, *Gold in the Black Hills*, p. 90; William C. Sherman, *Prairie Mosaic: An Ethnic Atlas of Rural North Dakota* (Fargo: North Dakota Institute for Regional Studies, 1983), pp. 111–112.

32. Clifton Phillips, *Indiana in Transition: 1880–1920* (Bloomington: Indiana Historical Society, 1968), p. 369; John Baskins, *New Burlington, Ohio: The Life and Death of an American Village* (New York: W.W. Norton Co., 1976), p. 73; Robert S. Lynd and Helen Merrell Lynd, *Middletown: A Study in Contemporary American Culture* (New York: Harcourt, Brace, and Co., 1920), pp. 293 and 363; Mary Deasy, *The Hour of Spring* (New York: Arno Press, 1976). Persistence of anti-Irish prejudice is recorded in Helen Hooven Santmyer's novel, . . . *And Ladies of the Club* (New York: G.P. Putnam, 1984); see *Newsweek* (June 18, 1984): 93.

33. Roger C. Kennedy, *Men on the Moving Frontier* (Palo Alto, Calif.: American West Publishing Co., 1969), pp. 114–117; Roger Clements, "British Investment and American Restrictions," *Mississippi Valley Historical Review* 42, no. 4 (September 1955): 207–228; Frederick C. Luebke, *Immigrants and Politics: The Germans of Nebraska, 1880–1900* (Lincoln: University of Nebraska Press, 1969), p. 97.

34. Vinyard, *The Irish on the Urban Frontier*, Table X–2, p. 316; Frank P. Donovan, *Mileposts on the Prairie: The Story of the Minneapolis and St. Paul Railway* (New York: Simmons Boardman, 1948), p. 238; *The Daily Herald* (Clinton, Iowa) (December 9, 1895).

35. Michael Funchion, *Chicago's Irish Nationalists, 1881–1890* (New York: Arno Press, 1976), pp. 10–11.

36. John Corrigan, "How the Irish Built Chicago," *Irish-American News* (Chicago) (November 1979).

37. M.L. Ahern, *The Great Revolution: A History of the Rise and Progress of the People's Party in the City of Chicago and the County of Cook* (Chicago: Lakeside Publishing Co., 1874), pp. 1–60; Ellen Skerrett, *The Irish Parish in Chicago, 1880–*

1930 (South Bend, Ind.: Cushwa Center for the Study of Catholicism, University of Notre Dame), series 9, no. 2 (Spring 1981), pp. 1–16.

38. John Corrigan, "How the Irish Built Chicago" *Irish-American News* (Chicago) (July-August 1979).

39. Funchion, *Chicago's Irish Nationalists*, p. 14.

40. William Hard, "Making Steel and Killing Men—Unnecessary Accidents in the Steel Mills," in Arthur and Lila Weinberg, eds., *The Muckrakers: The Era in Journalism That Moved America to Reform, 1902–1912* (New York: Capricorn Books, 1961), pp. 342–358.

41. Michael Funchion, "Irish Chicago: Church, Homeland, Politics and Class—The Shaping of an Ethnic Group, 1870–1900," in Peter D'A. Jones and Melvin G. Holli, eds., *Ethnic Chicago* (Grand Rapids: William B. Eerdmans Publishing Co., 1984), pp. 26–28; Allen F. Davis, *The Social Settlements and the Progressive Era* (New York: Oxford University Press, 1967), pp. 114 and 139; Victor Hickes, "The Virden and Pena Mine Wars of 1898," *Journal of the Illinois Historical Society* 52, no. 2 (Summer 1959): 263–279.

42. Ibid., pp. 16–21.

43. Ibid., p. 24; Michael Funchion, ed., *Irish-American Voluntary Organizations* (Westport, Conn.: Greenwood Press, 1983), pp. 74–92.

44. Funchion, "Irish Chicago," pp. 12–20; James W. Sanders, *The Education of an Urban Minority: Catholics in Chicago, 1833–1965* (New York: Oxford University Press, 1977), passim.

45. Stephen Longstreet, *Chicago: 1860–1919* (New York: David McKay Co., 1973), pp. 200–205; Lloyd Wendt and Herman Kogen, *Lords of the Levee* (New York: Bobbs Merrill Co., 1943), pp. 20–41.

46. St. Clair Drake and Horace R. Cayton, *Black Metropolis* (New York: Harper and Row, 1945), pp. 1–100; Roger Biles, *Big City Boss in Depression and War: Mayor Edward J. Kelly of Chicago* (De Kalb: Northern Illinois University Press, 1984), pp. 153–159.

47. Bill Gleason, *Daley of Chicago: The Man, the Mayor and the Limits of Conventional Politics* (New York: Simon and Schuster, 1970), p. 367.

48. Kathleen Whelan Fitzgerald, *Brass: Jane Byrne and the Pursuit of Power* (Chicago: Contemporary Books, 1981), p. 38.

49. Dennis T. Flynn, ed., *On Irish Themes* (Philadelphia: University of Pennsylvania Press, 1982), pp. 1–34; Marcus Klein, *Foreigners: The Making of American Literature, 1900–1946* (Chicago: The University of Chicago Press, 1981), p. 214.

50. Robert Conot, *American Odyssey*, pp. 389, 447–452.

51. Jo Ellen Vinyard, *The Irish on the Urban Frontier*, pp. 130–141; Conot, *American Odyssey*, pp. 18–22.

52. Alan Brinkley, *Voices of Protest: Huey Long, Father Coughlin and the Great Depression* (New York: Alfred A. Knopf, 1982), pp. 143–169; Charles J. Tull, *Father Coughlin and the New Deal* (Syracuse: Syracuse University Press, 1965), pp. 89–92, 170.

53. Steve Babson, "Pointing the Way: The Role of British and Irish Skilled Tradesmen in the Rise of the UAW," *Detroit in Perspective* 7, no. 1 (Spring 1983): 75–96.

54. Ed Cray, *Chrome Colossus: General Motors and Its Times* (New York: McGraw-Hill Co., 1980), pp. 496–497.

55. Dennis A. O'Neil, *A Whale of a Territory: The Story of Bill O'Neil* (New York: McGraw-Hill Book Co., 1966), pp. 107–215.

56. Howard P. Chudacoff, *Mobile Americans: Residential and Social Mobility in Omaha, 1880–1920* (New York: Oxford University Press, 1972), pp. 63–65, 142; Frederick C. Luebke, *Ethnicity on the Great Plains* (Lincoln: University of Nebraska Press, 1980), pp. 214–218.

57. O'Neill, *A Whale of a Territory*, p. 250.

58. Robert C. Nesbit, *Wisconsin: A History* (Madison: University of Wisconsin Press, 1973), pp. 210–221; Richard S. Davis, "Milwaukee: Old Lady Thrift," in Robert S. Allen, ed., *Our Fair City* (New York: The Vanguard Press, 1947), p. 193; Sidney Fine, *Frank Murphy: The Detroit Years* (Ann Arbor: University of Michigan Press, 1975), pp. 30–120; Peter K. Eisinger, *The Politics of Displacement: Racial and Ethnic Transition in Three American Cities* (New York: Academic Press, 1980), pp. 60–61; Vinyard, *The Irish on the Urban Frontier*, pp. 140–142.

59. Robert Griffith, *The Politics of Fear: Joseph R. McCarthy and the Senate* (Lexington: University of Kentucky Press, 1970), passim.

60. The Irish-American Cultural Institute publishes a quarterly, *Eire-Ireland*, and its newsletter *Ducas* details its activities.

9 CATTLE, MINES, AND MOVIES— THE FAR WEST

In their sweep to the Rocky Mountains and beyond, the Americans galloped into a luminous legendry of their own pioneer achievements. For the Irish-Americans the Western frontier provided the most liberating influence in their experience of the new land. The melancholy background of the old country, the ghetto confinement of the Eastern cities, and the uncertainties of minority status were all transcended in the adventures of the Far West. There were miseries in plenty on the high plains and in the passes of the Rockies, but the mentality of daring and gambling for high stakes that colored the lifestyle of the West seems to have given a new impulse to the Irish rovers as they moved beyond the Mississippi. Nowhere on the American scene was the national vitality, emphasized by George Santayana, so expressively present as in the West. It is little wonder that journalist John O'Sullivan was inspired to proclaim it in a term reverberating with energy when he pronounced its power a "manifest destiny." It was the life force of a people high in the saddle, and the Irish rode headlong into the West as part of the panorama.

The Western frontier was many frontiers, but the first was the world of the trader and fur trapper. Of all the New World fauna—bison, mountain lion, bear, and antelope—none was as influential as the little swimming beaver. The most valuable fur-bearing creature on the continent, the dam-building, tree-chewing, prolific beaver lured trappers into forbidden regions where loneliness, death, and peril surrounded each day's labor. Having found beaver water and built a shelter, the trapper slid through the lake or stream in a canoe or worked along its shore, setting traps just below water level and chaining them to small posts or logs. Baited with beaver scent the traps did their job, and the trapper returned to gather his pelts. Up canyons, across torrents, past glaciers, and through icy streams and mountain swamps the trappers sought their prey with an obsessive energy. Before they knew it they too had been trapped by the rigors and the beauty of the Sierras, the Rockies, and the Cascades.

It is difficult to believe that men could be so hardened, stubborn, and aggressive as to dare what the mountain men dared. Indians, of course, had keen wilderness skills, yet they also had a superstitious avoidance of environmental challenges that were not necessary. The white Americans leaped to such challenges, and in many cases did so with limited wilderness training. They learned as they leaped to the mountains. Kentuckians John and Benjamin O'Fallon, working out of Fort Leavenworth with the Missouri Fur Company, compiled a spectacular record of exploration, trading, and dealing with the Indians. John Fitzgerald fought through hair-raising scrapes with Indians along with Jim Bridger as tribal war parties sought to plunder their furs and equipment. Robert P. Campbell in 1829 fought a five-hour battle with Indians that resulted in the loss of seven members of his party. In the 1840s Joe Doyle began a career of trading with tribes in the Colorado Territory and eventually became a territorial legislator.[1] Perhaps the most colorful of all mountain trappers was "Bad Hand" Tom Fitzpatrick from County Cavan. His nickname came from a hand injury suffered when his rifle blew up in a red-hot Indian fight. Fitzpatrick served as a guide to both the Southwest and Oregon. Whether it was true that he had miraculously survived being scalped by one swipe of a grizzly bear's paw, thus attaining a revered status in the eyes of Indians, and whether he actually had seven Indian wives, his extraordinary Rocky Mountain travels and contests with man and nature are the very essence of frontier adventure.[2]

Not all the Irishmen pursued the beaver in the awesome mountains. Dr. Henry Connelly married into a Mexican family in Santa Fe and became a pioneer trader there. Gervais Nolan, born of an Irish father and a French mother in Canada, went to New Mexico in 1824 and married Maria Dolores Lalande, built up a large mining fortune, and purchased over 800,000 acres in Colorado. The Santa Fe trade could make men rich, and in 1847 E.C. McCarty took the first big wagon train to Santa Fe from Kansas City to bring back Mexican wool and hides. It had been a hazardous trail through Comanche territory for years ever since Captain Ben Riley had escorted wagons through attacks in 1829. The Plains Indians after adapting to the horse developed superb skills as mounted warriors, as Indian agent W.J. McGee was one of the first to point out.[3] For some of the trappers and deserters from trading parties there was no wealth to be had, only death, and their grisly end is recounted in the journals of the trading parties led by Ben O'Fallon and Tom Fitzpatrick.

In popular perception it is the trail-herding cowboy who is the personification of the West, and yet his primacy lasted only a few decades after the Civil War. The romance of his reign, however, has triumphed over the realities of dirty range life and his nemesis, barbed wire. The challenge of trail driving came young for some. James M. Dougherty was only sixteen when he had to assume responsibility for driving 1,000 head of cattle hundreds of miles. The distances of the drives were astonishing. After Joe McCoy established Abilene, Kansas, as the first railhead market for cattle in 1867, the long drives from Texas drew thousands of young men into herding. Con Shea herded cattle from Texas all the way to Oregon and Idaho. Andy Adams, son of a Northern Ireland man, was still riding herds on long treks in the 1880s with companions Jim Flood, Bob Quirk, Barney McCann, and Pete Slaughter.[4] The skills of working with rope and whip and all the gear of the cattle trade were largely Mexican, but David Dary traces the term *cowboy* itself to the Irish. The image and adventure of range life, however, were as American as the tumbleweed.[5]

The railroad, barbed wire enclosure of the plains, and new patterns of beef distribution soon made the longest drives obsolete. More knowledge made ranching elsewhere more practical. The Texas cattle barons flourished through the 1880s as markets for beef expanded. Big ranchers like Daniel Sullivan, Thomas O'Connor, and Michael O'Connell shipped beef by rail out of San Antonio. Martin Kelly, a Galwayman in Corpus Christi, shipped his beef by cattle boat. By the 1880s the cattle industry reached from these places far to the north to Wyoming where the stockmen practically conducted their own exclusive government. It was not sedentary ranch life that made the boot and saddle legend, though; it was the rough, roving life of the cowpoke, free and strenuous.

To the mountain man and the cowboy must be added the hard-rock miner if we are to see the cast of Western drama complete. Far less attractive than the other two occupations, the miner's labor was more definitive for the ultimate shape of the West. With the miner came the mechanisms and concerns of industry and growing opportunities for stable settlement. The Irish as the archetypal diggers of America were involved in Western mining from the beginning, carried from place to place by the intermittent crazes for gold and silver that sent men clawing the earth at all points of the compass.

The great gold fever that compelled people to race to California in 1849 was simply one of a whole cycle of mining rushes that seethed across the Western states in the nineteenth century. Gold may have been the lure, but other minerals proved to be more important. Almost invariably the working and living conditions in the mining camps were primitive in the extreme. In the Grass Valley in California in 1860 the Irish quartz miners had at first to contend with deadly nitroglycerin fumes. Later the mine owners switched to a system of dynamiting, equally dangerous but calculated to eliminate miners' jobs. So there was a labor strike with all the attendant suffering. This was the scenario in scores of mining situations.[6]

Mine managers often cared little about their immigrant miners. One manager in Utah reproached his brother for hiring "Irish and Dago" miners, and another in Arizona resented "Irish Mexican greasers" in his mine.[7] Rock falls in mine shafts were a constant hazard. Drilling and loading holes with explosives made daily care imperative. As the years passed the dangers did not greatly decrease, for the pressure to speed excavation, load ore, and cut costs increased. Thus in the Telluride, Colorado, Smuggler Mine in 1901 twenty-five men died in a tunnel fire. These men had worked for $3 a day. Even outside the mines in the rugged mountain terrain perils abounded. Cripple Creek, Colorado, got its name because of the crippling accidents that occurred there. Snow slides, avalanches, flash floods, blizzards, and forest fires all fell upon Leadville, Colorado, in addition to the mine mishaps for which the town was noted.[8]

In a mining camp like Virginia City, Nevada, bachelor miners lived in bunkhouses or rude boardinghouses for a dollar a day, but rent was higher if a bonanza was under way. Cots were often rented for an hourly "sleep rate" and were kept in continuous use in frame flophouses for miners working in day and night shifts. The Irish-born miners, who were often one-third of the work force in the Western gold, silver, lead, and copper fields, were joined by thousands of American-born men of Irish background, so that the mine camps often had a lively Irish character. There were conflicts with Cornish miners, but there were also happier occasions such as St. Patrick's Day celebrations in the 1860s in various camps.[9]

From the 1860s on the Irish led most of the activity to form unions. In 1879 Mike Mooney worked in Leadville to organize for the Knights of Labor, seeking to bring Italians along with the Irish in the effort. He was believed to have "an almost magical influence over his supporters." Mine unionists usually had to face bitter opposition from mine owners, and the famous Marcus Daly, an Irishman who became a "Copper king" in Montana, was a fierce foe of organized labor. L.W. Callahan was an extraordinarily dedicated organizer for the Western Federation of Miners in Idaho and Oregon, and he performed feats like hiking eighty miles through the Cascade Mountains to organize miners in remote diggings. The mine conditions and exploitations made some Western miners wildly radical, and the Industrial Workers of the World found ready adherents among them. Bill Whalen caught their spirit in his chorus for "The Prison Song" to be sung to the tune of "Tramp, Tramp, Tramp, the Boys are Marching":

> Are you busy, Fellow Workers?
> Are your shoulders to the wheel?
> Get together for the cause
> And some day you'll make the laws,
> It's the only way to make the masters squeal.[10]

The strength of feeling against the mining interests which also often controlled the railroads and the towns in the mountain and desert West can only be understood if it is recalled that the dreadful working and living conditions persisted in one boom town after another from the 1850s right into the twentieth century. And through this long span of time the Irish continued to migrate to Leadville, to Butte, and to other mining centers. In Leadville alone in 1873 over $4 million in gold, silver, copper, and lead was extracted, and by 1879 this had swelled to over $18 million worth of ore, but the miners saw little of it in their wages. Peter Hanratty led what is probably the longest coal strike on record in the Oklahoma Indian Territory from 1899 to 1903 to gain bargaining rights—and won.

One of the most famous struggles for labor recognition was the Coeur d'Alene "Mining War" in Idaho in 1892. Tom O'Brien, Peter Breen, P.C. Sullivan, J.J. Tobin, and other miners formed a miners' union for the workings around the town of Gem. O'Brien had served in the Union Army in the Civil War and had been a miner in Nevada, California, and Montana. He was not a firebrand, but a steady, persistent labor man. When a strike was called by the union, the mine owners imported nonunion labor. Fighting with rifles broke out in July at the Frisco mine, and that mine's mill was dynamited. The union miners rounded up the imported labor and sent them packing, but the "scabs" were fired on as they straggled to the steamboat near Gem. Martial law was declared. Hundreds of union miners were jailed and their leaders got stiff terms in prison as the Idaho governor sided with the mine owners. The entire incident and its Irish-led militancy had a strong influence on spurring greater mine union organization.

Organizing spread, as did fighting against strike breakers, and in Colorado John H. Murphy, attorney for the Western Federation of Miners, battled for both Irish and Italian miners in 1904 as the governor of the state compliantly sent troops to overcome the union.[11]

These penetrations of the Irish into the unexplored mountains, into the trail herding of the prairies, and later into the mining of the West were, of course, simply part of the broader flow of population beyond the Mississippi. It was the settlers who would bring stability to these new territories as they fenced their homesteads, built their towns, and pitted themselves against the roaring storms and summer heat of the land. Richard Bartlett notes that the Irish were substantially represented in this settlement flow. By 1870 California had 54,000 Irish-born, and they were scattered through the frontier forts and dusty towns from Montana to Texas.[12] In Wyoming by 1870 they were in Sweetwater, Carbon, and Albany counties, and in Montana in Deer Lodge and Jefferson counties. They moved west from the big Irish concentration in Missouri and scattered like the tumbleweed.[13]

The trek west was an epic of discomfort, and later romantic views of it do the reality a disservice. As a boy Charles O'Kieffe left Nebraska with his parents and eight brothers and sisters in 1884. The father later disappeared and the family traveled 500 miles westward to homestead in a sod house in territory still roamed by the Sioux. No boy could forget such an experience.[14] Surely they felt themselves to be like those earlier explorers, men like Lieutenant Tom Sweeney in Colorado or Captain Charles Murphy leading 49'ers to California. But the wagon trek saga is misleading. The settlement was a mixture of transportation modes, with railroads, steamboats, and carts all playing a role.[15] It was chaotic and dirty, plagued by disease and a hapless misfortune for many of those who tied their hopes to the journey. Dr. Helen Doyle MacKnight practiced pioneer medicine in primitive conditions and remembered the case of a half-Indian, one Johnny Lynch, who had been cut open badly in a knife fight and whose "gizzards" had been tucked in as he was sewn up by his friend, bartender Kelty Jim. Health hazards, poverty, and fearful weather changes were all part of the migrant experience that thousands suffered. But they could not be deterred, for they were subject to a rhetoric of popular confidence. Dillon O'Brien in his novel of pioneer life published in 1866 fixed the Irish outlook. The United States was a place where "the spirit of republicanism has at length found a land worthy of her temple." And a companion sentiment went with that premise: "He who is forgetful of his native land is ever ready to be a traitor to that of his adoption."

People from humble backgrounds truly believed these premises. One such couple from Irish beginnings became the parents of perhaps the West's most symbolic figure, William F. Cody, the "Buffalo Bill" who, after killing his first Indian in a skirmish at age eleven, went on to become the trapper, scout, and hard-riding guide who was the hero of millions of American youngsters.[16]

John D. Unruh has made clear in his fine study *The Plains Across*, in which numerous Irish are mentioned, that violence in the westward movement was predominantly initiated by white men, although the war cults of the Indians such as the Sioux, Comanche, and Apaches did produce deadly struggles. Unruh tells of one "white Indian," a white named James Tooly disguised as an Indian, who led a band that attacked a wagon party near the Humboldt River, where Tooly was shot and killed. Fanny Kelly in Wyoming had the ghastly experience of seeing her husband killed by Indians and her baby daughter almost saved but at length killed, and then she was taken captive for five months by the Sioux. The grieving frontier woman wrote these lines of Victorian maternal grief for the dead child:

> No simple stone e'er marks the spot
> Where Mary sleeps in dreamless sleep,
> But the moaning wind with mournful sound
> Doth nightly o'er it vigils keep.[17]

The military were part of the violence of the West and frequently were not forces for peace but rather forces of provocation. The Irish with large numbers of young males and with poor economic prospects made up a heavy complement of the army, especially after the Civil War. One estimate places the Irish-born alone at a level of twenty percent in the army from 1865 to 1874. It was a harsh and rudely conducted army. Each year between twenty-five and forty percent of the personnel could be turned over due to death, discharge, and desertion. Irish noncommissioned officers were the backbone of the regiments in the heavily Irish forces stationed in such lonely forts as Fetterman, Russell, and Steel in Wyoming. An officer of the Fourth Cavalry Regiment put his view succinctly: "I preferred the Irish—they were more intelligent and resourceful as a rule." They soldiered along with Black units in the Indian frays and promoted extension of American authority into the desolate corners of barely explored territory. At Fort Phil Kearney in northern Wyoming there was a desperate struggle with the Indians in 1866, where Private Patrick Smith, full of arrows and scalped, crawled a half mile to a blockhouse, only to die later in the massacre that annihilated everybody in the fort.[18] Thirty-one Irish were killed with Myles Keogh and General Custer at the Little Big Horn, and their fate can be taken as symbolic of that of many others as part of the toll of military violence in the West.

Other kinds of violence, however, were more common than that of the military. Range wars, saloon fights, mining claim disputes, and vigilante escapades spilled blood on the raw frontier, and here the Irish were involved prominently as well. Robert Hine sees vigilante violence directed by political and business interests at Indians and at the Irish as well in Montana and California and in San Francisco in 1856 when thirty Irishmen were rounded up and deported.[19] In Oklahoma, which came into the union late in 1907, there was a delayed but wild chapter of this frontier disorder. The case of desperadoes was especially rampant there with Emmett Dalton, Mike and Bill Doolin, Morris and Pat O'Malley, and Cattle Annie McDermott set against federal marshals. It is little wonder that the half-Indian chief of the Choctaws, Green MacCurtain, joined other tribes in an abortive attempt to set up a separate Indian state called Sequoyah.[20]

Violence involving that storied figure, the gunfighter, might have assumed mythic proportions but the characters giving rise to the legends were real enough. Whether there was more six-gun killing on the frontier than murder in the major cities has never been calculated, but the imagination of America was captured by the Western gunmen. Henry McCarty, alias Billy the Kid, killed Frank Cahill in 1877 as his first victim. The list is very long from there. "Kid Curry," it was said, would ride 1,000 miles to kill a man. Brothels, dance halls, and gambling saloons spawned a horde of characters like "Chuck-a-luck" Johnny Gallagher who cut men's throats as they bent their heads back to drink the whiskey he bought them.

Kansas was the terminus of the trail herd drivers, and life was wild when their drives were finished. In the 1870s men like Sheriff Ed Hogue of Ellsworth, Kansas, had the problem of losing prisoners to lynch mobs. Flame-haired Kate O'Leary, as tough as she was good-looking, ran a saloon and sporting house in Dodge City. In addition to fighting Indians when she was a girl and shooting dead an overly active cowboy on her doorstep, she was not above keeping order in her establishment with a few well-placed shotgun blasts. Jack Callahan's whorehouse in Cimarron was so dangerous that the whole town got together one day and chased Callahan and drove his gunmen out once and for all. James Kenedy, a Texan, tried to assassinate Mayor James "Dog" Kelly at Dodge City after several shoot-outs in Ellsworth. Michael Meagher was made marshal of Wichita after seven others had held the job for only brief periods, so active was the gunplay. Two-gun desperado Bill Mulvey challenged the wrong man when he met Bill Hickock and met his end right there. Saloon girl Molly Brennan figured in a dispute in Sweetwater, Texas, when she was fatally shot shielding Bat Masterson.[21] It was all demented mayhem and gory murder that became transformed by Owen Wister's novel *The Virginian* and then endlessly mythologized by Zane Grey, Ernest Haycox, Max Brand, and the movie makers of a plethora of cow town epics.

An old poem published in a Denver newspaper forecast the romanticized power of the lonely gunslinger:

The Two-Gun Man

One day, rode forth this man of wrath,
  Upon the distant plain,
And ne'er did he retrace his path,
  Nor was he seen again;
The cow town fell into decay;
  No spurred heels pressed its walks;
But, through its grass-grown ways, they say,
  The Two-Gun Man still stalks.[22]

The gunfighter myth was the logical extension of the extremes of the disorder, freedom, casual ways, and intense individualism of the Western experience. There is something there as well of Irish frustration, reckless bravery, and defiance of unwanted law.

Texas, among other extraordinary attributes, shares the cultures of the South, the desert Southwest, and the range culture of the cattle drovers in the nineteenth century. The sad fate of the Irish colonies headed by James McGloin, James Power, and James Heweston near Corpus Christi, which were chartered by Mexico in the 1820s, are a reminder of the terrible toll the frontier exacted. Cholera, Comanches, and the war of Texas with Mexico in 1836 all but wiped out these "Refugios." That did not stop the influx of Irish into Texas, though, because men like Martin McHenry Kenny in Austin County had great schemes for the dry flatlands of the state. New colonists came to the San Patricio colony on the Nueces River in 1846. By 1850 there were groups of Irish in Galveston, Houston, Austin, and San Antonio, and their numbers tripled in the next decade. Cornelius Cahill was alderman and judge in Corpus Christi and led his community in 1852. Daniel and Thomas Hickey did the same in Galveston. John Kennedy made a $100,000 fortune by 1860 in Houston as the town's baker.[23]

The Civil War split Texans but the majority supported the Confederacy. Robert Loughery became renowned as the fighting editor of the Marshall *Texas Republican*. Having fought the anti-Catholic Know-Nothings, he fought the Yankees as well in his fiery columns. His radicalism supported opposition to high-handed railroads after the war, but eventually he joined the board of directors of the Southern Pacific. Loughery was the type of free-swinging controversialist for which Texas became famous, and only one of hundreds who made the state's politics vividly contentious. By 1887 the state census showed 18,000 Irish-born in Texas. They were a boisterous part of the Lone Star State.[24]

Texas boasted it was more boisterous than other states, but it was a claim hard to sustain. Butte, Montana, proclaimed itself "The World's Greatest Mining Town," and though Father J.J. Callaghan early organized a decent school, the rough-and-ready character of the place was the great instructor of its youth. Sheriff Jere Murphy had a tough time keeping order among the hardy miners. When they didn't like one of John Maguire's theatrical representations, they mounted the stage and beat up the actors. Wild-eyed Charlie Collins roved the town orating about his schemes to make a gold strike, amass a fortune, and finance an Irish revolution. When Carrie Nation, renowned foe of all booze, came to town, May Maloy chased her right out of her saloon into the street, and Carrie gave up her ideas of breaking up saloons with a hatchet.[25]

Denver was the metropolis of the mountain West. Edward Orpen had organized a Fenian Brotherhood circle there in 1866. Most of the Irish in the city were poor, but they contributed to buy uniforms for their marching society, the Mitchel Guards, and they gave to the Land League in the 1880s. By the 1890s there were some 4,000 who were Irish-born in Denver and twice that of Irish background. They improved their lot only slowly, lagging behind the Germans and others, with fifteen percent still laborers in 1900.[26]

This slow progress was obscured by the success of a few. M.J. MacNamara owned the biggest department store in the city in the 1880s, but fortunes could be made and lost quickly. Pat Casey, a wagon freighter, discovered a rich quartz vein. He could not read or write, but he amassed $200,000, which he lost in bad investments, so he went back to New York and contented himself with operating a saloon. The most spectacular case of get-rich-quick success, however, was that of J.J. Brown and his wife, Molly Tobin Brown. He got rich as a mine manager and she, a former waitress in a clapboard hash house, became a legendary social climber. Her story is widely known through her own passion for publicity and from the popular musical comedy based on her life, "The Unsinkable Molly Brown." Her career of spending, posing, and social ambition really shows the hunger for acceptance of the Irish nouveau riche, who were frequently excluded from local socialite circles even in the more democratic cities of the West.[27] It was difficult to gain acceptance when famous saloons like that of the Flaherty brothers were full of brawling miners, and when characters like Prairie Dog O'Byrne were still around. O'Byrne made a bit of money and bought two great antlered elk which he taught to pull his carriage. He insisted on driving them up the hill to the state capitol, frightening every horse in sight and scandalizing those who by 1890 were trying to make Denver a dignified major city.[28]

It must be remembered that migratory Irish miners often came to the West to make a stake to take back to the old country. Some had loftier motives than buying a cottage and farm in Ireland. Young James Marron from County Cavan emigrated to New York, worked as a laborer on the Brooklyn Bridge, that wonder of the age, and then went to Colorado. He worked a decade in the mines to save enough money to be a priest. With his earnings he started back to Ireland but was robbed of his savings in Brooklyn. Back to the mines he went and toiled and saved again. At last he had enough money. He returned to Ireland and put himself through Maynooth Seminary. He lived to age ninety-nine, riding through his parish on horseback in the 1950s, a renowned old priest full of tales of America.

Utah certainly represents a special dimension of Western life and it has traditionally been accorded a status of cultural distinctiveness in the Rocky Mountain belt. Mormon history and exclusiveness marked Utah early, but the years following the arrival of the adherents of the Church of the Latter-Day Saints saw the expansion of their influence into parts of Colorado and Idaho as well. Sociologist Thomas O'Dea in the mid-twentieth century found the Mormons still a "highly self-conscious sub-culture."[29] The accession of this outcast religious group to power in their region of mountain and desert is a unique American story of evangelism and frontier turbulence, polygamy and religious dissent, state authority and minority freedoms.

The sovereign position of the Church of the Latter-Day Saints in Utah, growing as it did out of the expulsion of the group from its Illinois settlements, was only assured after a time of migration, trials, and conflict. Attempts by federal authorities to impose territorial law in Utah were one source of conflict. Non-Morman settlers and emigrants who provoked Indian hostility and threatened Mormon holdings were another problem. The Mormons did not take kindly to such men as Superintendent of Indian Affairs John C. O'Neill, so he was displaced. In 1857 the most sensational incident of conflict occurred when John Doyle Lee, a Mormon leader, led a group attacking an emigrant wagon train in the notorious Mountain Meadows Massacre in which men, women, and children were slaughtered. Relations with non-Mormons were not made any better when men like James Lynch halted their journey leading a party to Arizona and testified against the Mormons responsible. Even in the restrained legal prose of official testimony, the horror of the event is movingly perceptible.[30]

Some Irish people were involved as associates of Brigham Young, and the Mormons did attempt to proselytize in Ireland. But for the most part the Irish came to Utah as miners and railroad workers, and their presence was not comfortable. An 1860 census shows them in Carbon County, and they were in the mines at Ophir, Park City, and Silver Reef, which soon became ghost towns when their ore ran out. William McGroarty was one of the few men to challenge the Mormons politically, which he did as a miners' candidate in 1867, but he was hopelessly outnumbered.[31]

The tense period in the 1850s when the Mormons challenged federal authority over their polygamy practices and other issues led to the dispatch of army units to Utah. The disturbances known as the "Mormon rebellion" were viewed as treason by Col. Patrick Connors in charge of the army in the Salt Lake Valley. Brigham Young had boasted that given a decade of peace he would build an empire that would not have to suffer the authority of the United States. Connors was sent to Fort Douglas to keep vigil over the "City of the Saints," and the presence of his largely Irish troops may be one reason the Mormons were wary of Irishmen. It was this dispute between what the Mormons saw as an occupying army and the federal officials that was resolved by Thomas L. Kane, an adept lawyer originally from Philadelphia.[32]

Father Edward Kelly was the priest permanently placed in Salt Lake City in 1866. By 1871 there was a Catholic school and shortly thereafter St. Mary's Academy and Holy Cross Hospital. Irish-born Father Lawrence Scanlan in charge of the territory in 1875 had to face the fact that his flock consisted of 800 Catholics scattered across 87,000 square miles of Utah.[33] The restoration of civil authority led to a long period of diligent development. A few Irish moved to Ogden and Eureka, but the need for water was a ready barrier to use of much of the land.

In the 1880s an Irishman appeared in the Salt Lake Valley who would change its entire physical prospects. He had been a coal miner in England, so he knew about digging and tunnels. His name was Patrick Moran, and he teamed up with construction boss Frank Gawan to bring fresh water to Salt Lake City. He built the huge Cottonwood Conduit from the mountains, and it was said that every Salt Lake maiden thereafter took a bath thanks to Pat Moran. His water pipelines made possible the cultivation of 40,000 acres in the valley. In 1910 he built the Bishop Creek Dam, further expanding the water supply. What had been desert and salt flat became verdant cropland, a green oasis due to Moran.[34]

The West that shaped all of these events, the West into which the Irish streamed with all the others, was starkly and dramatically beautiful. Photographer Timothy O'Sullivan, who traveled with the U.S. Geological Expedition in 1867, has left us a record of its barrenness and its magnificence. Stunning silver lakes, towering escarpments of rock in shimmering ice, the surreal formations of Pyramid Lake in Nevada, and the roaring glory of Shoshone Falls were all captured by O'Sullivan's camera, as well as the burning sand wastes, wretched mines, and ramshackle settlements such as Hogan Springs and Curry's Mill near Virginia City in Nevada. With the acute eye of his camera, O'Sullivan revealed for those who would not dare the West the scenes confronting those who did.[35]

California was "west of the West" as the saying went, but in its earliest years under American control it was very much part of the mining and range culture of the trans-Mississippi region. Irish sailors and ship masters came to the Pacific coast early on American and Chilean vessels. In 1800 "Honest Joe" O'Cain in the eighteen-gun ship named after himself was trading otter skins with Aleuts and Russians on the coast. Along with the Spanish priests of Baja California, Jose O'Donoju came among the troops to the mission at Los Angeles in 1834, and various other Irishmen were surveyors, ranchers, and explorers before the American invasion in 1848. As early as 1814, John Milligan, a beached sailor, is recorded as teaching the Indians to weave near Salinas.[36]

The war with Mexico and the wild gold rush of 1849 brought throngs of Irish to the Pacific's edge. Charles Boyle's diary said he came to California to "eradicate the detested sin of being poor."[37] Others came in search of sin, not to eradicate it. The innocent had to mingle with mountebanks, chiselers, quack medicine men, gold-mad zealots, religious fakers, and outright bandits on the trek overland. The overland trail across blinding deserts and stupendous mountains produced sensational tales, none more bizarre than that of the Donner party in which a number of Irish families traveled. In 1844 an overland party, half of which was made up of the huge Martin Murphy family, had tried to cross the Sierra Mountains and had been snowed in at Truckee Pass, but eventually made it through to California. Their fate was an ill omen for the Donner party. In 1846 the Donner brothers, Jacob and George, from Illinois began the most disastrous wagon journey ever to trail to California. Seeking to use an untried Sierra route, they were snowed in and forty of the eighty-seven emigrants perished. Some of those who lived survived by eating the flesh of those who had frozen or starved in the snowbound huts thousands of feet above sea level in the wintry passes. Patrick Breen, head of a family from County Cavan, kept a diary of the ordeal. The November blizzards created walls of snow everywhere. Desperate attempts to escape on snowshoes earned snow blindness, exhaustion, and hallucinations. Breen recorded the starvation, the death of children, the weakness of all the party, bears stealing the scant food left, and the terror of relentless desolation in the frozen mountains.[38]

The thousands of emigrants who sailed to Panama, hiked through the jungle isthmus, and shipped north to California had other adventures, but nothing to rival the saga of the Donner party. In places they found some Irish living with close ties to the Mexican families whose sway had been ended by American conquest. Bernard Murphy married Annie McGeoghagan and their large Rancho Pastoria de las Barregas was one of the old Spanish Crown grants.[39] Not all the settlement was tolerant by any means, and the grisly record of white versus Indian conflict was extended right up to the shores of the Pacific. The California Indians who represented over a hundred tribal groups, some of which were very primitive, were faced with forces of white invasion that were all but genocidal. In the Round Valley in northern California 100 Wailakee Indians—men, women, and children—were killed in a single massacre in which the outlaw range hands directed by cattle baron George White swept down upon them. Few of the 11,000 Yuki Indians in the area survived this kind of persecution. Jasper O'Farrell in a report to the governor of California blamed the whites for the violence and sought reservation territory for the Yuki, but the land-hungry whites overran all such plans.[40]

It was in San Francisco that the Irish first established a large community. There were some 4,000 of them there by 1852, almost half of them laborers. About one-third of these Irish-born people had resided in Eastern or Southern states. James Walsh has noted that San Francisco at one end of the continent grew in less than a decade to a size that Philadelphia on the East Coast took 150 years to achieve.[41] R.A. Burchell in a model study of the San Francisco Irish compiled copious detail to demonstrate the special conditions that permitted rapid Irish success in the city. The youth of the city, the lack of an Anglo upper class, and the favorable economy of a swiftly developing state all made opportunities abundant. The fact that a great many of the Irish immigrants were young, came in families, and had previous urban experience added to the prospects. By 1860 the Irish community was already organized, active, and involved with the Fenian Brotherhood, church and school construction, and a plenitude of careers. There was antagonism against the Irish, but it was not as severe as in the East. The Chinese population in the city in an indirect way aided Irish mobility, for it occupied the lowest social and labor position in which the Irish were usually to be found in the nineteenth century. The Irish were able, despite rancor with the Chinese and others, to legitimize their own presence and move quickly to positions of political power and economic advancement.[42]

Four senators from California were Irish in the nineteenth century and one of them, David Broderick, son of a stone mason, established the San Francisco Democrats' Irish-dominated machine. Chris Buckley, the phenomenal "Blind Boss," exercised control lasting till the end of the century. The labor movement was a potent element in this control and carpenters' union head P.H. McCarthy was the most notable of a long line of labor leaders who set standards for labor activity in California.[43] The Progressive movement split the San Francisco Democrats when James G. Maguire, a single tax enthusiast, fought Boss Buckley's cohorts, and this was just one of many irregular political departures for which the state became famous. There were antiwar dissenters in World War I, labor radicals like Tom Mooney and Frank Roney, and Charlie Kelly's coast-to-coast march of the unemployed in the 1930s began in San Francisco.[44]

The sophistication of San Francisco and its cosmopolitan orientation that gathered in people from Asia, Russians expelled by the Bolsheviks, a French colony, and Italian wine growers made it a fitting terminus for all that dynamism and calculating emigration that had traversed the continent. The wealth it drew from mining alone created fabulous residences in its socialite corona on Nob Hill. The "Bonanza Four," a quartet of Irishmen who controlled the Bonanza properties that yielded them all fortunes in gold and silver, drove splendid carriages to mansions on that hill. It is estimated that James Fair, John Mackay, J.C. Flood, and William O'Brien made over $60 million in the two decades after 1867.[45] It was not the golden success of such men that was the most important feature of the Irish adaptation in California, but rather the good living that ordinary families could enjoy.

The achievements of California were so compelling that they drew the desert state of Nevada into the larger state's orbit. Political activity by early miners briefly gave a semblance of local control under such men as O.B. O'Banion, but absentee ownership of mines and cattle soon created "a great rotten borough." It was not until the twentieth century that Senator Patrick McCarren came to represent the influence of Nevada itself. By turns a supporter of the New Deal and then a foe of President Franklin Roosevelt, a strident nationalist but then an isolationist, McCarren, the fiery anti-Communist, bespoke the maverick Western spirit. His sponsorship of the McCarren-Walter Immigration Act in 1952 was a watershed in American policy toward immigrants, and ironically began a process by which Irish immigration would be definitively choked off after two centuries.[46]

Los Angeles, developing later than the Golden Gate city, grew slowly until the twentieth century. The key to growth was water in the arid hills that lay between the coast and the inland desert, and the key to water was a bold contractor whose vision literally transformed the dry landscape and made a modern city possible where the mission of Nuestra Señora de Los Angeles was located. William Mulholland was born in Ireland and made his way in manhood to the Pacific coast in 1877. He arrived with $10. Mulholland began various small water projects, and then conceived a vast hydraulic system that would draw water from the Sierra Nevada Mountains. Grandiose schemes were always being proclaimed, and the desert swallowed most of them. Mulholland's was different. He was a shrewd, tireless, and hard-driving master of engineering projects. He designed enormous pipelines reaching to the Sierras, blasted tunnels through the mountains, and tapped the pure waters from the annual snow melts 200 miles from Los Angeles. The city of Los Angeles, amazed that the feat was achieved, began a career of water imperialism that assured its future. In the great real estate boom of the 1880s James and Robert McFadden built up communities such as Newport Beach, F.G. Ryan developed Santa Monica, and John G. Downey platted 20,000 acres in the Los Angeles area.[47]

The familiar pattern of Irish community elaboration was less pronounced among the palm trees of Los Angeles. The ties were looser. There was more individual amplitude and less need for ethnic solidarity. The city at first had a Southern flavor and Irish Catholics were vaguely related in their religion to Mexicans, and this was not a positive factor. Following the Dublin Rising of 1916 the local Irish came together to campaign for Irish independence. In his tour of the United States in 1919 to plead for this goal, young Eamon DeValera made Los Angeles one of his stops. The local American Legion opposed his visit in the interest of a "Pure Americanism" that admitted no ethnic causes. The flag of the new Irish Republic was torn down. Irish rallies were picketed and Irish organizers were threatened and abused. That did it. The blood was up. The Irish came together in a way they had not been united previously, with attorney Joseph Scott as their leader. They linked up with the stronger Irish community in San Francisco led by crusading Jesuit priest, Father Peter Yorke.[48] The Los Angeles Irish thereafter maintained their own profile of nationalist and cultural activities and became part of the larger Hibernia on the American scene.

The historic link between the prairie and mountain West and California became more tenuous as the state developed its urban, suburban, and special coastal regional culture. The "Pacific South" culture in the early twentieth century was still somewhat amorphous, but as it took on its own ambient character it became prolific of an entire lifestyle notably different from that of other areas. It shared this later with Arizona, but Arizona had no magnificent ocean edge. The California of the Southern sun was more motorized, stylish, outdoor-oriented, and youthful than other regions. It was also more experimental and subject to fads in religion, politics, and leisure. California gave the rest of the nation surfing, the one-floor suburban "ranch house," bizarre cemeteries, and, above all, the motion picture industry. The latter served to sum up the American experience for popularized consumption as did no other medium, and ethnic groups were part of the summarization, the Irish among them. Similarly northern California had a scenic grandeur like Oregon, less sun, and a settled ambience.

But only southern California had that hothouse of dreams, Hollywood, and the movie world's lights and shadows shone on the Irish as stars and bit players. For the Irish, as for other groups, the American motion picture has, unfortunately, been a strange melange—part fiction, part folk drama, and part reality. The complex world of ethnic subcultures has been reflected only confusedly on the shimmering screen. And since ethnic subcultures have been deeply influential and dynamic in American life, it is important to understand how the extraordinarily powerful motion picture has dealt with them.

Creative Irish participation in American films came from their rich theatrical tradition which was welcomed by the booming entertainment industry as a whole. The American film and stage producers had to battle continuous and rigorous Protestant sanctions imposed as part of the puritanical strain in the country's culture, in some ways dating back to the seventeenth century. The Irish in the theater had no such moral qualms about the movies or the stage. They were part of a culture rich in music, folk dancing, and story telling, and these proved happy assets to the stage and screen as the country gradually accepted popular dramatic entertainment as something other than a desecration to the soul of an essentially Protestant society. Besides, since the immigrant Irish were a socio-economic "out-group" anyhow, they could not afford to reject paying livelihoods in such fields as the theater, no matter what alleged moral taint may have been involved.

The historical range of Irish-American theatrical stereotypes and stock characters was extensive indeed. From the British theatrical tradition the American stage had inherited a series of stock Irish characters. The bumbling servant, the braggart fortune seeker, the reckless lover, and the wild Irish girl were all standard Irish types utilized by playwrights from Sheridan to Shaw.[49] That these types did not reflect the range and human dimensions of Irish character did not trouble British authors or audiences, and Americans were troubled even less, for theatrical license was accorded such portrayals since they did not offend the dominant Anglo-Saxon group in either nation.

When the making of films arose as a more hectic aspect of theatrical enterprise, the Irish stereotypes, still very much in cultural currency, were carried over into the new medium. The drunken "boyo," the braggart greenhorn, "Brigid" the clumsy maid, "Tim" the dumb cop, and "Paddy" the burly laborer were standard characters with a century of repeated "Pat and Mike" jokes behind them. The Irish themselves as troupers still disported to their own mockery, though giving the audience what it wanted often included debasing one's own identity.

Crude silent films like *The Cohens and the Kellys* (1926) actually developed into an equally crude but profitable talking picture series, and along with such early sound films as *Abie's Irish Rose* (1929, 1946) played upon intergroup feelings to produce pluralist harmony by stereotyping both the Jews and the Irish as boorish, loud, stubborn, and given to humorous mishandling of the English language. Such film characteristics were part of the distorted image of minority group behavior and usually did not occur in the portrayals of younger "born-in-America" offspring of the feuding families, such as Abie Levy and Rosemary Murphy of *Abie's Irish Rose*. Unfortunately, both poor Abie and Rosemary lost any semblance of their respective Jewishness and Irishness.

The tradition of the stereotyped stage Irishman continued through the studio's heyday, and even during their decline it was never really expunged. One interesting early exception to the "buffoon" Irish stereotype was James O'Neill, the stage matinee idol who played the title role in a silent adaptation of *The Count of Monte Cristo* (1912). He had toured the country for many years in a melodramatic stage version of the Dumas novel and always lamented the wasting of his talents in the same part for so long. His son Eugene, America's Nobel Prize–winning playwright, would use him as the model for James Tyrone, the bitter patriarch of *A Long Day's Journey into Night* (1956), which was filmed successfully in 1962. The Tyrone family members, of course, were not "stage Irishmen" in the stage or screen versions.

Though portraits of the Irish in the film studios' products were stereotypical, they were seldom consciously offensive. They also demanded a large number of actors and actresses whose background and names would be Irish or pseudo-Irish. The star system had to meet the expectations of all kinds of groups, the Irish among them. Never mind that the careers of some of these performers declined from time to time; their portrayals of Irish roles would remain nonetheless as the recognizable though stereotyped representations of the Irish to generations of American moviegoers. If their recognizably Irish names went upon movie house marquees for a while, that was enough for promotional purposes.

Even a partial list of performers with Irish names indicates the extensive "Irish" presence in American films. Among the silent film performers were Nancy Carroll, Maurice Costello, William and Dustin Farnum, Lloyd Hughes, Alice Joyce, Gregory Kelly, Edgar Kennedy, May McEvoy, Thomas Meighan, Colleen Moore, Tom Moore, Jack Mulhall, George O'Brien, Mary Philbin, and Hal Skelly. Talking films, through several generations of Hollywood, featured such names as Sara Allgood, Ed Begley, Peter Boyle, Walter Brennan, George Brent, Art Carney, Walter Connolly, Dolores Costello, Bing Crosby, Brian Donlevy, James Dunn, Irene Dunne, Richard Egan, Barry Fitzgerald, Errol Flynn, William Gargan, Jackie Gleason, James Gleason, Richard Harris, Helen Hayes, Jack Haley, Grace Kelly, Patsy Kelly, Paul Kelly, Arthur Kennedy, Frank McHugh, Erin-O'Brien Moore, Victor Moore, Lloyd Nolan, Edmond O'Brien, Margaret O'Brien, Pat O'Brien, Carroll O'Connor, Donald O'Connor, Maureen O'Hara, Dan O'Herlihy, Dennis O'Keefe, Ryan O'Neal, Maureen

O'Sullivan, Peter O'Toole, Tyrone Power, Tom Powers, Anthony Quinn, Ronald Reagan, Mickey Rooney, Robert Ryan, Arthur Shields, Margaret Sullavan, Spencer Tracy, and many others with Irish surnames, real or assumed. The length and fame of this list suggest the appeal of Irishness in a business that was preoccupied with profits and often oblivious to ethnic sensitivity.

While scriptwriters, directors, and production and financial organizers were behind the scenes, it was the movie scenes themselves on the screen that captured the public's imagination. The film product had to be compatible with popular presumptions. In the calculations of Hollywood, a strategy was developed to cater to the mainstream of Anglo-America and yet patronize and celebrate the various immigrant traditions also. Irish and Irish-sounding names for performers had a special significance. While Jews, Poles, and others often sought to adopt Anglo names for screen careers, Irish names, whether real or assumed, were acceptable on movie billboards. The Irish were common coin in the country, and their names were generally pronounceable. Thus, their transfer from vaudeville and their recruitment for Hollywood were facilitated because of an advertising peculiarity relating to American group attitudes.

But Hollywood was an industry involving far more than performers. The constant generation of scripts was one of the major preoccupations of the industry after "talkies" were introduced. From the subcultural stream of Irish-American writers some luminous talent became available. Eugene O'Neill, though wary of film versions of his plays, did applaud Paul Robeson's title role in the film version of *The Emperor Jones* (1933),[50] but Lionel Barrymore as Nat Miller in *Ah, Wilderness!* (1935) and William Bendix as Yank in *The Hairy Ape* (1944) appeared in mediocre versions of O'Neill and confirmed the playwright's pessimism about Hollywood's capacity to cope with serious drama. John O'Hara's *Butterfield 8* (1960) and *Pal Joey* (1957) were more adaptable, and O'Hara, F. Scott Fitzgerald, George Kelly, and many lesser Irish-American writers participated directly in the creation of dialogue for the screen. Script writing, however, was usually only a money-making venture for major authors and never drew sufficient exercise of talent or attention to bring to the screen the keen realities of Irish-American experience as distilled in novels and plays.

The writers themselves were not hired to portray Irish-American life, but to provide stock scripts, often ordered by studio moguls on an almost-whimsical basis. Neither Kelly nor Fitzgerald ever worked on the screen adaptations of their own works, and, indeed, they were often given scripts to write that had little or nothing to do with their particular subject interests. Kelly, an expert at realistic dramatizations of the middle class, was once required to do a screenplay for Wallace Beery, a rural comedy called *Old Hutch* (1936); Fitzgerald's last writing assignment was a college comedy set in Dartmouth in the thirties, titled *Winter Carnival* (1938). Such writers played the game for what it provided—ready cash—and reserved their serious efforts for their plays or novels. It is worth noting that O'Hara, Kelly, and Fitzgerald, obviously of Irish descent, virtually ignored the immigrant Irish in their literary output, concentrating instead on the American middle and upper classes. Novelist James T. Farrell, whose Studs Lonigan trilogy is the classic portrayal of the world of the urban Irish, never wrote at all for Hollywood.

The making of movies, like so much of the country's economic enterprise, grew into a full-blown business in a very disorderly fashion. Motion picture companies were a blend of theater, new technology, swift finance, and production facilities that were jerry-built and chaotic. The day of the organizer could not long be delayed. Movie companies could not run multi-million dollar businesses like one-man garment factories. Irish-Americans entered Hollywood behind the scenes, both as picture directors and as business managers. John Ford, John Huston, and Raoul Walsh directed dozens of movies during the heyday of the American film industry. Above all Hollywood directors, Ford attempted, though not always successfully, to present valid portraits of the Irish, such as those in the 1935 Academy Award–winning film, *The Informer*.[51] Too often, however, the artistic direction of films was constrained and crude, while the business direction of the industry was an arena for boisterous energy and expansion. This was especially true during the 1920s. It was during this period that Joseph P. Kennedy came to Hollywood. In 1928 he began a thirty-two-month whirlwind career as film financier that would net him $5 million. He began by promoting the talents of Gloria Swanson in an unreleased silent film titled *Queen Kelly* and swiftly moved through a series of ventures that culminated in the organization of the RKO Corporation. Such organizational feats reflected not only individual virtuosity, but the potential ability of Irish-Americans to manipulate their own and other ethnic colleagues and interests and to maneuver skillfully in an American culture with which they were highly conversant.[52] As in politics, the Irish were frequently to be found in roles as interpreters and intermediaries.

Although the Irish as part of the great American movie audience saw themselves portrayed on the screen for decades, and although their tastes and preferences were carefully adverted to by filmmakers with respect to certain moral views, the limitations of film-making culture did not really permit trenchant presentations of key themes of the Irish-American experience. A pleasant musical biography of George M. Cohan such as *Yankee Doodle Dandy* or *The Great Victor Herbert* (1939), based on the life of the Dublin-born composer of operettas, could be entertaining, but such movies really did not relate to the social realities most Irish people knew. *Old Chicago* (1938) with Tyrone Power and a butchered version of James T. Farrell's fine novel *Studs Lonigan* (1956) were typical of the wide-of-the-mark movies about the urban Irish. War movies touched on a broadly shared Irish-American experience in military service, but these movies invariably misrepresented the realities of war with mock heroics and cheap propaganda. Because of Catholic taboos about sex, Irish family life was difficult to deal with on the screen, and the conservative American Catholic hierarchy would tolerate no films that would treat with real insight problems within its ranks; the studios obliged with the charming, inoffensive Bing Crosby–Barry Fitzgerald "nice priest" genre. No movie even tried to comprehend the huge subject of Irish immigration and its implications, and *The Quiet Man* portraits of Ireland itself only lent lovely natural scenery as a background for more stereotyping of Irish characters.

Nevertheless, there were a few Hollywood films that showed something of the social trauma of first- and second-generation Irish families. James Dunn and Peggy Ann Garner made *A Tree Grows in Brooklyn* memorable, and *The Subject Was Roses* (1968) caught the Irish lifestyle in the Bronx with keen accuracy. Spencer Tracy in *The Last Hurrah* (1958) gave the Irish politician credibility. Probably the best of the movies showing the Irish in social contexts would include a product of Warner Brothers, *City for Conquest* (1940) with James Cagney, Anne Sheridan, Frank McHugh, Anthony Quinn, and Arthur Kennedy as the sons and daughters of working-class families caught in the toils of urban frustration, and even this was a mediocre movie. Later, *The Molly Maguires* (1970) with Sean Connery and Richard Harris was a grimly appropriate recollection of the Irish in Pennsylvania mining towns of the 1800s. One of the best, but most depressing, views of the Irish as victims of American urban conditions was *On the Waterfront* (1954), with Marlon Brando as an exploited Irish dockworker and one-time pugilist. The picture was a seamy depiction of waterfront American life of which even O'Neill would have approved.

After the breakup of the big studio system that dominated the movie industry until about 1950, the formulas for making films changed, and the depiction of the Irish on the screen changed as well. The accepted stock images of the Irish faded, partly because they had become hackneyed, but also because the profile of the group in American life was changing with many fewer Irish immigrants and much greater social diversity for the Irish-Americans. The new wave and individualist filmmakers who emerged after the demise of the big studios portrayed the Irish—if at all—in an increasingly fragmentary fashion. Individual portraits might stand out, as in Robert Shaw's fine acting of an iron-jawed Irish gangster in *The Sting* (1973), but basically there was no longer an easily defined social context for presentations of the Irish that most filmmakers could perceive. What remains are adventure flops like *Murphy's War* (1970), or insubstantial, noisy shooting plots like *Kelly's Heroes* (1970) or *The Wild Geese* (1978). The old Irish stereotypes are less and less applicable; it is hard to fix a commonly acceptable image of the Irish when the group's imagery reaches from Brendan Behan to John F. Kennedy, from Princess Grace of Monaco to Bernadette Devlin. And one must ruefully admit that since the Irish have become more assimilated into the American mainstream, it is just possible that they may have lost some of their individuality and their color—two qualities essential for any dramatic medium.

In the 1970s Fellini, Truffaut, and others provided films surpassing the best that America produced. International influences, the revolution in candor about sex, and more explicit portrayals of violence broke inhibitions in one movie after another. The Irish-Americans remained, however, a conservative opinion bloc, flushed with bourgeois success and skeptical of the "new morality." There were also among them supporters of the fevered anti-Communism that was expounded in the 1950s by Senator Joseph McCarthy which resulted in the blacklisting of Hollywood writers and actors because of their political beliefs.[53] They were unable themselves to update their image or project a new characterization of themselves, and even on fierce subjects such as the struggle in Northern Ireland they have remained dramatically and tragically mute. The British, closer to Irish talent, might cast well such films as *Ryan's Daughter* (1970), but America had to wait for more than a decade after the Ulster problem erupted to view a movie made from the widely read novel *Cal* by Bernard McLaverty.

Finally, it might be expected that Ireland itself and the brilliant drama it produced in the twentieth century would have had a substantial impact on American filmmakers. After all, the Irish drama was in English. However, the transfer from Ireland to America and from stage to film was simply not effected. On the whole, American films missed the gritty compactness, witty inventiveness, and historic content of Irish life here and abroad. The American film industry just moved too fast and too superficially to reveal the depth of Irish motives and mores. Part of the explanation for Hollywood's failure to assert the racy and moody drama of Irish life in the movies was because of the nature of the medium itself. Writers wrote genre films, but seldom anything specifically Irish enough to require cultural fidelity. When John Ford sought to film O'Casey's *The Plough and the Stars*, studio officials refused to permit the kind of casting or accurate dialogue that would have respected the integrity of the play.[54] Films culturally explicit about the Irish would be too risky at the box office, it seemed. Because of the breadth, the complexity, and the springing ambiance of the Irish tradition, Hollywood was not able to capture more than a bit of its comic surface or a few chords of its sonorous seriousness.

It is unfortunate, but perhaps culturally inevitable, that such a refulgently oral and prodigally rich literary people as the Irish would be incompatible with American films. They figure in "entertainment" films, but very rarely in films with insight and passionate revelations of the human condition. American films would have to grow still more mature before they could adequately interpret the Irish, an ancient people addicted to contradictions beyond the simplicities on which American films have largely been based.

In summary, the Irish mark on American films was essentially creative as expressed through performers and writers, but repressive as manifested in the Production Code and McCarthyite witch-hunting. The Irish might have been a more powerful force in filmdom, but they were ultimately handicapped by their failure as a group to transmit adequately the literary and dramatic tradition native to Ireland to the peculiarly American cultural medium of films. The tragedy of Ireland's own intellectual and historical frustrations is in part responsible for this failure, for from a broken culture the Irish brought to America only such fragments as emigrants can bear away. The sad result has been that the "stage Irishman" and his screen brother have really emerged as identical twins.

To the California sun fest of growth must be added the even more exotic evolution of Hawaii. As early as 1794 Irishmen had set foot on the gorgeous islands whose indigenous people were to be so badly treated by American government and business enterprises. The domineering Protestant missionaries on the islands actually drummed Father Patrick Short down to the dock and out of Hawaii in 1834, so rabid was their abhorrence of Irish Catholics. The plutocracy of consecrated exploiters with nasty racist records overrode native Hawaiians and the Portuguese, Japanese, and Chinese immigrants with the aid of Washington, which doted on the military importance of the islands. Longshore leaders like Robert McElrath, a leftist, were the most effective foes of the fruit companies and big landowners. The chief figure in breaking the hold of the old autocrats, however, was John Burns, a Democratic politician who had begun his career as an official regulator of Hawaii brothels. By fighting the Anglo racism that infected the life of the islands and allying himself with the talented Japanese population, he won a Democratic landslide for the territory in 1954 and brought programs like those of the mainland New Deal to Hawaii. He also worked ardently for statehood for Hawaii by collaborating with Representative Leo O'Brien of New York, chairman of the House of Representatives' Committee on Interior and Insular Affairs. He even took a hula girl, Leilani O'Connor, to visit congressmen in his campaign. In 1959 statehood was conferred on Hawaii, but Burns lost power when William F. Quinn became the first governor with promises to distribute unused public lands to the islands' land-poor citizens. Mingled with the population of Asian ancestry, a whole array of Irish came into prominence in this period in a further demonstration of Irish hyperadaptability.[55]

The entirety of the Western dimension of American life reaching from the primitive world of the mountain men through the adventurous migrations of range settlement and right up through the creation of technological urbanism is an amazing transition. It is little wonder that as Western folkways receded, Western mythology grew and was replayed for America in film. It was difficult to cope with all this change psychologically without myth. The frontier tradition extending across the prairies, reaching a crescendo in the rockies and a finale in California, was like a movie in its swiftness. The Rocky Mountain belt with its early disorder and competing, class-conscious corporate mining and railroad elites was to climax in California in an epilogue of the postfrontier experience that forecast a wholly new kind of Pacific coastal style. It had a rapid growth and youthful orientation but was laced with contradictions because the new cultural style clashed with the actual problems of daily living where work always outweighs leisure.

For the Irish who rode west in the individualist frontier spirit, the migration was an anomaly of liberation. As people set forth from a stricken society in Ireland, and from conditions of social constraint in the East, the gamblers' choices for success in the West fitted their opportunist emigrant tradition. By taking part in the epic of westward movement they created for themselves their own ethnic legendry of hard times and high adventure. But the fluid nature of the western migration, the swiftness and casualness of it, undercut the Irish need for a community basis to maintain their own subcultural tradition. It is rare to find a Western community in the second half of the twentieth century, except for San Francisco, where the Irish maintain group traditions. The Irish are commemorated in the deeds of individuals—very colorful individuals—but have only a recollective community presence. For the Irish as a social and cultural group, the West is a ghost town.

In the high-tech world of computerized services, instant high-rise downtowns, and a lifestyle characterized by loosening family ties and secularized social distance, the Irish in the "New West" have a diminished presence, as do all the ethnic groups with the exception of Hispanics and American Indians. There is irony in the re-emergence of these two groups that were displaced by the onrush of Anglo and European immigrant invasion. The Indian and Hispanic, despite generations of repression, now displace those Irish who have repressed themselves. The lack of new emigration from Ireland, the depletion of Irish presence, and the recession of the older aggressive Irish profile is part of an ethnic displacement that has been caused by the erosion of the settler-created West. As Jim Robbins has written,

The Western ranching sub-culture, the source of America's most powerful and pervasive myths of freedom, democracy, romance and brutality, still retains much of its traditional character . . . [but] . . . ranchers, farmers and small town residents are finding thread after thread of their agrarian fabric unravelling in the face of absentee corporate power, ever-increasing land prices and interest rates, poorer livestock markets and decline of family enterprises.[56]

The ranching subculture along with the hard-rock mining tradition is being overcome by what Lawrence Larsen calls "the Urban West at the End of the Frontier."[57] Educated, administrative, responsive to the pervasive national mass media, this new West shimmers with the digital images of the computer age. It is attuned to the present and only somewhat toward a defined future. It is ahistorical, conscious of the past only as an amusement. The people who preceded it are film images. The Irish are statistical curiosities without group significance today in the vast American expanse where "the West was won."

NOTES

1. Dale Morgan, *Jedediah Smith and the Opening of the West* (Lincoln: University of Nebraska Press, 1953), pp. 59–61, 97, 295–296; LeRoy R. Hafen, *The Mountain Men and the Fur Trade of the Far West*, 10 vols. (Glendale, Calif.: Arthur H. Clark Co., 1966), vol. 3, p. 89.

2. Morgan, *Jedediah Smith and the Opening of the West*, pp. 108–115.

3. Hafen, *The Mountain Men and the Fur Trade of the Far West*, vol. 4, p. 225; Henry Pickering Walker, *The Wagonmasters: High Plains Freighting from the Earliest Days of the Santa Fe Trail to 1880* (Norman: University of Oklahoma Press, 1966), p. 76; Ray Allen Billington, *The Far Western Frontier: 1830–1860* (New York: Harper

and Row, 1956), p. 37; Walter Prescott Webb, *The Great Plains* (New York: Grosset and Dunlap, 1931), p. 47.

4. Chris Emmett, *Shanghai Pierce: A Fair Likeness* (Norman: University of Oklahoma Press, 1953), pp. 84, 239–251; Mary Eloise DeGarmo, *Pathfinders of Texas: 1836–1846* (Austin: Von Boeckmann-Jones Co., 1951), p. 157; Louis Pelzer, "A Cattleman's Commonwealth on the Western Range," *Mississippi Valley Historical Review* 13, no. 1 (1926–27): 30–50; Andy Adams, *The Log of a Cowboy: A Narrative of the Old Trail Days* (Lincoln: University of Nebraska Press, 1967), pp. 13–47.

5. David Dary, *Cowboy Culture: A Saga of Five Centuries* (New York: Avon Books, 1981), pp. 83, 171, 235, 241. Examples of Irish cattlemen are given by Lewis Atherton, *The Cattle Kings* (Bloomington: University of Indiana Press, 1971), pp. 9, 17, 62, 85, 162.

6. Ralph Mann, *After the Gold Rush: Society in Grass Valley and Nevada City, California, 1849–1870* (Branford, Calif.: Stanford University Press, 1982), p. 184; and Roger D. McGrath, *Gunfighters, Highwaymen and Vigilantes: Violence on the Frontier* (Berkeley: University of California Press, 1984), p. 109.

7. Ronald C. Brown, *Hard-Rock Miners: The Intermountain West, 1860–1920* (College Station: Texas A and M Press, 1979), pp. 30–31.

8. John Stevens Roberts, "The Telluride Labor Dispute of 1903–04" (Master's thesis, Western State College, Denver, 1970); Sandra L. Myres, *Westering Women and the Frontier Experience* (Albuquerque: University of New Mexico Press, 1982), p. 264; Brown, *Hard-Rock Miners*, pp. 28–29.

9. Ibid., p. 28; Mark Wyman, *Hard-Rock Epic: Western Mines and the Industrial Revolution; 1860–1900* (Berkeley: University of California Press, 1979), p. 162.

10. Wyman, *Hard-Rock Epic*, pp. 46, 253–254; Industrial Workers of the World, *Songs of the Workers* (Chicago: IWW, 1970), p. 55.

11. Robert Wayne Smith, *The Coeur d'Alene Mining War of 1892: A Case Study of an Industrial Dispute* (Corvallis: Oregon State College Press, 1961), pp. 30–126; John Barnhill, "Triumph of Will: The Coal Strike of 1899–1903," *Chronicles of Oklahoma* 65, no. 2 (Spring 1983): 80–89; George Suggs, Jr., "Strike Breaking in Colorado: Governor James H. Peabody and the Telluride Strike, 1903–04," *Journal of the West* 5, no. 3 (July 1966): 454–468.

12. Richard Bartlett, *The New Country: A Social History of the American Frontier, 1776–1890* (New York: Oxford University Press, 1974), p. 151; James F.X. McCarthy, "Irish Movers and Managers: Montana, 1875–1900," in Kevin M. Cahill, ed., *The American Irish Revival: A Decade of the Recorder, 1974–1983* (Port Washington, N.Y.: Associated Faculty Press, 1984), pp. 382–394.

13. Ronald Vern Jackson, ed., *Wyoming 1870 Territorial Census Index* (Salt Lake City: Accelerated Indexing Systems, 1978), pp. 23 and 49; Ronald Vern Jackson, ed., *Montana 1870 Territorial Census Index* (Salt Lake City: Accelerated Indexing Systems, 1979), pp. 62, 76, 155, 161; William F. Parish et al., *Missouri: Heart of the Nation* (St. Louis: Forum Press, 1980), p. 153.

14. Charles O'Keefe, *Western Story: Recollections of Charley O'Kieffe, 1884–98* (Lincoln: University of Nebraska Press, 1960), passim.

15. David Lavender, *Colorado River Country* (New York: Dutton Co., 1982), p. 53; John Francis McDermott, ed., *The Frontier Re-Examined* (Urbana: University of Illinois Press, 1967), p. 30.

16. Christiane Fischer, ed., *Let Them Speak for Themselves: Women in the American*

West, 1849–1900 (Hamden, Conn.: Archon Books, 1977), p. 193; Dillon O'Brien, *The Dalys of Dalystown* (St. Paul: Pioneer Publishing Co., 1866), pp. 8, 448; John Burke, *Buffalo Bill: The Noblest Whiteskin* (New York: G.P. Putnam's Sons, 1973), pp. 1–17.

17. John D. Unruh, *The Plains Across: The Overland Emigrants and the Trans-Mississippi West, 1840–1860* (Urbana: University of Illinois Press, 1979), p. 197; Fanny Kelly narrative, *Annals of Wyoming* 28, no. 2 (1956): 168–172.

18. Robert M. Utley, *Frontier Regulars: The United States Army and the Indian, 1866–91* (New York: The Macmillan Co., 1973), p. 23; Dee Brown, *Fort Phil Kearny: An American Saga* (Lincoln: University of Nebraska Press, 1962), pp. 124–125; Paul Andrew Hutton, *Phil Sheridan and His Army* (Lincoln: University of Nebraska Press, 1985), pp. 37 and 95.

19. Robert V. Hine, *The American West: An Interpretive History* (Boston: Little, Brown and Co., 1973), Chapter 6.

20. Glen Shirley et al., *West of Hell's Fringe: Crime and Criminals and the Federal Peace Officers in Oklahoma Territory, 1889–1907* (Norman: University of Oklahoma Press, 1978), pp. 53, 115, 410–411; Danney Goble, *Progressive Oklahoma: The Making of a New Kind of State* (Norman: University of Oklahoma Press, 1980), pp. 209–211; Edwin C. MacReynolds, Alice Marriott, and Estelle Faulconer, *Oklahoma: The Story of Its Past* (Norman: University of Oklahoma Press, 1975), p. 223; Patrick J. Blessing, *The British and Irish in Oklahoma* (Norman: University of Oklahoma Press, 1980), pp. 30–33.

21. Joseph G. Rosa, *The Gunfighter: Man or Myth?* (Norman: University of Oklahoma Press, 1969), pp. 43–46, 79, 98, 99, 144–148, 155; James D. Horan, *Across the Cimarron* (New York: Bonanza Books, 1956), pp. 94–106, 174–190.

22. Rosa, *The Gunfighter*, p. 219.

23. Roy Miller, "The Irish Progenitors of Texas," *Frontier Times* 3, no. 12 (September 1926): 1–8; Hobart Huson, "The Refugio Colony and Texas Independence," *Frontier Times* 14, no. 5 (February 1937): 187–192.

24. Charles W. Ramsdell, "Martin McHenry Kenny," *Texas Historical Quarterly* 105, no. 4 (April 1907): 341; Ralph A. Wooster, "Foreigners in the Principal Towns of Ante-Bellum Texas," *Southwestern Historical Quarterly* 66, no. 2 (October 1962): 208–220; DeGarmo, *Pathfinders of Texas*, pp. 50, 186, 209; Max S. Lale, "Robert W. Loughery: Rebel Editor," *East Texas Historical Journal* 21, no. 2 (1983): 3–15; Terry G. Jordan, "The Forgotten Texas State Census," *Southwestern Historical Quarterly* 85, no. 4 (1982): 404; Norman D. Brown, *Hood, Bonnet and Little Brown Jug: Texas Politics, 1921–1928* (Austin: Texas A and M University Press, 1984), passim.

25. Works Progress Administration Writers Project, *Copper Camp: Stories of the World's Greatest Mining Town, Butte Montana* (New York: Hastings House, 1943), p. 72; Lambert Florin, *Ghost Town Album* (New York: Bonanza Books, 1962), p. 177; Dee Brown, *The Gentle Tamers: Women of the Old Wild West* (Lincoln: University of Nebraska Press, 1958), p. 279.

26. P. Guptil, ed., "The Colorado Fenians," *Eire-Ireland* 9, no. 2 (Summer 1969): 7–17; Steven J. Leonard, "The Irish, English and Germans in Denver, 1860–1890," *Colorado Magazine* 54, no. 2 (Spring 1977): 126–154.

27. Maria Davies McGrath, *The Real Pioneers of Colorado*, 3 vols. (Denver: The Denver Museum, 1934), vol. 1, p. 233; Caroline Bancroft, *The Unsinkable Mrs. Brown* (Boulder, Colo.: The Denver Public Library and State Historical Society, 1963), passim.

28. Inez Hunt and Wanetta W. Draper, *Prairie Dog O'Byrne* (Denver: Sage Books,

1960), pp. 102–109. The social status of the Irish is shown in Thomas Noel, *The City and the Saloon: Denver* (Lincoln: University of Nebraska Press, 1982), pp. 56–57; Patricia McGivern, "Owen J. McGolderick: The Career of a Denver Irishman," in Cahill, ed., *The American Irish Revival*, pp. 395–404.

29. Helen Z. Papanikolas, ed., *The Peoples of Utah* (Salt Lake City: State Historical Society, 1976), p. 100.

30. Norman F. Furniss, *The Mormon Conflict* (New Haven, Conn.: Yale University Press, 1960), p. 97; Juanita Brooks, *The Mountain Meadows Massacre* (Norman: University of Oklahoma Press, 1950), pp. 279–282. Wallace Stegner, *Mormon Country* (Lincoln: University of Nebraska Press, 1970), p. 284, tells of some of the Irish-American outlaws in the area.

31. Brigham Madsen, "The Colony Guard to California in 1849," *Utah Historical Quarterly* 5, no. 1 (Winter 1983): 5–29; Ronald Vern Jackson, *Utah 1860 Territorial Census Index* (Salt Lake City: Accelerated Indexing Systems, 1979), p. 375; Wyman, *Hard-Rock Epic*, p. 46; Robert J. Dwyer, *The Gentile Comes to Utah: A Study of Religious and Social Conflict* (Salt Lake City: Western Epics, 1971), pp. 46 and 156.

32. Furniss, *The Mormon Conflict*, p. 231; Papanikolas, *The Peoples of Utah*, p. 102; Billington, *The Far Western Frontier*, pp. 216–17.

33. Dwyer, *The Gentile Comes to Utah*, pp. 156–170; Francis J. Weber, "Catholicism among the Mormons," *Utah Historical Quarterly* 44, no. 2 (Spring 1976): 141–148.

34. William L. Moran, "A Dam in the Desert: Pat Moran's Last Water Venture," *Utah Historical Quarterly* 50, no. 1 (Winter 1982): 22–26.

35. James D. Horan, *Timothy O'Sullivan: America's Forgotten Photographer* (New York: Bonanza Books, 1966), pp. 151–214.

36. Ralph J. Roske, *Everyman's Eden: A History of California* (New York: The Macmillan Co., 1968), pp. 131–133; Hubert H. Bancroft, *California Pioneer Index: 1542–1848* (Baltimore: Regional Publishing Co., 1964), pp. 264–265.

37. Unruh, *The Plains Across*, p. 96.

38. James Hewitt, ed., *Eye-Witnesses to Wagon Trains West* (New York: Charles Scribner's Sons, 1973), pp. 75–116.

39. Francis J. Weber, *California: The Catholic Experience* (Hong Kong: Libra Press, 1981), pp. 44–52.

40. Lynwood Carranco and Estte Beard, *Genocide and Vendetta: The Round Valley Wars in Northern California* (Norman: University of Oklahoma Press, 1981), pp. 102–120. McGrath, *Gunfighters, Highwaymen and Vigilantes*, discusses robber gangs and lynching.

41. R.A. Burchell, "The Gathering of a Community: The British-born of San Francisco, in 1852 and 1872," *Journal of American Studies* 10, no. 3 (December 1976): 279–312; James P. Walsh, "The Irish in Early San Francisco," in James P. Walsh, ed., *The San Francisco Irish: 1850–1876* (San Francisco: Irish Literary and Historical Society, 1978), p. 21.

42. Louis Bisaglia, "The Fenian Funeral of Terence Bellew McManus," *Eire-Ireland* 14, no. 3 (Fall 1979): 45–64; R.A. Burchell, *The San Francisco Irish: 1848–1880* (Berkeley: University of California Press, 1980), pp. 179–185.

43. L.A. O'Donnell, "From Limerick to the Golden Gate: Odyssey of an Irish Carpenter," *Studies* 67, nos. 269–270 (Spring-Summer 1979): 76–91.

44. Donald E. Walters, "The Feud between California Populist T.V. Cator and Democrats James Maguire and James Barry," *Pacific Historical Review* 27, no. 3 (August

1958): 281–289; Donald McMurry, "The Industrial Armies and the Commonweal," *Mississippi Valley Historical Review* 10, no. 3 (Summer 1923): 215–252.

45. R. A. Burchell, *The San Francisco Irish: 1840–1880* (Berkeley: University of California Press, 1980), pp. 186–187.

46. Gilman M. Ostrander, *Nevada: The Great Rotten Borough, 1859–1969* (New York: Alfred A. Knopf, 1966), p. 24; Von V. Pittman, "Three Crises: Senator Patrick McCarren in Mid-Career," *Nevada Historical Quarterly* 24, no. 2 (1981): 221–234.

47. Glenn S. Dumke, *The Boom of the Eighties in Southern California* (San Marino, Calif.: Huntington Library, 1944), pp. 5, 73–74; David Clark, "Los Angeles," in Richard M. Bernard and Bradley R. Rice, eds., *Sunbelt Cities: Politics and Growth since World War II* (Austin: University of Texas Press, 1983), pp. 274–275.

48. Timothy J. Sarbaugh, "Irish Republicanism vs. 'Pure Americanism': California Reaction to Eamon DeValera's Visits," *California History* 60, no. 2 (Spring 1981): 172–185.

49. The above material on the movies appeared in longer form in William Lynch and Dennis Clark, "Hollywood and Hibernia: The Irish in the Movies," in Randall Miller, ed., *The Kaleidoscopic Lens: How Hollywood Views Ethnic Groups* (Englewood Cliffs, N.J.: Jerome Ozer, Publisher, 1980), pp. 98–113. Awareness of a kind of "second-class citizenry" of an ethnic and professional nature may well account for the arrogant defensiveness as well as the creative drive of a personality such as playwright George M. Cohan, whose grandparents emigrated from County Cork. Cohan, though he made but two films, was the most versatile figure in the history of the American stage. He was also the subject of a memorable biographical film, *Yankee Doodle Dandy* (1942). The stereotypes of the Irish are discussed in Stephen Garrett Bolger, "The Irish Character in American Fiction: 1830–60" (Ph.D. diss., University of Pennsylvania, 1971).

50. Louis Schaeffer, *O'Neill: Son and Artist*, 2 vols. (Boston: Little, Brown and Co., 1973), vol. 2, p. 352.

51. Ford's difficulties with his studio, RKO, in presenting honest Irish portraits are recorded in Lewis Jacobs, *The Rise of the American Film: A Critical History* (New York: Harcourt, Brace and Co., 1967), p. 483. Even Ford was forced into Irish stereotypes in films such as *The Quiet Man* (1952).

52. Richard J. Whalen, *The Founding Father: The Story of Joseph P. Kennedy* (New York: The Founding Father, 1964), p. 99.

53. Jack Vizzard, *See No Evil: Life Inside a Hollywood Censor* (New York: Simon and Schuster, 1970), pp. 49–50. Vizzard's book is an amusing and informative account of Hollywood film "censorship" during the sound era. For a good discussion of the Legion of Decency see also Garth Jowett, *Film: The Democratic Art* (Boston: Little, Brown and Co., 1976), especially pp. 241–242, 246–256, 416–418; William V. Shannon, *The American Irish: A Political and Social Portrait* (New York: The Macmillan Co., 1963), pp. 380–381. Shannon vividly describes and explains the perverse attraction of McCarthy to the Irish-American electorate. See also John W. Caughey, "McCarthyism Rampant," in Alan Reitman, ed., *The Pulse of Freedom* (New York: Norton, 1975), pp. 139–141. Caughey gives a close account of the effects of McCarthyism on Hollywood.

54. Joan Mellen, in *Big Bad Wolves: Masculinity in the American Film* (New York: Pantheon Press, 1977), pp. 41–42, sees John Ford and his Irish heroes as extolling Irish "macho types" in war and Western movies.

55. Nancy and Jean Francis Webb, *The Hawaiian Islands: From Monarchy to Democracy* (New York: Viking Press, 1956), pp. 62–65; A. Grove Day, *Hawaii and Its*

People (New York: Meredith Press, 1968), p. 44; Gavin Daws, *Shoal of Time: A History of the Hawaiian Islands* (New York: The Macmillan Co., 1968), p. 89; Francine Du Plessix Gray, *Hawaii: Sugar-Coated Fortress* (New York: Random House, 1972), pp. 92–96; Paul C. Phillips, *Hawaii's Democrats: Chasing the American Dream* (Washington: University Press of America, 1982), p. 86; Perry E. Hilleary, ed., *Men and Women of Hawaii, 1954* (Honolulu: Honolulu Star Bulletin, 1954), pp. 104, 153–155, 236, 483–486, 515, 592.

56. Jim Robbins, "Range War in the Rosebud Valley," *The New York Times Magazine* (May 6, 1984): 82.

57. Lawrence H. Larsen, *The Urban West at the End of the Frontier* (Lawrence: The Regents Press of Kansas, 1978).

10 CACTUS CELTS— THE SOUTHWEST

One way of describing the interior Southwest consisting of New Mexico, Arizona, and parts of west Texas and Nevada is to say that they are the total climatic opposite of Ireland. Yet even in these dry, brown, sandy, sun-bleached states, the Irish from their rain-soaked green land found a place. Their earliest appearances in the desert territory are in the eighteenth century as soldier and priest. Commandant Col. Hugo O'Conor rode the Rio Grande and battled Indians for the Crown of New Spain in a legendary career of fighting and strenuous placement of settlements in the 1770s. He struggled to maintain fifteen forts from the Gulf of Mexico to California. At San Agustin del Tucson, O'Conor found "water, pasture and wood" and brief respite, but he rode and fought himself into an early grave in his militant defense of the northern outposts of New Spain.[1]

A more reflective tour of this same frontier was carried out by the priest Don Pedro Alonso O'Crouley y O'Donnell. Taken to Spain as a child from Limerick as were others dedicated to a priesthood forbidden in Ireland, he was educated at Cadiz and became an historian. His journal of his travels in California and the Southwest was compiled in sadness and indignation about the cruelties of the servants of Spain to the Indians, the greed and hoarding of the rich in their haciendas, and the lack of protection for the weak afforded by the distant power of the Crown. He foresaw the ruin of an empire that was rotted with abuse, and prayed in the desert for its victims.[2]

Thus, before Anglo-America had turned its mounted rovers and wagons toward these desert sands and wind-worn mountains, the Indian and Hispanic cultures had already fought an epic of exploration, ecological ingenuity, and conflict over land and religion. The Indian, the Latin, and the Anglo-American cultures, as Paul Horgan has written, each had "particular social backgrounds which gave to the three cultures their violently distinct characters." The first settlers of the American penetration of those dry lands had "an instinctive fondness for the reckless, savage life, alternately indolent and laborious, full and fasting, occupied in hunting, fishing, feasting, intriguing, amours, interdicted by no laws or difficult morals. . . . "[3]

Mingled with this rude confrontation to the two older cultures was a sprinkling of that Irish energy that showed itself wherever the Americans went. They were included in the first probes into the Southwest from the United States. Augustus Magee led a filibustering "foreign legion" into the area in 1812 and was promptly driven out by the servants of Spain. James McLanahan did the same kind of thing and was happy to emerge alive two years later after suffering in Mexican prisons. The failure of such ventures was not a deterrent, however, and the adventurers kept coming up to and after the war with Mexico. In the 1850 census of New Mexico there were Irish in Santa Fe and Albuquerque, and in 1870 in Story County, Nevada, there were O'Tooles, O'Rourkes, O'Learys, O'Connors, and O'Donnells.[4] As miners, drovers, and traders they had sought out the trails to Mexico.

In the empty wilderness cut by dry arroyos and seared by an eternal sun, humans became as fierce as the landscape. Apaches and renegade whites raided, stole, and contended for the scarce resources of the untamed Southwest. Men like Captain James Callahan became border fighters for most of their lives. Riding out of San Antonio, he and his irregulars would pursue escaped slaves into Mexico and battle Indians and blacks led by Chief Wild Cat, sometimes winning, sometimes losing. Callahan's tough rangers were fought right out of Piedras Negras one day by Blacks and Mexicans, and he was killed in 1856 in a family feud.[5]

Irish Catholics were not fully accepted in an area where Catholicism was identified with Mexicans, and Mexicans were identified with opposition to American ambitions. Sam Huston and his Protestant Irish friends James W. Flanagan and F. M. Dougherty were sympathetic to the anti-Catholic Know-Nothings. The intensity of the antagonism toward the Irish Catholics was made morbidly apparent by the famous incident in the Mexican War involving the San Patricio Battalion. Generals Winfield Scott and Zachary Taylor had an army that had almost half of its regulars and even more of its volunteers made up of the foreign-born. Both men were harsh disciplinarians. During the war desertion was a serious problem and over 6,000 soldiers deserted. The Mexicans were offering bounties and land to deserters, and ordinary distaste for military life, cruel disciplinary practices, disenchantment with the war, and the representation in the army of misfits and criminals added to the problem. There is evidence, too, that the foreign-born were treated unfairly in disciplinary matters. It was an army shot through with discontents, the first American army to fight a war since 1812. The suspicion that the Irish Catholics were easily subverted by Mexican priests and were of dubious loyalty anyway was widely held by Yankee officers.[6]

Deserters in Mexican uniforms first appeared handling Mexican artillery at the Battle of Matamoros. The San Patricio Battalion with a harp of gold on a green flag that had been formed by Mexico was really only two companies of about 200 men. At the Battle of Churubusco approximately eighty-five were taken prisoner after the Mexican surrender. Thirty-five had been killed in the battle. Seventy-two of the San Patricios were tried as deserters in courts martial presided over by Colonel Bennet Riley, an Irish Catholic. Thirty of the prisoners were condemned to death in one group of trials, but three had sentences reduced to being branded and receiving fifty lashes. They had iron yokes forged around their necks for their period of servitude at hard labor. On September 10, 1848, sixteen of the condemned men were hung. Only seven professed to be Catholic and were comforted by priests. On September 13 thirty more San Patricios were hung, including one man who had lost both legs in the battle and who was dragged out of the hospital to the gallows. In all, although the records are confused, a total of fifty San Patricios were executed and others branded, lashed, and put to brutal labor.[7] The incident deeply moved many Mexicans. It was not clear that the executed soldiers were deserters, and in the minds of Mexicans this made little difference. The San Patricios did not go over to the Mexicans for religious reasons, but for a complex of motives. The violence of war and the brutality of the frontier were mixed in the misfortunes of the San Patricios. The hapless soldiers in the incident were part of an Irish famine generation steeped in tragedy, and this was simply one more grim incident, so the event did not markedly impress either the Irish or the Americans at the time. Along with the Mollie Maguire hangings in Pennsylvania in 1877, however, these executions probably were the largest mass executions in American history, one military and one civilian, if Blacks and Indians are excepted, and in both cases the Irish were the victims of grievously malign conditions.

The misfortunes of soldiering, however, did not deter Irish enlistment. Unemployment and the lure of adventure were the recruiter's great allies, so that at forsaken outposts like Fort Union in the desert in New Mexico, Irish-American soldiers were plentiful as the army kept vigil among Mexicans and hostile Indians. Boredom, fighting, and an occasional lynching marked the days of the army men. Dr. John Byrne, medical officer at Fort Union, was appalled by the sixty cases of venereal disease in his post hospital, and the commander of the outpost chased away the Mexican women who were the chief attraction of the local saloons.[8]

The Indian wars were full of ferocity. In 1864 the Kiowas and Cheyennes killed 200 settlers and soldiers and reduced the New Mexico settlements to starvation. Patrick O'Neill took wagons of supplies from Denver to New Mexico across 350 hair-raising miles of mountain and desert to feed the survivors.[9]

It took two generations after the Civil War for the old Southwest to settle down. The cowboys did indeed ride in, get drunk, and shoot up the town. James Cook recounts how Chuck McCarty from Ben Slaughter's ranch drank too much at Milligan's store and could hardly hit anything in town when he fired and was ignominiously arrested by a Mexican deputy sheriff. In Arizona Sheriff Jim Doran was a very busy man running down robbers regularly, and he complained the task was too tiring in its regularity. More serious than the random violence were range wars that occurred when the interests of powerful cattlemen clashed.

"The Lincoln County War" in New Mexico at the end of the 1870s is an example. J. J. Dolan, a well-to-do rancher, got into a dispute with an Englishman named Tunstall over an insurance debt. Peter McSween took Tunstall's side. Sheriff William Brady sided with Dolan, as did Judge Lawrence G. Murphy. Dolan's men shot and killed Tunstall. McSween retaliated and in a shoot-out killed three of the Dolan group and Sheriff Brady. Things went from bad to worse thereafter and for several years rustlers and badmen took over Lincoln County and great stretches of the territory.[10]

The cure for this kind of social turmoil was the militia posse that acted as a wide-ranging law enforcement cadre. Such a posse went after John Kinney, a former soldier and hired gun who led a rustling gang in the 1880s. The posse, riding hard and fast, caught Kinney, killed five of his gang, and arrested twenty others. The posse was law enforcement at its most primitive, and its pursuits of such notorious characters as Kinney are as much part of the folklore of the Southwest as the desert itself.[11]

One of the larger-than-life figures of Arizona was William "Buckey" O'Neill, who came to the territory from St. Louis. He was the essence of the desert frontier in its final period of rampant vitality. As editor of Arizona's leading newspaper he declaimed tirelessly the wonders of his beloved Arizona. As a builder he worked in practical ways to give it structures to replace the sand-blasted board ramshackle that passed for towns. As a horseman he was the admiration of every youngster who dreamed of dashing through the mesquite on a fine quarter horse. O'Neill was mayor of Prescott and head of a cavalry outfit called the Milligan Guards. When the Spanish and American War broke out, he joined the explosive outpouring of patriotic effusion and headed off with the Milligan Guards to follow Teddy Roosevelt to Cuba. He was killed in the charge up San Juan Hill, the very personification of Irish-American daring as extolled by the popular press of the day. The Arizona sun still shines down on a mounted statue of "Buckey" O'Neill as he rides in memorial glory the dream of a West that is no more.[12]

The relentless search for minerals that accompanied increasing industrialization brought prospectors by the thousands to Nevada, New Mexico, and Arizona. In the blazing deserts and treeless mesa country they gouged the earth not only for silver and gold, but for copper, which was ever more valuable as its use in electrical systems grew. Mining claims were snatched up by one promoter after another, and greed never took a holiday. One A. J. Shotwell in the 1890s browbeat and chiseled various Arizona Indians, subsistence farmers, and failed prospectors into giving up their copper mining rights in the area of Ajo, Arizona. He hoped to use his ties to St. Louis bankers to open a big copper mining enterprise. He met a man named Fred McGahan who claimed he had invented a vacuum smelting machine that would smelt any grade of ore. Shotwell jumped at the scheme only to lose $34,000 to the rascally McGahan who had never invented anything but swindles, having previously bilked two mining companies in St. Louis. For once a swindler, Shotwell, got swindled.[13]

Mining copper was like mining everything else. It was dangerous, dirty, cyclical, and conducted by get-rich-quick operators for whom the labor force involved was a disposable commodity. In Arizona in the 1890s the Western Federation of Miners under Secretary Treasurer James Maher took up the cause of the Irish, Mexican, Cornish, and Italian miners. Maher and Edward Kennedy squared off against the giant Phelps-Dodge Corporation in the mines at Bisbee to establish a union, and a strike ensued in 1896. Reverend Harvey Shields, an Episcopal minister, opposed them and rallied the storekeepers and landlords in the area in behalf of the company. It was a bitter episode, but Maher won the right to unionize, part of a protracted struggle over wages, working conditions, and layoffs that would continue for over two generations in Arizona.[14]

As the interior Southwest settled down it became more and more attractive to Americans captivated by the dramatic scenery and Indian and Hispanic past of the region. The Catholic past became a tourist attraction as the old Spanish missions were restored. There had grown up a tradition of Irish missionaries serving in the area and this continued through much of the twentieth century. Speaking Spanish and providing educational and social services to Indians and Chicanos long excluded from mainstream progress, these immigrant priests and nuns were part of the institutional development of the region that had begun in the 1860s when Sister Catherine Mallon and her companion Sisters of Charity had journeyed there to work as nurses among the sick, injured, and unemployed in the Irish railroad camps.[15] In the 1960s such figures as Monsignor William Bradley, born in Derry in Ireland, continued this tradition in Catholic charities, and he also campaigned forcefully through his newspaper columns and speeches for a resolution of the Northern Ireland problem that would remove the British from control of his native city.[16]

The same transformation that had overtaken California reached into the Southwest in the mid-twentieth century. Tourist centers, health resorts, retirement colonies, and artists' retreats dotted the deserts, and venerable cities like Santa Fe took on new life. Georgia O'Keefe brought to American art the rich ochre beauty of the sun-seared rocks and ancient brown aridity of the desert's magnificence. But the new technology of urbanism, antithetical to the beauty of the region's natural endowment, unfolded plastic, air-conditioned cities and suburbs across the cactus-studded land. In Nevada William B. Byrne, head of the Las Vegas Convention and Visitors' Bureau, contrived the legislation that literally made a city and an industry from nothing more substantial than the evanescent human quirk of playing hunches. He created the gambling mecca of America in all its incongruous, garish, and absurd grotesquerie when he devised the legislation that set up the state gaming commission in the 1950s.[17]

The long repression of Mexican-Americans and the protracted overlordship that whites exercised over Indians perpetuated the triad of cultures in the Southwest. Irish priests and nuns might work with Mexican-Americans, but there would be no true fusion or absorption of one group by the other. Similarly, the Indian remained a man apart. Efforts by bureaucrats to erase Indian beliefs and practices, such as Commissioner of Indian Affairs Charles Burke's inane effort in 1923 banning all Indians under fifty years of age from taking part in Indian dances, were part of an arrogant policy that the Irish above all should have seen as similar to what they themselves had suffered.[18]

The swift rise of the sunbelt cities and their prosperity brought Irish-Americans from other parts of the country to the glowing new office towers of Tucson and Phoenix. They brought with them their consciousness of identity and often a continuing attachment to Catholicism. There was sufficient Irish interest in the region to stimulate cultural activities related to the national networks sponsoring lectures, musical groups, and visits by government figures from Ireland. The challenge of rising Hispanic consciousness and political power was bound to cause a competing reaffirmation of Anglo-American history and tradition in the region. As that occurred the Irish-American contribution would also be reaffirmed as part of the Southwest's cultural mosaic, as colorful and distinctive as the Indian sand paintings that portrayed the events of generations past in a land where the sun reigns supreme.

NOTES

1. Jay J. Wagoner, *Early Arizona* (Tuscon: University of Arizona Press, 1975), p. 327.

2. Don Pedro Alonso O'Crouley y O'Donnell, *The Kingdom of New Spain, 1774* (San Francisco: John Howell Publishers, 1977), pp. 117–119.

3. Paul Horgan, *The Heroic Triad: Essays in the Social Energies of Three Southwestern Cultures* (London: William Heinemann Ltd., 1971), pp. xi and 184.

4. Ronald Vern Jackson, ed., *New Mexico 1850 Census* (Salt Lake City: Accelerated Indexing Systems, 1978), pp. 29 and 320; Ronald Vern Jackson, ed., *Nevada 1870 Territorial Census* (Salt Lake City: Accelerated Indexing Systems, 1979), pp. 362–365; Lynn I. Perrigo, *The American Southwest* (New York: Holt, Rinehart and Winston, 1971), p. 98.

5. *Southwestern Historical Quarterly* 70, no. 4 (April 1967): 574–585.

6. Ralph Wooster, "An Analysis of Texas Know Nothings: 1851–55," *Southwestern Historical Quarterly* 70, no. 3 (January 1967): 414–423; Dennis Joseph Wynn, "The San Patricios and the United States–Mexican War, 1846–1848" (Ph.D. diss., Loyola University, 1982), pp. 36–47, 96–147.

7. Wynn, "The San Patricios and the United States–Mexican War," pp. 135–147.

8. Chris Emmett, *Fort Union and the Winning of the Southwest* (Norman: University of Oklahoma Press, 1965), pp. 142–143, 397.

9. David Lavender, *Bent's Fort* (Garden City, N.Y.: Doubleday and Co., 1954), pp. 356–519.

10. James H. Cook, *Fifty Years on the Old Frontier* (Norman: University of Oklahoma Press, 1954), pp. 223–226; Joseph Miller, ed., *Arizona Cavalcade* (New York: Hastings House, 1962), pp. 95–97; Howard Roberts Lamar, *The Far Southwest* (New Haven, Conn.: Yale University Press, 1966), pp. 156–158.

11. Larry D. Ball, "Militia Posses: The Territorial Militia in Civil Law Enforcement in New Mexico, 1877–83," *New Mexico Historical Review* 55, no. 1 (January 1980): 45–69.

12. Ralph Keithby, *Buckey O'Neill* (Caldwell, Idaho: Caxton Printers, 1949), pp. 1–45.

13. David Lavender, *The Southwest* (New York: Harper and Row, 1980), p. 271.

14. James D. McBride, "Gaining a Foothold in the Paradise of Capitalism: The Western Federation of Miners and the Unionization of Bisbee," *Journal of Arizona History* 23, no. 3 (Autumn 1982): 299–316. In the bitter strike of 1984 against the same company, Dr. Jorge O'Leary, the company physician, joined the strikers on the picket line.

15. Thomas Richter, ed., "Sister Catherine Mallon's Journal," *New Mexico Historical Review* 52, no. 2 (April 1927): 135–147.

16. William J. Bradley Papers, Balch Institute for Ethnic Studies, Philadelphia.

17. *The New York Times* (April 13, 1984).

18. Edward H. Spicer and Raymond A. Thompson, eds., *Plural Society in the Southwest* (Albuquerque: University of New Mexico Press, 1972), p. 177.

11 ROADS TO THE KLONDIKE—THE NORTHWEST

After the trials of the overland treks on the prairies, the struggles and splendors of the Rockies and the Sierras, and then the magnificence of California, it would be an excess of expectation to believe that there was more to the American land to be sought out. But there was. In the Northwest there were the heart-lifting Cascade Mountains and exhilarating forests, more gold to be mined, and the thrilling scenery of the Oregon country. Francis Parkman on the Oregon Trail listened avidly as a trader named McCluskey told him of the Sioux war fever and how a chief called "The Whirlwind" led his men against the whites. Indians or not, the trekkers increased year by year to set up homesteads and ranches to the west and west again.[1]

The most renowned pioneer figure of the Northwest was Doctor John McLoughlin. Born of an Irish father and a Scotch mother in Canada, he studied medicine in Scotland and France. Intrepid and six feet four inches in height, he was named chief factor for the Hudson Bay Company in Oregon in 1821, where the Indians were so hostile that the company men had to mount guard day and night. McLoughlin skillfully changed this and developed trade with the Indians, so that by 1828 30,000 beaver skins worth $250,000 were traded in that year. Through his promotion of agriculture and his pacification of relations with the Indians, McLoughlin made a lasting imprint on a territory teeming with natural opportunities.[2]

The Irish emigration to the Northwest was a repetition of their penetration of the Rockies, a combination of soldiering, mining, and then settlement. In 1850 most of the Irish in Oregon were army troops according to Daniel O'Neill's census. William P. Dougherty was one of the first emigrants to the territory, but it was a lonely wilderness then. In 1855 Lieut. Col. James Kelly defeated the Walla Walla Indians. His regimental surgeon pickled the ears of their defeated chief as a memento of the victory. Miners poured into the Northwest as soon as the army broke Indian resistance. James O'Meara, who came up from San Francisco, was an early Democratic leader and publisher of the Oregon newspaper, *The Standard*, but editorial opinion was laughably marginal in this frontier territory. In 1843 James O'Neill and Robert Moore had drawn up an Oregon code of laws, and the rudiments of civil order were established, but it would be a generation before authority was really organized.[3]

Capt. Christopher Power Higgins and his troops came to the Hell Gate district in Washington in 1850. Higgins and another Irish-born pioneer, W. F. Seely, had a slight disagreement, which they settled with an epic bare-knuckled battle, and then the two of them became fast friends. As leaders in the settler world of the Northwest they had a wide influence on Indian affairs, settlement policy, commerce, and legislation. Higgins served in the legislative assemblies of both Montana and Washington territories. Similarly, Maj. Peter Ronan as a pioneer newspaper editor, Indian agent, and agricultural specialist was very active. His work in behalf of the Indians amid cultural conflicts with whites, fishing and hunting disputes, tribal combats, and contradictory government policies was carried out with skill and dedication.[4]

Parts of the Northwest were appallingly barren, a seeming penalty of nature for the glorious landscapes of other parts. When a newspaperman, John Finerty, traveled the Powder River country with General Cook's exploration column, he wrote that "the soil looked like the surface of a non-atmospheric planet, hard, repulsive, sterile."[5] The thin grassland of other states was one reason cattlemen moved Northwest. Stockmen on the ranges above the Upper Flathead River in the 1870s included a number of ambitious Irish ranchers: Thomas McGovern, John O'Leary, Thomas Lynch, John Dooley, and W. J. Egan. In the Kootenai River area David and James Boyle, Thomas Quirk, and John P. Wall ran herds. Successful ranching meant more land, and land was cheap in Idaho and Oregon so the tendency was to expand that way, especially as the railroads reached west from Milwaukee and other Eastern rail centers. Thomas Shaughnessy, president of the Canadian Pacific, and others raced for the rights to Northwest routes. When there were mining strikes, big companies like the Sullivan Concentrating and Mining Company took over and gobbled up the claims of the restless prospectors.[6]

By the 1870s the Irish were trooping into Oregon to colonize whole sections of it. Concentrations grew up in Portland and across the mountains around Riley and Burns. In Morrow County in the northern Oregon country was an especially interesting group. William Hughes arrived in 1870 and Charlie Cunningham homesteaded on Butter Creek in 1876. Others followed, practically all directly from Ireland. In 1890 John Kilkenny and James Carty began to bring in their extensive families. Kilkenny was from County Leitrim. His parents had gone to America to make money to support their families in the poor mountains of Leitrim, and then returned to Ireland. Their son made his way to Umatilla, Oregon, and worked on the Oregon R and N Railroad. He and Carty borrowed money and went into the sheep business. Leitrim was a sheep county in Ireland, for little else could be raised on its rugged heights. The bunch grass was so plentiful in Morrow County that there was no need for winter feed, and Kilkenny prospered on his sheep ranch. Brothers, cousins, and other Leitrim families were "brought over." Greyhounds were important to chase the coyotes away from flocks, and on Sundays the ranchers rode fine strong horses out with their hounds to worry the wily coyotes. Sheep ranchers versus cattle ranchers provoked range wars, and Kilkenny fought it out with the cow men near Indian Creek. He became a bank director and chairman of the local school board. His ranch lands expanded to over 20,000 acres by 1914, with 12,000 sheep and 250 head of cattle. Deep water wells, powered windmills, and finally electricity were installed.

What grew up around John Kilkenny and his friends was a big Irish colony of Cartys, Dohertys, Farleys, Flanagans, McDaids, McEntires, Sheridans, and dozens of others. It was a rough and ready immigrant community on the last frontier with strong bonds and a strenuous spirit. As they sang:

> The fun and the frolic, prevented the colic,
> In the immigrant Irish of yore.
> Inborn was their mirth 'twas with them
>   since birth,
> And was bred in the bone to the core.

They hunted, built homes, settled quarrels with their fists, brewed their own potables, and danced at the Ancient Order of Hibernians affairs. Though mostly Catholic, there were Protestants among them, but there was no religious friction. The forty-year migration of families into this community was not too much different from hundreds, indeed thousands, of other Irish family-based settlement patterns. The Morrow County Irish, however, were among the last settling on open homestead land and sharing the frontier experience.[7]

Even in the 1880s vast areas of the Northwest remained unexplored. Twenty-two-year-old Lieut. Joseph P. O'Neil of the 14th Infantry was detailed by the army to explore the area "east of Puget Sound" and into the stupendous Olympic mountain range. Fresh out of the University of Notre Dame, O'Neil gathered men like Lieut. Thomas P. Bradley and a motley cadre of guides, trappers, and tough old prospectors and set out on a government mapping and exploring expedition. His pack mules and party penetrated areas no white man had seen and mapped routes through the elk-filled valleys and mountain magnificence of one of the world's most dramatic wilderness areas.[8]

The Irish in the cities of the Northwest came into political activity early in the region's history, but they did not develop the kind of communal politics that characterized the groups in the East and Midwest. Leaders like Judge Thomas Burke who became chief justice of the Washington Territorial Supreme Court had followers, but they relied largely on their own talents. The politics of the area were dispersed, discontinuous, and with a strong streak of radicalism. The Western Federation of Miners fought bitter strikes in Idaho. The internal fights in the federation itself led to furious disputes as when J. J. O'Neill, editor of the *Miners' Magazine*, squared off against an Industrial Workers of the World (IWW) faction, and Paddy Mulloney shot the leader of the other group. The Northwest became the battleground for labor radicals in contest with mine, railroad, and lumber magnates. By the 1890s the agitation was widespread. The Irish were in skilled spots in the highly dangerous lumbering camps in the Northwest. J. J. Donovan was one of the biggest timber barons in the Northwest and he helped set a pattern of militant anti-union activity. At the time of World War I he was pitted against the IWW in a violent strike, and U.S. Army troops were used to break the strike and move the lumber.[9]

IWW organizers fought fiercely with the Western Federation of Miners led by Charles Mahoney, but conditions in the lumber camps were so bad that lumberjacks would follow anybody to fight the lumber companies. Largely migratory, the lumber workers were often isolated in the deep forests far away from any government protection, though there was little of that since the timber companies dominated state governments thoroughly. IWW organizer Red Doran testified that "camps were insanitary, abominable places. . . . Many times there was not any hay, let alone mattresses. The grub . . . was mighty poor, little or no provision was made for bathing and dirty, filthy animal life was in abundance; animal life you had to pack with you."[10] These conditions prevailed for fifty years for the lumbering workers. IWW recruiting led to prosecution of unions all through the area. Employer-paid vigilantes even lynched organizers. In Everett, Washington, in 1916 a group of 300 IWW lumber workers crossed Puget Sound from Seattle and were met in the town by police and vigilantes who opposed their landing. John Looney and others were killed. Tom Tracy, an IWW man, was charged with starting the affray. He and seventy-three others were freed after a trial, one of the most sensational of the IWW cases arising out of the group's organizing attempts.[11]

Seattle was the metropolis of the Northwest, but it was owned by absentees. The Northern Pacific Railroad acquired a land grant in the nineteenth century of 47 million acres, an area larger than New England. This legalized robbery of the whole landscape began absentee domination of the Washington economy. Timber, fishing, mining, shipyards, and, above all, transportation were controlled by outside powers. Seattle was the control point. The city could not shake its ramshackle, gambling pioneer past beneath this corporate dominance until twenty-nine-year-old Jerry O'Connell came to town in the 1930s. O'Connell had proved too radical for Montana politics, so he moved to Seattle and by 1939 headed the Seattle Democratic Committee. His politics were left-wing and stormy. He sent Hugh DeLacy to Congress to oppose Franklin Roosevelt's "imperialist war." In the uproarious war years when Washington and Oregon were close behind California in population increase, O'Connell fought "big interests" continuing the regional grudge fight.[12]

The New Deal of Franklin Roosevelt brought the nation's greatest hydroelectric projects to the Northwest. The taming of the Columbia River was to the Northwest what the transcontinental railways were to the nation's midlands. It opened the way for the development of agriculture on an unprecedented scale, growth of aluminum and steel industries, and further expansion of lumber processing through cheap electrical power. The Grand Coulee Dam was an awesome conception, a structure 400 feet high and 4,000 feet long to cordon the waters of a river that had roared its torrents through the mountain passes since time began. The first proponent of this stupendous project was an Irish engineer, James O'Sullivan, and unlike the designers of other great wonders of human construction, he did not have to wait several dynasties to see the scheme fulfilled. It was built with all the energy of America behind it, a monument to the nation's conquest of resources—and to O'Sullivan's vision.[13]

Perhaps it was the life-wrenching experience of emigration that endowed some of the Irish with an intrepid disposition that led them undaunted into situations that are true-life adventure stories. The case of Michael MacGowan is an example. Born into an impoverished family in 1865 in Donegal, he was taken as a child to a "hiring fair" where he was hired out to hard work for tough farmers. Tiring of that he conspired to get to America and did so, arriving in Pennsylvania among relatives who got him a job in a steel mill. Soon enough the wanderlust recurred, and he was off to the silver mines in the mountains of Montana. When the great gold strikes occurred in the Klondike, MacGowan, now a skilled miner, took off with two friends for Alaska. Speaking Irish among themselves, they fought the elements on the road to the Klondike. They suffered severely in their struggle up the Yukon to reach Dawson. Starving and exhausted, they encountered in the frozen wilderness a Corkman named Con O'Kelly, who saved them and gave them access to his food and cabin above the Arctic Circle. Gradually MacGowan secured enough gold to permit him to return to Ireland after an absence of eighteen years. He wrote his tale of adventure in Gaelic and it is read today in Irish schools as one of the most popular emigrant recollections.[14]

Long before the Klondike gold rush two Irishmen founded Alaska's first newspapers, the *Sitka Times* and the *Alaska Times*, to lure settlers. The wild journey to the Klondike lured thousands of Irish from mining jobs, lumber camps, and railroad gangs. One was Klondike Mike Mahoney, a teamster who contracted with a theatrical troupe, the Sunny Sampson Sisters Sextet, in February 1898 to lead the party and their equipage from Skagway to Dawson in forty-five days. He performed the unbelievable feat of taking a piano over the Chilkoot Pass. This hellish pass was notorious for costing the lives of hundreds of horses and scores of men. It ascended the frozen mountains at a forty-five degree angle, was torn by blizzards and winds, and offered only torturous footing every inch of the way. A famous photograph of it shows an endless line of burdened men struggling up its trail in slowly plodding peril. Mahoney somehow hauled his freight and the painted but half-frozen ladies of the troupe, plus their piano, up and over that pass in February, and on to Dawson in the allotted time, a deed recounted with amazement by the sourdoughs of Dawson and Skagway for years.[15]

Living in Alaska was a bit like living in Ireland, except that the mountains were higher and the climate was worse. The resources catalogued by the Harriman Expedition in 1899 when scientist Thomas Kearney and the survey party sailed the coastline in Capt. Peter Dolan's ship were kept in almost feudal control by the Seattle banks, shippers, and commercial interests. Alaska railroad contractors like Dan Donovan, and Doherty and Company and James O'Neill had to import every scrap of equipment at exorbitant rates from "the lower forty-eight."[16] This continued relentlessly until enough population and enough political anger grew to liberate the territory from the economic groups that exploited it from the south. A key figure in this change of status was William Egan, a native Alaskan born at Valdez in 1914. He was elected to the territorial legislature in 1940 and fought to have a referendum held on making Alaska a state. He guided the Alaska Constitutional Convention in 1955 and became the new state's first governor in 1959; he served three terms wrestling with tough problems of resource development, environmental control, and apportionment of political power among Aleuts and Indians previously excluded from politics.[17]

In the Northwest and in Alaska nature overcame culture, so that after the frontier color faded community life tended to be more like the settled Midwest. The late development of this tremendous area gave it a socially ineffectual character. The mountain barriers divided it severely. It remained culturally anemic well into the twentieth century despite the labor and dissident challenges to its dominant conservatism.

For the Irish these areas were a bold promise on the far side of the frontier, if the harsh economic forces could be turned to advantage. They blended into the area's social life but yet preserved a token separate identity. In 1939 in Portland, Oregon, the All-Ireland Cultural Society replaced the old Ancient Order of Hibernians chapter and fostered a broad social and cultural program, and it strengthened in the next generation.[18]

Still, as ethnic groups, American Indians and Japanese were probably as prominent and it is doubtful that a distinctly Irish profile will be present in the region's affairs in another generation.

NOTES

1. Francis Parkman, *The Oregon Trail* (New York: Random House, 1949), p. 121; Lancaster Pollard, "The Pacific Northwest," in Merrill Jensen, ed., *Regionalism in America* (Madison: University of Wisconsin Press, 1965), pp. 187–214.

2. C.E. McGuire, ed., *Catholic Builders of the Nation: A Symposium of the Catholic Contribution to the Civilization of the United States* (Boston: Continental Press, 1923, pp. 359–362.

3. Jesse Douglas, "The Population of Oregon in 1850," *Pacific Northwest Quarterly* 41, no. 4 (January 1950): 95–108; Malcolm Clark, *Edenseekers: The Settlement of Oregon: 1818–1863* (Boston: Houghton Mifflin Co., 1981), pp. 280–281, 291–293; LeRoy R. Hafen, *The Mountain Men and the Fur Trade in the Far West*, 10 vols. (Glendale, Calif.: Arthur H. Clark Co., 1966), vol. 3, p. 85.

4. Helen Addison Howard, *Northwest Trail Blazers* (Caldwell, Idaho: Caxton Printers, 1963), pp. 205, 227–245.

5. Edgar I. Stewart, ed., *Penny an Acre Empire in the West* (Norman: University of Oklahoma Press, 1968), p. 257.

6. Flora May Bellefleur Isch, "The Importance of Railroads in the Development of Northwest Montana," *Pacific Northwest Quarterly* 41, no. 4 (January 1950): 19–29; Dorothy O. Johansen, *Empire of the Columbia: A History of the Pacific Northwest* (New York: Harper and Row, 1967), p. 323. Jensen, ed., *Regionalism in America*, pp. 208–209, shows that the Irish were the second largest foreign-born group in Oregon and Washington in 1880.

7. John F. Kilkenny, *Shamrocks and Shepherds: The Irish of Morrow County* (Portland: Oregon Historical Society, 1981), pp. 5–20.

8. Robert L. Wood, *Men, Mules and Mountains: Lieutenant O'Neil's Olympic Expedition* (Seattle: The Mountaineers, 1976), pp. 45–96.

9. Edmond S. Meany, "Judge Thomas Burke," *Washington Historical Quarterly* 17, no. 1 (January 1926): 34; Robert Ficken, "The Wobbly Horrors: Pacific Northwest Lumbermen and the I.W.W., 1917–28," *Labor History* 24, no. 3 (Summer 1983): 325–341; Robert E. Pike, *Tall Trees, Tough Men* (New York: W.W. Norton Co., 1967), pp. 51, 127, 132–133, 144.

10. Patrick Renshaw, *The Wobblies: The Story of Syndicalism in the United States* (New York: Doubleday and Co., 1968), pp. 60–64, 70, 84–87.

11. Ibid., p. 93.

12. Richard L. Neuberger, "Seattle: Slave and Master," in Robert S. Allen, ed., *Our Fair City* (New York: The Vanguard Press, 1947), pp. 330–331.

13. Johansen, *Empire of the Columbia*, p. 515.

14. Michael MacGowan, *The Hard Road to the Klondike* (translated from the Irish *Rotha Mor an t' Saoil* by Valentin Iremonger) (London: Routledge and Kegan Paul, 1962), pp. 14–108.

15. Clarence Hulley, *Alaska: Past and Present* (Westport, Conn.: Greenwood Press, 1980), p. 206; Harold Merritt Stumer, *This Was Klondike Fever* (Seattle: Superior Publishing Co., 1978), pp. 111–121.

16. William H. Goetzman and Kay Sloan, *Looking Far North: The Harriman Expedition of 1899* (Princeton, N.J.: Princeton University Press, 1982), pp. 75–80; *Alaska Railroad Record* 1, nos. 4 and 7 (1916): 26, 54, 175.

17. *The New York Times* (May 8, 1984).

18. Michael F. Funchion, ed., *Irish-American Voluntary Organizations* (Westport, Conn.: Greenwood Press, 1983), pp. 7–9.

12 ST. BRENDAN'S MANY ISLES

The great legend of Brendan the Navigator who sailed with his fellow monks into the Atlantic unknown in the sixth century beguiled Europe in the Middle Ages. Brendan's adventures took him to a wondrous archipelago and to *Tir na nOg*, the Land of the Young. In all the wandering fantasy of the Brendan saga there is the deep human yearning for a new place, a new beginning. In the emergence of modern America, that journey to a strange and exciting new world has been enacted by Brendan's own people. In America the Irish have discovered many isles full of marvels, and they are still seeking to understand how this discovery has changed their history. Similarly, we in America are also seeking to evaluate this multicultured peopling amid the contrasts of our land.

In New England the Irish encountered that original model of the new American society, the contractual community. Based on a form of freely devised religion, the Puritan vision was actualized as a civil compact that brought Biblical codes into daily local life. Rousseau's social polity and Locke's schemes for government were outpaced by the actual practical formation of the New England covenant. John Locke's civil formulation was full of concern for property, but the property of rocky New England's settlers was God.

The Irish had no part in the Puritan covenant. They were not parties to the original contract and were excluded from its provisions, yet they continued to migrate into the communities of its godly elect. Their own religious heritage was not only different, but it would flourish as the New England covenant waned. As division and alteration diminished the Protestant vigor of the New England region, the Irish Catholic foundation burgeoned. Protestant power established in the seventeenth and eighteenth centuries declined as Irish Catholic institutions rose in the nineteenth and twentieth. Though parochial in many ways, this Catholicism was Mediterranean and cosmopolitan in others. The religion of the Irish became an expansive influence that took them beyond considerations of New England's heritage of contractual Protestant communion. The Irish social and political emergence was a powerful influence that changed the basic character of the region.

In contrast, New York was to be an unprecedented phenomenon for which there were no lasting covenants, no models, and no Godly sanction. The new metropolis surged outward and upward with startling energy. It was the consummate alternative to the ruralism of Ireland. At one point there were more Irish-born in it than in Dublin, Ireland's leading city. All of the forces of technology and urban complexity that America could muster were concentrated in New York, and from 1860 to 1960 the Irish became the specialists for its negotiation and governance. Coursing among its medley of ethnic groups they made a special reputation for themselves as dealers, interpreters, intermediaries, and directors. From labor leader Michael J. Quill's rule over the subway men who roared through the darkness below its streets to Mayor William O'Dwyer's political sway in the board rooms of its corporate towers, the Irish were its power brokers. The alacrity with which they policed the city, organized its votes, and pursued its wealth was testimony to the hunger for status that they brought from Ireland. These people from a small island with only rudimentary opportunities were stimulated to unheard-of competition by the spirit of New York. They did not need covenants, for in the polyglot earnestness of the place they relied on their own sharp affinity to combine for their own interests. The urban colonies they lived in looked to St. Patrick's Cathedral, Tammany Hall, and Irish organizational leaders for guidance. New York and its rich hinterland were an American experience beyond the prophecies of Puritans or any other colonizers. Through it the Irish were made brazen in the fire of an incalculable urbanism, and they became the grass roots political mentors of America.

Beyond the enormous whirligig of Gotham the Irish dug their way to Lake Erie across the richly treed state of New York. Let that achievement, which elevated New York and diminished proud Boston and Philadelphia, stand for all the Irish labor that helped to open the Republic's resources. As the communications systems of the country grew the Irish rode them to a fare-thee-well. The communications arteries of scores of districts channeled business and talent to New York City, and Manhattan became the media mecca of the nation. Placed as they were at its center, the Irish were drawn into all of the circuits of information and entertainment that were concentrated there. As much as the urban epicenter itself, this involvement with New York's communications nucleus was a bonus for the Irish, for it eventually placed them in the midstream of American discourse in a media-addicted nation.

The ports of the placid Delaware served as the entry points for Pennsylvania, and that region was the marshaling place for journeys that initiated the Irish into definitive American experiences. If New England was too constricted ideologically to foster pluralism from the outset, and if New York was too hectic to formalize it, Pennsylvania proclaimed it from the beginning as a Quaker ideal. The reality was more ambiguous. Bloody conflict with Indians, irascible relations with stubborn Pennsylvania Dutch, and competitions as varied as the mountain ranges that cleaved the state formed a challenge to schemes of peaceful polity. Into this segmented commonwealth the Irish Protestants and Catholics entered as forest fighters and traders who battled their way through the wilderness to open the Appalachian interior that would breed the intrepid frontiersmen for the first westward thrust to the heartland. James Fenimore Cooper's Natty Bumpo and Owen Wister's Virginian would be outrun by Pennsylvania-born Daniel Boone, who was no fictional creation but reality grown into legend.

The Revolutionary heritage of Philadelphia where the nation was conceived was replete with Irish activists. The secretary of the Continental Congress, the printer of the Declaration of Independence, the founder of the American Navy, and a whole phalanx of Washington's generals were all part of the Revolution's Irish cohort. They imprinted themselves on the country's early history with sufficient force to make their role part of the local hagiography, but this also had implications for the history of the Irish in the future of the nation. What happened in Philadelphia became the focus of the patriotic credo, and Irishmen were included in its genesis. Thereafter, when the group was attacked as alien and unwelcome, they could strongly retort that they too had championed the infant Republic's cause. In a country full of pluralist strains, where democracy cast up intermittent tempests of hostility, this was considerable political advantage.

It was in industrial Pennsylvania beginning in the 1830s, however, that the Irish faced a further test of their survival on the American scene. For a century thereafter the mines, railyards, ports, and factories of the state were the battlegrounds for Irish workers hard pressed to maintain any human dignity amid grueling lives of work and social disability. Pennsylvania was the great trial ground of the industrial revolution for America, and the Irish were bound to the smoking wheels of industry in Pittsburgh and Philadelphia and all the collieries, steel towns, and mill centers in between. The industry that would bridge the nation, triumph over the Confederate secession, and make America a world power eagerly used immigrants once the Irish had proven valuable workers. It also abused them mercilessly. It was only through a tough courage that Irish families survived the industrial regime, and in doing so they created a hope for others that humane values could be defended against technological and economic exploitation. By the late nineteenth century industry ruled America, and the Pennsylvania Irish derived a hard-won social lesson: In a land of powerful industry, those without organization are mere victims. John Siney, Mary O'Reilly, and Terence Powderly took this message to workers across the land, and the country is the better for their labor militancy.

Beyond the mountain ranges of the East the northern bosom of the country lured settlement for two centuries. Prairie lands, river empires, and whole systems of lakes made the Midwest penetrable. But the Midwest was to grow to have two minds and a persistent cultural duality. One was to produce the archetypal small town, the bucolic community that would be the reverie world for generations of novelists and tale spinners. Huckleberry Finn, that rambling youth with the Irish surname, inhabited such a town, as did generations of boys who represented unspoiled America. Along the rivers and the shores of the Great Lakes was another Midwest of industrialized power. Machines for a thousand uses poured out of its mills, and men struggled to remember who they were amid the roar of manufacturing. If the rural Midwest represented archetypal community, the industrial Midwest created social implosions in which community was lost. As the effects of the industrial society penetrated the smaller Midwestern cities and towns, the idyll of the trusting prairie community faded. In the 1920s Robert Park analyzed the anomie of Chicago's masses, and not long after Robert and Helen Lynd found the same malady in industrializing "Middletown" in Indiana. As material abundance grew, the old values of community declined. Immigrants became nonimmigrants, and nonpersons all too often.

The Irish in the Midwest imitated this pattern. In the cities they found community for a longer period than in the prairie towns, but in both environments they were winnowed in the currents of change. The land that was supposedly settled was merely populated. It was "restless, vigorous, not yet settled into permanence."[1] On the Great Plains, institutions were in a continuous process of revision. Workmanship, farming, and law all were in redefinition as the myth of small-town solidity declined.[2] And even in the bigger cities the Irish had to force their memories to maintain their tradition.

The South was for the Irish a region of special travail. The subtropical climate of its rivered expanse with its fevers and diseases took a horrendous toll of the emigrants of the eighteenth and nineteenth centuries. The Irish, Northern Europeans vulnerable in this climate, were placed even more at risk by poverty, crowding, and relegation to slum lowlands. This helped to frustrate the growth of Irish coastal and river communities. In the mountain districts geographic factors hemmed the early Irish into isolation and, again, poverty and kept later immigrants from joining earlier ones to form that bond of continuity that would have maintained an active identity.

Still, in cities such as New Orleans, Memphis, and Charleston, and in that partly Southern and partly Western metropolis of the Mississippi, St. Louis, Irish communities did persist. In tiny scattered Catholic enclaves and in Scotch-Irish outposts in North Carolina a continuity based on especially intent family consciousness was sustained. Throughout the region, however, the social impasse of its racial codes and the quick intolerance of its popular nativistic religious dispositions markedly curtailed Irish influence. In a region where the phenomenon of immigration was restricted, acceptance of the foreign-born was limited. The distinctiveness of Southern culture itself acted as a solvent dissolving group ethnicity, except in the case of Blacks against whom a special paranoia prevailed among native and immigrant alike. The hierarchical structure of Southern life did permit the entry into upper-class levels of those who were fortunate enough to succeed economically, for even the South shared the general characteristic of fluidity that pervaded a new country. Irishmen did enter the plantation elite, and the family-revering sentiment of the South permitted these individualist achievers to blend their names with those who were the custodians of the region's special historical memory.

Beyond the cultivations of the East, the South, and the Midwest was that sprawling range of empires of novelty and adventure—the West—half a continent for exploration and conquest. "What do we want with this vast worthless area, this region of savages and wild beasts, of deserts, shifting sands and whirlwinds of dust, of cactus and prairie dogs?" asked Daniel Webster in 1838.[3] Americans soon answered: beaver, buffalo, gold and a score of precious ores, adventure, free range, and land, land, land. Into the vastness of the West they went, and the raucous cavalcade took a century to settle its own dust. It was an especially American mixture of undeveloped institutions and advancing technology, of cosmopolitan fragments amid primitive conditions, of wealth and destruction. The Irish were distributed both at the edges and in the middle of the movement west, their presence added to the violence and the elation. As a former subject people, the West for them was the apotheosis of their liberation.

For marginal men in a new society, the Western frontier was especially appropriate for the Irish. There the repressions and cramped civilities of Anglo society were discarded. A democratic companionship of trial, toil, and daring replaced them. The Irish as a group had to prove themselves in America, and the West was the place to do it with flair—high in the saddle and hard for the ride. Thus it was that the Irish figured vividly in the creation of the myth of the West, the nation's epic tale of pioneering, democratic mission, and struggle with disorder.

In the Southwest the stubborn Protestant Irishry of former Kentuckians, sons and grandsons of the first Kentuckians, is memorialized in the lists of those who fell at the Alamo. In a more peaceful sequel, the Irish Catholics allied with Hispanic Catholics of the Southwest to conserve a whole regional culture of missionary achievement. In the Northwest, Alaska, and Hawaii the rewards of the frontier struggle were extended, and Irish participation in the settlement of these areas was an expression of the normative role they had made for themselves on the American scene.

As America became more conscious of itself it invented a literature that expressed its own distinctiveness and made it aware of the diversity within its borders. The writings of the Irish-Americans would reflect this differentiation. The Boston novels of Edwin O'Connor and those about Albany from the extraordinarily gifted pen of William Kennedy are rich with local flavor, and the fiction of Betty Smith, Elizabeth Cullinan, and Mary Gordon is both vivid and redolent of New York, but all are distinctly of the Northeast. Jack Dunphy's fine novel, *John Fury*, and Tom McHale's *Farragan's Retreat* are especially keyed to Philadelphia, as the comic satire of Finley Peter Dunne and the naturalistic classics of James T. Farrell are keyed to Chicago. The South of Harnett T. Kane and Flannery O'Connor is as different from the Pennsylvania "Gibbsville" of John O'Hara as the Midwestern Irish Catholicism of Mary Deasy and

J. F. Powers is from the zany recklessness of Thomas McGuane's novels of Montana. John Gregory Dunne's *True Confessions* has a California crime story perspective that is a clear contrast to George V. Higgins' accounts of the Boston underworld. Whether in the archly intellectual prose of Mary McCarthy or the hard-bitten firefighting novels of Dennis Smith, the different social worlds of the American scene are manifest. Paul Horgan's tales of the Southwest with their verity of historical coloring are thoroughly different from the urban seaminess of New York in the stories of Joe Flaherty and Jimmy Breslin. The literature of the Irish-Americans alone reveals the extent of their regional coloration.[4]

What is the larger meaning of the populous Irish infusion into American life that has been recounted here? What is its meaning within the framework of our national history? Its meaning is central to the exemplification of the American idea. The regional transplantation grafted the Irish onto the continental American tree of liberty. Indeed, it grafted Ireland itself to America for generations in a persistent sentimental and demographic affiliation. The mocking lesson of the historic conjunction could not have been missed by imperial England: Those whom she had sought to banish to oblivion had bounded the Atlantic to freedom, and they looked back on their oppressors with contempt from the rich heights of democratic achievement.

Yet, while all this regional adaptation was proceeding, the Irish also assumed a national status by establishing their kinship across the entire continent. They did this by threading among and across the regions of the country networks of affinity and affiliation that linked them in a rambling fraternity and projected for them a social presence that became part of the national folklore and imagery. A basic element of this affinity was family consciousness and the bonds of family memory and emigration. With this intimate familial sharing was carried a cultural interlacing that embraced an inherited body of folkways, a musical tradition full of vitality and a religious development that provided a framework for personal and family values.[5]

From the Irish religious traditions that were permitted to flourish on the American scene there emerged an extraordinary charitable and educational hegemony that served and was served by many thousands of the most talented people of this ethnic group. Congregations of nuns, such as the Sisters of Mercy, the Sisters of St. Joseph and the Sisters of St. Francis, with mother houses in the Eastern states fanned out across the country establishing clinics, hospitals, hospices, schools, and vocational training facilities. Their health and medical work led to a notable conjunction of the efforts of physicians and nursing personnel beginning in the 1880s. By 1912 there were fifteen Catholic hospitals in the Northeastern states, fifteen in the Midwest, eleven in the South, and nineteen in the western half of the country.[6]

Similarly, in the field of primary and secondary education there arose a virtual school empire that grew from the first feeble efforts in the country's infancy. Irish Protestants set up a precocious chain of frontier schools. The Irish Catholics, after having been divested of most of their Gaelic heritage and subjected to colonial educational experiment under British rule, undertook to vindicate their own educational commitment in America with alacrity from the 1830s onward. Irish Franciscan priests in Brooklyn, Irish Christian Brothers in New York and Baltimore, and Sisters of Mercy in scores of locations from Philadelphia to Iowa founded immigrant-serving schools. The pace of establishment must appear today to be almost obsessive as the pastoral letters of bishops in 1833, 1837, 1840, and 1843 pleaded for schools. The Plenary Council of Catholic bishops in 1852 stated, "We are following the example of the Irish hierarchy who are courageously opposing the introduction of a system based on the principle which we condemn." That principle was state-dominated schooling with a powerful anti-Catholic bias.[7]

The Irish succeeded in turning European religious congregations into their own ethnic fraternities in America. The Christian De La Salle Brothers, who originated in France, for instance, began work in 1815 in New York. By 1864 an Irishman headed a congregation that was largely Irish with schools from New England to St. Louis. By the 1880s most major cities all the way to California had Christian Brothers' schools after John P. Murphy from Tipperary and John McMahon from Mayo expanded this work further.[8] Yet the Christian Brothers were only one of a score of such congregations vitalized by Irish members who by 1915 had built 1,266 secondary schools and thousands of primary schools across the country.[9]

In higher education the dimensions of the achievement were equally impressive. Irish leadership played the dominant role in no fewer than 167 Catholic colleges and universities built by 1900, and Irish Protestants achieved a smaller but still remarkable record. These institutions became a mixture of classical curriculum and Victorian religious rigor, but ironically they did not transmit a distinctive cultural heritage from the homeland, since new American influences shaped them definitively.[10]

All of this work of social service and education emanated from a group that was heavily weighted with disabilities due to disruption of life patterns through emigration, poverty, minority status, and social discrimination. It was enacted with a commitment, morale, and style that were distinctively Irish, and formed an alliance of relationships that were fully expressive of ethnic pride and behavior. It constituted an interface of kinship that was informal yet purposeful, infused with a folk spirit yet cosmopolitan in its engagement with novel American opportunities.

In the field of journalism the group sought to express its own goals and to maintain nationalist and social ties. *The Shamrock* in New York in 1815 and *The Erin* in Philadelphia in 1823 showed the way for the later New York *Irish World and Industrial Liberator* and *The Boston Pilot*. Editors, correspondents, and publishers, key figures in a democracy, arose in throngs to fill the pages of such papers as *The Celtic Cross and Western Irishman* in Colorado and *The*

Dove of Ireland magazine, and Irish newspapers from Kansas and Tennessee to Montana and Oregon. These papers bound the Irish together with news of nationalist struggle, local political gossip, and homely tidings of the Old Country.[11]

Occupational and labor relationships were also strong bands of Irish-American exchange. Dockworkers, bricklayers, miners, and railroadmen each had their own lore and cameraderie. Ideologies such as socialism and syndicalism created devoted cadres of Irish followers. A semimigratory occupation such as bridge building and iron and steel erection developed labor union bonds amid fierce employer opposition, strikes, and grim records of work accidents. Irish-American delegates from Boston, Chicago, Buffalo, New York, and Cleveland assembled in the International Association of Bridge and Structural Iron Workers in 1896, and by 1900 there were 6,000 largely Irish members.[12]

From dozens of such associations the labor movement grew to include conservative as well as radical factions pitted against extremist capitalist leaders who had police and political allies who were also Irish. Female leadership grew more slowly but included a heartening roster of Irishwomen in unions of shirt and garment workers, clerks, teachers, and telephone workers. The pioneering efforts of Annie Fitzgerald of the American Federation of Labor, Hannah O'Day of the Women's Trade Union League, Catherine Goggin of the teachers' federation, and Bridget Kenney of the telephone workers were prodigious.[13]

In the theater and entertainment fields the musical and declamatory traditions of the group stimulated a penetration of American theatrical life from its earliest days. In the 1820s Irish plays were being given in New York and New Orleans. By the 1850s Irish troupes ranged coast to coast, but it was in the second half of the nineteenth century that Irish participation in commercial theater became a major part of theatrical life as the plays of Dion Boucicault and Edward Harrigan drew huge audiences. Below the commercial circuits were energetic amateur dramatic and musical societies in Irish communities everywhere. Even on the frontier the Irish had their own theater promoters and troupes on the "Silver Circuit" in Colorado, Utah, and Wyoming, and Irish plays were given from the mining camps of Tucson to the ornate theaters of San Francisco.[14]

This broad ethnic subculture composed of these and numerous other networks underlay the more familiar political and nationalist interests of the Irish-Americans. It had both a convivial sociability cultivated in saloons and taverns wherever the group congregated and a more serious communal and ethnic expression that sought pluralist status and historical recognition for the Irish in American life.[15] Although the social bonds and group identity were an imported creation deriving from Ireland, the techniques of group perpetuation and the structures for interaction were the products of the ingenuities of American experience. Like the regional adaptations of the group, the nationwide overarching ties they cultivated manifested a capacity and resilience that had been completely unanticipated by the social critics of the nineteenth and early twentieth centuries.

The Irish emigration was not only a transition from an old rural society to a new and technological one; it was also an opening to the tremendous diversity that the great geographic scale of America offered. It was many emigrations, repeated emigrations, a continued exploration of regions, differences, and opportunities, while the identity related to the old country was still retained. It is this continued and sequential character of the immigrant experience for various groups that we have only partly realized.

In the psychological realm the dynamics of the emigrant flow involved more than the immediate impulses of poverty and oppression and the attraction of American abundance. For an ancient people like the Irish the process generated a myth that was resonant with hope. It was the myth of a second chance.[16] Ireland—conquered, beaten, wracked by storms of misfortune—had always looked back to the dream of a golden age. It could be a pre-Christian Celtic age, a medieval Christian age, or the brief eighteenth-century taste of liberty under Henry Grattan's Parliament. In the nineteenth century, however, there arose a new dream, one of political and social deliverance focused on America. It was an aspiration for redemption through emigration, and it reached into the meanest hovels on the island. It touched multitudes and gave them the revelation that there could be a second life, a new life of promise in America. The myth would be traduced in a tragic manner for great numbers of the Irish, but that did not negate its power. And because it was a popular belief, one that became part of the folk tradition of the people, it could not be exorcised or discredited even when priests and patriots railed against it in the interest of keeping the young at home to rebuild the country.

For the emigrants the ways of America became a means to stabilize themselves in the face of historic stress. The old traditions of Ireland were reduced by war, famine, and dislocation. The Irish language, the vessel of the old culture, was declining rapidly. The religion of the countryside was being modernized. The rural world of subsistence farming, limited grazing, and craft skills was being changed forever by land consolidation, enclosure of tracts for cattle herds, and commercialism.[17] In America a refuge could be found, and a transitional culture formed that was an asylum for several generations until the damages of affliction and disruption could be repaired. By partly fusing with the dominant American culture and partly retaining that which was Irish, the emigrants both pursued their new dispensation and kept a sustaining identity. It was this transitional medium that was Irish-America.

The confusing mixture of old and new, the mingling of foreign and native dispositions, at once crude and subtle, was typical of the modern age of intensified mobility and communications. The same process would be unleashed for masses of Europeans in the eighteenth and nineteenth centuries, and for Africans and Asians in a later period. What resulted was a vast crosscurrent of cultural exchange. The ability of the Irish to maintain their identity in this changing current of habit and invention was part of their broader effort to define their national image and character after centuries of derogation and repression. Not all peoples

were as fortunate. Scores of ethnic nations with their long cultural treasuries
were dispersed or submerged by modernization as technology, genocide, and
change worked their ways upon them.

For the Irish abroad, especially those in America, the revolution of communications and travel meant that they could transmute their parochialism into a
sort of folk internationalism. It is one of the contradictions of modern history
that the process through which imperialist elites forced themselves onto other
societies should be utilized by conquered groups to evade domination and sub-
jection. British and French, Dutch and Spanish adventurers established imperial
control by setting up their national customs and values as structures for mastery
of other societies. London merchants, Parisian royalists, Dutch seafarers, and
Castilian dynasts all propagated their cultural presumptions as imperial justifi-
cations. With quixotic fortune, the Irish exported their own parochialism and
made it the vehicle for an emigrant cult that rescued them by the hundreds of
thousands and contributed to their survival as a nation.

The synthesis of this long Irish-American experience for the group itself was
a tradition, strongly self-defined, that conferred on the Irish the attributes of
survival beyond suffering, achievement against hostility, and cultural autonomy
mingled with power and success.[18] Was this ethnic view accurate? Did the Irish-
Americans delude themselves? It is essential to question the validity of this set
of beliefs for they are central to how history is popularized in this country. First
it must be stated that the success image of the Irish-Americans can only be
sustained if the most gross measures of contemporary lifestyle and attainments
are accepted as criteria. The past is far too full of the ghosts of failure and the
evidence of the results of exploitation to be exorcised. All of the social mobility
of the group, which has doubtless increased in the twentieth century, has to be
evaluated for its significance for the group's tradition and future. Affluence was
repeatedly attained by Irish-Americans and even came to be expected as the
twentieth-century American economy produced an unprecendented environment
of goods, services, and consumer abundance. This was accompanied, however,
by influences in the mainstream culture that swiftly eroded the Irish-American
cohesion derived from a distinct identity, religious affiliation, and political and
organizational ties. These influences, combined with a precipitous decline in
immigration, rapidly altered Irish-American solidarity and affiliation after 1960.
Thus, the social mobility of Irish-Americans undercut their identity as an ethnic
group. As Norman Yetman has explained: "The decline of precisely those factors
that had initially separated them from the larger society was what contributed
to the decline of Irish ethnicity. Today the Irish have become fully respectable
and virtually indistinguishable from their non-ethnic American counterparts."[19]

In the face of this erosion of identity and advance to higher status in American
life, the Irish were not able to sustain their power. The dispersal of ethnic
residential clusters left them with diminished political influence, and their pluralist plying of the new kind of politics through the electronic media was not a
substitute that could maintain ethnic bonds. The values they had internalized in

family life, religious identification, and cultural distinctness were outpaced by the cycles of change that had become inherent in American society.[20] Among other effects, the traditional relationship to Ireland was reduced and the ability of the Irish-Americans to affect political life in Ireland curtailed. The construct of beliefs and affiliations that had served the group in the extension of its influence throughout American life from the age of Charles Stewart Parnell in the 1880s through that of John F. Kennedy in the 1960s dissolved. What was left was a history and a nostalgia, but in contemporary terms only an elusive and inchoate presence.

Even the highly touted social and economic success of the Irish-Americans was a phenomenon usually considered without adequate perspective. Looked at over the full minority career of the group extending from colonial to contemporary times, the acceptance and affluence of the Irish ''in the heel of the hunt'' were not that impressive. Too great a price in exploitation, prejudice, cultural loss, pathology, disorganization, and injustice had been paid not to be entered into the historical ledger to balance the latter-day attainments.[21] The satisfied view applauding Irish-American social upgrading has usually focused on the survivors in a shortened time frame, and almost never adverted to the nonsurvivors, those victims of destructive forces who in their multitudes would never be counted into the great American success story. The long chronicle of Irish-American vulnerability to social rejection and economic depradation, to living conditions rife with the worst rates of disease and mortality, to cults of violence both military and outlaw, and the flagrant records of a whole catalog of social problems over a very long period of time should sharply delimit the acclamation of more recent success. A review of ethnic history taking these factors into account would afford a much more realistic recollection of the past. James T. Farrell put the matter succinctly when he wrote:

I am a second generation Irish-American. The effects and scars of immigration are upon my life. The past was dragging through my boyhood and adolescence. Horatio Alger Jr. died only seven years before I was born. The ''climate of opinion'' was one of hope. But for an Irish boy born in Chicago in 1904, the past was a tragedy of his people.[22]

This was one kind of recollection of the tradition at one pole of opinion. The other pole was represented by the glorification of the Kennedy family as the symbol of Irish-American success. Both perceptions would have to be accommodated as the group's social position changed rapidly in the 1970s and 1980s.

The hiatus in the Irish-American tradition in the second half of the twentieth century had numerous causes. Decreased emigration, changes in the Catholic Church after Vatican Council II, decline of traditional roles for members of the group, displacement by other groups, and failure to renew organizational forms all contributed. The chief alteration in American life that affected this ethnic tradition, however, was the fact that the ''cultural apparatus'' had changed.[23] The ways of identifying oneself, the associations relating to group allegiance, the esteem of the tradition itself all changed. Tremendously influential mass media systems intervened to replace community-based social affiliations. Educational advances added whole new dimensions of comparison and contrast that put the old Irish-American cult into a new and narrower framework. These influences frequently did not directly derogate the Irish attachment: They simply ignored it, overbore it with attractive alternatives, or gave it an old-fashioned cast.

If the basis upon which the Irish had established their regional and national participation in American life had changed, what was to follow? Old social formulas do not suddenly end irrevocably. They tend to be transformed or gradually replaced. As the standards and directions of the country's life changed, the prospects for an altered Irish-American identity would depend upon further adaptation of the group's tradition.

Central to the reorientation of the Irish-Americans would be their own conception of their past. The preservation and presentation of the record of the Irish people in America will in the future require academic and popular undertakings that now occur only as random and marginal efforts. Celebrations and commemorations have their place in such efforts, but they should be planned so that some substantial contribution results. Study and publication programs, archival endowments, prizes to encourage research, and adoption of Irish projects by American institutions could all emanate from historical observances. The record is so extensive, so filled with the adventures and achievements of the Irish-Americans, that there should be little difficulty in finding occasions for such work. It is a challenge that is fundamental to the well-being of cultural traditions in a tempestuous world. The survival of traditions is linked to the hopes of developing peoples everywhere. That the children of Ireland, buffeted by misfortune and persecution, could move to a new world and succeed in making themselves part of a novel and extraordinarily dynamic society with unprecedented standards of material and liberatarian benefits, and that this could occur despite the wars, revolutions, oppression, and disruption that have plagued the last three centuries, should give hope to all who yearn for human betterment.

NOTES

1. Walter A. Rowlands, "The Great Lakes Cutover Region," in Merrill Jensen, ed., *Regionalism in America* (Madison: University of Wisconsin Press, 1965), p. 332.

2. Elmer Starch, "The Great Plains—Missouri Valley Region," in ibid., p. 352.

3. Cited in Alice Cowan Cochran, *Miners, Merchants and Missionaries* (Metuchen, N.J.: The Scarecrow Press and the American Theological Library Association, 1980), p. vii.

4. Daniel J. Casey and Robert E. Rhodes, eds., *Irish-American Fiction: Essays in Criticism* (New York: AMS Press, 1979), pp. ix-xii.

5. Dennis Clark, "Our Own Kind: Irish Folk Life in an Urban Setting," *Keystone Folklore* 23, no. 3 (1979): 28–40; Hasia R. Diner, *Erin's Daughters: Irish Immigrant*

Women in the Nineteenth Century (Baltimore: The Johns Hopkins University Press, 1983), pp. 158–167.

6. The Irish character of these congregations is clear from their records: Register of the Sisters of St. Joseph, 1847–1900, Archives of the Sisters of St. Joseph, Chestnut Hill College, Philadelphia; biographies and analysis of Sister M. Adele Gorman, O.S.F., June 13, 1983, Sisters of St. Francis of Philadelphia Archives, Glen Riddle, Penn.

7. M. Joanna Regan, *Tender Courage: A Brief Sketch of the First Sister of Mercy* (Gwynned Valley, Penn.: Gwynned Mercy College, 1978), pp. 1–12; Rev. J.A. Burns, *The Growth and Development of the Catholic School System in the United States* (New York: Benziger Brothers, 1912), pp. 48, 150, 162–172; Rev. J.A. Burns, "Catholic Secondary Education in the United States," *Catholic Education Association Bulletin* 11, no. 4 (August 1915): 64–66; Neil G. McCluskey, ed., *Catholic Education in America: A Documentary History* (New York: Columbia University Teachers College, 1964), p. 81.

8. Brother Angelus Gabriel, *The Christian Brothers in the United States, 1848–1948* (New York: Declan X. McMullen Co., 1948), pp. 155, 170–174.

9. Burns, "Catholic Secondary Education in the United States," pp. 64–66.

10. Edward J. Power, *A History of Catholic Education in the United States* (Milwaukee: Bruce Publishing Co., 1958), pp. 332–353. William F. Kelley, *The Jesuit Order in Higher Education in the United States* (Milwaukee: Wisconsin Jesuit Province, 1966), pp. 58–96, shows the strong Irish representation.

11. William Leonard Joyce, *Editors and Ethnicity: A History of the Irish-American Press, 1848–1883* (New York: Arno Press, 1976); Eugene P. Willging and Herta Hatzfeld, *Catholic Serials of the Nineteenth Century in the United States*, 2 vols. (Washington: Catholic University Press, 1968), vol. 1, pp. 16, 17, 75, 100, 105, 120, 158; vol. 2, p. 185.

12. Peter Carlson, *Roughneck: The Life and Times of Big Bill Haywood* (New York: W.W. Norton Co., 1983), pp. 35, 50, 162–163; John H. Lyons, ed., *An Informal History of the Ironworkers* (Philadelphia: International Association of Bridge, Structural and Ornamental Ironworkers, 1971), pp. 1–12.

13. Catherine Clinton, *The Other Civil War: American Women in the Nineteenth Century* (New York: Hill and Wang, 1984), pp. 195–196; Philip S. Foner, *Women and the American Labor Movement* (New York: The Free Press, 1979), passim.

14. Mari Kathleen Fielder, "Green and Gold Reconsidered: The Identity and Assimilation Dilemma of the American Irish as Reflected in the Dramas of Edward Rose" (unpublished paper, April 1983). Ms. Fielder has compiled a full documentation of this theater experience, and I gratefully acknowledge her sharing it with me in correspondence of January 23, 1984.

15. Dennis Clark, *The Irish Relations: Trials of an Immigrant Tradition* (Rutherford, N.J.: Fairleigh Dickinson University Press, 1982), pp. 61–75; Perry Duis, *The Saloon: Public Drinking in Chicago and Boston, 1880–1920* (Urbana: University of Illinois Press, 1983), passim; Michael F. Funchion, ed., *Irish-American Voluntary Organizations* (Westport, Conn.: Greenwood Press, 1983), pp. 22–26, 40–41, 147–149.

16. Warren I. Susman, *Culture as History: The Transformation of American Society in the Twentieth Century* (New York: Pantheon Books, 1984), pp. 10–13.

17. Kevin O'Neill, *Family and Farm in Pre-Famine Ireland: The Parish of Killashandra* (Madison: University of Wisconsin Press, 1984), pp. 187–194.

18. Examples are John O'Hanlon, *Irish-American History in the United States* (New

York: P. Murphy Co., 1907), and John M. Campbell, *History of the Society of the Friendly Sons of St. Patrick and the Hibernian Society* (Philadelphia: The Hibernian Society, 1892), passim.

19. Norman Yetman, "The Irish Experience in America," in Harold Orel, ed., *Irish History and Culture: Aspects of a People's Heritage* (Lawrence: University of Kansas Press, 1976), pp. 369–370.

20. Such Irish political strongholds as Boston were by the 1980s of variable ethnic character. *The New York Times* (July 7, 1983). In the catalog of groups in power, the Irish often were not even mentioned. Alex Barbrook and Christiana Bolt, eds., *Power and Protest in American Life* (New York: St Martin's Press, 1980), passim.

21. Donal O'Donovan, *Dreamers of Dreamers: Portraits of the Irish in America* (Dublin: Kilbride Books, 1984), pp. 1–7 gives the congratulatory view of Irish-Americans. Henry George wrote in 1879 as the industrial revolution began transforming life for working people, "It is true that wealth has been greatly increased, and that the average of comfort, leisure and refinement has been raised, but these gains are not general. In them the lowest class do[es] not share." Howard Zinn, *A People's History of the United States* (New York: Harper and Row, 1980), p. 258.

22. *The New York Times* (August 23, 1979).

23. C. Wright Mills, *Power, Politics and People* (New York: Balantine Books, 1963), p. 406. Herbert J. Gans sees the prospect for a "symbolic ethnicity" persisting in American life for an indefinite period. Herbert J. Gans, "Symbolic Ethnicity," in Herbert J. Gans et al., eds., *On the Making of Americans: Essays in Honor of David Reisman* (Philadelphia: University of Pennsylvania Press, 1979), pp. 193–233. Similar views are held by Rudolph J. Vecoli, "Return to the Melting Pot: Ethnicity in the United States in the Eighties," *Migration, 1974–1984* (Turku, Finland: Institute of Migration, 1984), pp. 117–132.

BIBLIOGRAPHY

ARCHIVES

American Catholic Historical Society, Philadelphia
American Irish Historical Society, New York
Balch Institute for Ethnic Studies, Philadelphia
Denver Public Library, Western History Collection
Eleutherian Mills—Hagley Museum and Library, Greeneville, Del.
Houston Public Library, Texas History Collection
Minnesota Historical Society, Archives of the Northern Pacific Railroads, St. Paul, Minn.
Union Pacific Museum, Archives of the Union Pacific Railroad, Omaha, Neb.

CENSUS MATERIALS

First Census of the United States, 1790, North Carolina Heads of Families (Washington: U.S. Government Printing Office, 1908)
Iowa Territorial Census of 1836 (Bountiful, Utah: Accelerated Data Systems, 1976)
Kansas Territorial Census Index, 1860 (Bountiful, Utah: Accelerated Data Systems, 1978)
Kentucky, Second Census of (Frankfurt, Ky.: privately published, 1954)
Lincoln County, Georgia, An 1800 Census for (Atlanta: R.J. Taylor Foundation, 1977)
Montana 1870 Territorial Census Index (Salt Lake City: Accelerated Indexing Systems, 1979)
Nevada 1870 Territorial Census (Salt Lake City: Accelerated Indexing Systems, 1979)
New Mexico 1850 Census (Salt Lake City: Accelerated Indexing Systems, 1978)
Utah 1860 Territorial Census Index (Salt Lake City: Accelerated Indexing Systems, 1979)
Wyoming 1870 Territorial Census Index (Salt Lake City: Accelerated Indexing Systems, 1978)

NEWSPAPERS

Catholic Star Herald (Camden, N.J.)
Daily Herald, The (Clinton, Iowa)

Evening Bulletin, The (Philadelphia)
Irish-American News (Chicago)
Irish Edition, The (Philadelphia)
Irish Nation, The (New York)
New York Times, The (New York)
Pennsylvania Gazette (Philadelphia)
Philadelphia Daily News, The
Public Ledger, The (Philadelphia)

JOURNALS AND MAGAZINES

Alaska Railroad Record
American Catholic Historical Review
American Historical Review
Annals of Iowa, The
Annals of Wyoming
Arkansas Historical Quarterly
California History
Catholic Education Association Bulletin
Catholic Educational Review
Chronicles of Oklahoma
Colorado Magazine
East Texas Historical Journal
Eire-Ireland
Florida Historical Quarterly
Frontier Times
Georgia Historical Quarterly
Illinois Catholic Historical Review
Irish Sword, The
Journal of American History
Journal of American Studies
Journal of Arizona History
Journal of the American Irish Historical Society
Journal of the Illinois Historical Society
Journal of the West
Journal of Urban History
Keystone Folklore
Labor History
McClure's Magazine
Maine Historical Society Quarterly
Marxist Perspectives
Maryland Historical Magazine
Mississippi Valley Historical Review
Nebraska History
Nevada Historical Quarterly
New England Quarterly
New Mexico Historical Review
New York Review of Books, The

New Yorker, The
Ohio History
Pacific Historical Review
Pacific Northwest Quarterly
Palimpsest
Pennsylvania History Magazine
Pennsylvania Magazine, The
Pennsylvania Magazine of History and Biography
Records of the American Catholic Historical Society
Southwestern Historical Quarterly
Studies
Tennessee Historical Quarterly
Texas Historical Studies
Theater History Studies
University of Arizona Bulletin
Utah Historical Quarterly
Vermont History
Washington Historical Quarterly
Western Pennsylvania Historical Magazine
William and Mary Quarterly

DISSERTATIONS

Allen, John Adams. "A Historical Study of the Legitimate Theater in Cripple Creek, Colorado, 1897–1907." Master's thesis, Northern Illinois University, 1967.

Browning, Richard James. "A Record of the Professional Theater Activity in Fargo, Dakota Territory from 1880 through 1888." Master's thesis, North Dakota Agricultural College, 1957.

Donnelly, James F. "Catholic New Yorkers and New York Socialists, 1870–1920." Ph.D. diss., New York University, 1982.

Donovan, G.F. "Pre-Revolutionary Irish in Massachusetts, 1620–1775." Ph.D. diss., St. Louis University, 1931.

Gipson, Rosemary Pechin. "The History of Tucson Theater before 1906." Master's thesis, University of Arizona, 1967.

Leonard, Ira Marshall. "New York City Politics, 1841–1844: Nativism and Reform." Ph.D. diss., New York University, 1965.

Light, Dale B. "Class, Ethnicity and Urban Ecology in a Nineteenth Century City: Philadelphia's Irish, 1840–1890." Ph.D. diss., University of Pennsylvania, 1979.

Meagher, Timothy J. " 'The Lord Is Not Dead': Cultural and Social Change among the Irish in Worcester, Massachusetts." Ph.D. diss., Brown University, 1982.

Wynn, Dennis Joseph. "The San Patricios and the United States–Mexican War, 1846–1848." Ph.D. diss., Loyola University, 1982.

BOOKS

Akenson, Donald Harman. *Being Had: Historians, Evidence and the Irish in North America*. Ontario, Canada: P.D. Meany, Publisher, 1984.

Allen, Frederick Lewis. *Only Yesterday: An Informal History of the 1920's*. New York: Harper and Row, 1931.

Alvord, Clarence W., and Lee Bedgood. *The First Explorations of the Trans-Allegheny Region by the Virginians, 1650–1674*. Cleveland: A.H. Clark Co., 1912.

Arnow, Harriett Simpson. *The Flowering of the Cumberland*. New York: The Macmillan Co., 1963.

————. *Seedtime on the Cumberland*. New York: The Macmillan Co., 1960.

Avery, I.W. *The History of the State of Georgia: 1850–1881*. New York: Brown and Derby, 1881.

Bailyn, Bernard. *New England Merchants in the Seventeenth Century*. Cambridge: Harvard University Press, 1955.

Baldwin, Agnes Leland. *First Settlers of South Carolina, 1670–1680*. Columbia: South Carolina Tricentennial Commission, University of South Carolina Press, 1970.

Balsamo, Will, and George Carpozi. *Always Kill a Brother*. New York: Dell Publishing Co., 1977.

Baltzell, E. Digby. *The Philadelphia Gentlemen: The Making of a National Upper Class*. Glencoe, Ill.: The Free Press, 1958.

Barnhart, John D. *Valley of Democracy: The Frontier versus the Plantation in the Ohio Valley, 1775–1818*. Bloomington: Indiana University Press, 1953.

Barrett, John G. *The Civil War in North Carolina*. Chapel Hill: University of North Carolina Press, 1963.

Bartlett, Richard. *The New Country: A Social History of the American Frontier, 1776–1890*. New York: Oxford University Press, 1974.

Bayor, Ronald H. *Neighbors in Conflict: The Irish, Germans, Jews and Italians of New York City, 1929–1941*. Baltimore: Johns Hopkins University Press, 1978.

Bennett, William Harper. *Catholic Footsteps in Old New York*. New York: United States Catholic Historical Society, 1973.

Benson, Lee Harvey. *The Concept of Jacksonian Democracy: New York as a Test Case*. Princeton, N.J.: Princeton University Press, 1961.

Berthoff, Rowland. *An Unsettled People: Social Order and Disorder in American History*. New York: Harper and Row, 1971.

Biles, Roger. *Big City Boss in Depression and War: Mayor Edward J. Kelly of Chicago*. De Kalb: Northern Illinois University Press, 1984.

Billington, Ray Allen. *The Far Western Frontier, 1830–1860*. New York: Harper and Row, 1956.

————. *The Protestant Crusade, 1800–1860*. Chicago: University of Chicago Press, 1964.

Blessing, Patrick J. *The British and Irish in Oklahoma*. Norman: University of Oklahoma Press, 1980.

Brecher, Jeremy; Jerry Lombardi; and Jan Stackhouse, eds. *Brass Valley: The Story of Working People's Lives and Struggles in an American Industrial Region*. Philadelphia: Temple University Press, 1982.

Brown, Thomas N. *Irish-American Nationalism, 1870–1890*. Philadelphia: J.B. Lippincott Co., 1966.

Brownell, Blaine. *The Urban Ethos in the South, 1920–1930*. Baton Rouge: Louisiana State University Press, 1975.

Brownell, Blaine, and David Goldfield, eds. *The City in Southern History: The Growth of Urban Civilization in the South*. Port Washington, N.Y.: Kennikat Press, 1977.

Buenker, John D. *Urban Liberalism and Progressive Reform*. New York: Charles Scribner's Sons, 1973.

Burnet, Jacob. *Notes on the Early Settlement of the Northwest Territory*. Cincinnati: Derby, Bradley Co., 1847.

Butts, R. Freeman, and Lawrence A. Cremin. *A History of Higher Education in the United States*. New York: Henry Holt and Co., 1953.

Calhoon, Robert McClues. *The Loyalists in Revolutionary America, 1760–1781*. New York: Harcourt, Brace, Jovanovich, 1965.

Callow, Alexander. *The Tweed Ring*. New York: Oxford University Press, 1965.

Cappon, Lester J., ed. *Atlas of American History: The Revolutionary Era, 1760–1790*. Princeton, N.J.: Princeton University Press, 1976.

Carey, Mathew. *Address to the Wealthy of the Land*. Philadelphia: William Geddes, 1831.

———. *Exhibit of the Shocking Oppression and Injustice Suffered by John Randel of the Chesapeake and Delaware Canal*. Philadelphia: Mathew Carey, 1825.

Caro, Robert A. *The Years of Lyndon Johnson: The Path to Power*. New York: Alfred A. Knopf, 1982.

Carty, James. *Ireland from the Flight of the Earls to Grattan's Parliament*. Dublin: C.J. Fallon, 1949.

Casey, Daniel J., and Robert E. Rhodes. *Irish-American Fiction: Essays in Criticism*. New York: AMS Press, Inc., 1979.

Cash, W.J. *The Mind of the South*. New York: Vintage Books, 1960.

Chambers, Henry E. *Mississippi Valley Beginnings*. New York: Putnam's, Inc., 1922.

Clark, Dennis. *Irish Blood: Northern Ireland and the American Conscience*. Port Washington, N.Y.: Kennikat Press, 1976.

———. *The Irish in Philadelphia: Ten Generations of Urban Experience*. Philadelphia: Temple University Press, 1973.

———. *The Irish Relations: Trials of an Immigrant Tradition*. Rutherford, N.J.: Fairleigh Dickinson University Press, 1982.

Clinton, Catherine. *The Other Civil War: American Women in the Nineteenth Century*. New York: Hill and Wang, 1984.

Cochran, Alice Cowan. *Miners, Merchants and Missionaries*. Metuchen, N.J.: Scarecrow Press and the American Theological Library Association, 1980.

Cochran, Thomas C. *Railroad Leaders, 1845–1890: The Business Mind in Action*. New York: Russell and Russell, 1965.

Connolly, S.J. *Priests and People in Pre-Famine Ireland, 1780–1845*. Dublin: Gill and Macmillan, 1982.

Conroy, J. C. *A History of the Railways in Ireland*. London: Longmans, Green and Co., 1928.

Cooney, John. *The American Pope*. New York: Times Books, 1984.

Corry, John. *Golden Clan: The Murrays, the McDonnells and the Irish-American Aristocracy*. Boston: Houghton Mifflin Co., 1977.

Cray, Ed. *Chrome Colossus: General Motors and Its Times*. New York: McGraw-Hill Co., 1980.

Cronin, Sean. *The McGarrity Papers*. Tralee, Ireland: Anvil Press, 1972.

Curry, Jane. *River's in My Blood*. Lincoln: University of Nebraska Press, 1983.

Daniell, Jere R. *Colonial New Hampshire*. Millwood, N.Y.: KTO Press, 1981.

Davis, James A. *The History of the City of Memphis*. Memphis: Hite, Crumpton and Kelly, 1873.

Davis, William C. *The Orphan Brigade: The Kentucky Confederates Who Couldn't Go Home*. Baton Rouge: Louisiana State University Press, 1980.

Dawley, Alan. *Class and Community: The Industrial Revolution in Lynn*. Cambridge: Harvard University Press, 1976.

Degler, Carl. *The Other South: Southern Dissenters in the Nineteenth Century*. New York: Harper and Row, 1974.

Devol, George H. *Forty Years a Gambler on the Mississippi*. New York: Johnson Reprint Co., 1968. Originally published by the author in 1892.

Dickinson, John N. *To Build a Canal: Sault Ste. Marie, 1853–1854 and After*. Columbus: Ohio State University Press, 1981.

Dickson, R.J. *Ulster Emigration to Colonial America, 1718–1785*. London: Routledge and Kegan Paul, 1966.

Diner, Hasia R. *Erin's Daughters: Irish Immigrant Women in the Nineteenth Century*. Baltimore: The Johns Hopkins University Press, 1983.

Dolan, Ellen Meara. *Old St. Patrick's Church*. St. Louis: Old St. Patrick's Church, 1967.

Dolan, Jay. *The Immigrant Church: New York's Irish and German Catholics, 1815–1865*. Baltimore: Johns Hopkins University Press, 1975.

Donaldson, Scott. *F. Scott Fitzgerald*. New York: Congdon and Weed, 1983.

Donohue, Michael. *An Oral History: Starting Off from Dead End*. New York: Community Documentation Workshop, 1980.

Donovan, Frank P. *Mileposts on the Prairie: The Story of the Minneapolis and St. Paul Railway*. New York: Simmons-Boardman, 1950.

Doyle, David Noel. *Ireland, Irishmen and Revolutionary America, 1760–1820*. Cork, Ireland: The Mercier Press, 1981.

Doyle, David Noel, and Owen Dudley Edwards, eds. *America and Ireland, 1776–1976: The American Identity and the Irish Connection*. Westport, Conn.: Greenwood Press, 1980.

Ducker, James H. *Men of the Steel Rails: Workers on the Atchison, Topeka and Santa Fe, 1869–1900*. Lincoln: University of Nebraska Press, 1983.

Duis, Perry. *The Saloon: Public Drinking in Chicago and Boston, 1880–1920*. Urbana: University of Illinois Press, 1983.

Dunaway, Wayland F. *History of the James River and Kanawha Company*. New York: AMS Press, 1969.

Eaton, Clement. *The Freedom-of-Thought Struggle in the Old South*. New York: Random House, 1964.

Edwards, Ann. *Road to Tara: The Life of Margaret Mitchell*. New Haven, Conn.: Ticknor and Fields, 1983.

Ellsworth, Lucius F., ed. *The Americanization of the Gulf Coast, 1803–1850*. Pensacola, Fla.: Historic Pensacola Preservation Board, 1972.

Emmett, Chris. *Fort Union and the Winning of the Southwest*. Norman: University of Oklahoma Press, 1965.

Ernst, Robert. *Immigrant Life in New York City, 1825–1863*. New York: King's Crown Press, 1949.

Fallows, Majorie. *Irish-Americans: Identity and Assimilation*. Englewood Cliffs, N.J.: Prentice-Hall, Inc., 1979.

Ferrell, Mallory Hope. *Silver San Juan: The Rio Grande and Southern Railroad*. Boulder, Colo.: Pruett Publishing Co., 1973.

Ferris, Robert. *Founders and Frontiersmen*. Washington: U.S. Department of the Interior, 1967.

Fitzgerald, Kathleen Whelan. *Brass: Jane Byrne and the Pursuit of Power*. Chicago: Contemporary Books, 1981.

Flannery, John Brendan. *The Irish Texans*. San Antonio: Institute for Texas Cultures of the University of Texas, 1980.

Flexner, James Thomas. *Lord of the Mohawks*. Boston: Little, Brown and Company, 1959.

Flick, Alexander C. *Loyalism in New York during the American Revolution*. New York: Columbia University Press, 1901.

Foner, Philip S., *The Great Labor Uprising of 1877*. New York: Monad Press, 1977.

————. *Women and the American Labor Movement*. New York: The Free Press, 1979.

Fowler, Gene. *Beau James: The Life and Times of Jimmy Walker*. Clifton, N.J.: Augustus M. Kelley, Publisher, 1973.

Fox, Dixon Ryan. *Yankees and Yorkers*. New York: New York University Press, 1940.

Frisch, Michael. *Town into City: Springfield, Massachusetts, 1840–1880*. Cambridge: Harvard University Press, 1972.

Funchion, Michael F., ed. *Irish-American Voluntary Organizations*. Westport, Conn.: Greenwood Press, 1983.

Furnas, J.C. *The Americans: A Social History of the United States, 1586–1914*. New York: G.P. Putnam's Sons, 1969.

Gabriel, Brother Angelus. *The Christian Brothers in the United States, 1848–1948*. New York: Declan X. McMullen Co., 1948.

Gard, R. Max, and William H. Vodrey. *The Sandy and Beaver Canal*. East Liverpool: Ohio Historical Society, 1952.

Garrity, Richard. *Canal Boatman: My Life on Upstate Waterways*. Syracuse: Syracuse University Press, 1977.

Gastil, Raymond. *Cultural Regions of the United States*. Seattle: University of Washington Press, 1975.

Genovese, Eugene. *Roll, Jordan, Roll: The World the Slaves Made*. New York: Random House, 1974.

Gibson, Florence E. *The Attitudes of the New York Irish toward State and National Affairs, 1848–1892*. New York: Columbia University Press, 1981.

Glazer, Nathan, and Daniel P. Moynihan. *Beyond the Melting Pot: The Negroes, Puerto Ricans, Jews, Italians and Irish of New York City*. Cambridge: The MIT Press, 1970.

Glazier, Ira, ed. *The Famine Immigrants: Lists of Irish Immigrants Arriving at the Port of New York, 1846–1851*. 6 vols. Baltimore: Geneological Publishing Co., 1982-

Goldston, Robert. *New York: Civic Exploitation*. New York: The Macmillan Co., 1970.

Goodrich, Carter. *Government Promotion of American Canals and Railroads, 1800–1890*. New York: Columbia University Press, 1960.

Gray, Ralph D. *The National Waterway: A History of the Chesapeake and Delaware Canal, 1769–1965*. Urbana: University of Illinois Press, 1967.

Greaves, Desmond. *The Life and Times of James Connolly*. New York: International Publishers, 1961.

Green, Constance McLaughlin. *American Cities in the Growth of the Nation*. London: John DeGraff, 1957.

Griffin, Clyde and Sally. *Natives and Newcomers: The Ordering of Opportunity in Mid-Nineteenth Century Pougheepsie*. Cambridge: Harvard University Press, 1978.

Griscom, John H. *The Sanitary Conditions of the Laboring Poor of New York*. New York: J. Griscom, 1865.

Gudelmas, William A., and William G. Shade. *Before the Mollie Maguires: The Emergence of the Ethno-Religious Factor in the Politics of the Lower Anthracite Region, 1844–1872*. New York: Arno Press, 1976.

Guilday, Peter. *The Life and Times of John England, First Bishop of Charleston, 1786–1840*. 2 vols. New York: America Press, 1927.

Gutman, Herbert G. *The Black Family in Slavery and Freedom, 1750–1925*. New York: Pantheon Books, 1976.

————. *Work, Culture and Society in Industrializing America: Essays in American Working Class and Social History*. New York: Random House, 1977.

Hahn, Thomas F. *Pleadings and Testimony: The Delaware and Hudson Canal Company versus The Pennsylvania Coal Company*. 8 vols. New York: W.C. Bryant and Co., 1858.

————, ed. *The Best from American Canals*. York, Penn.: The American Canal Society, Inc., 1980.

Hale, Edward Everett. *Letters on Irish Immigration*. Boston: Phillips and Samson, 1852.

Hammack, David C. *Power and Society: Greater New York at the Turn of the Century*. New York: Russell Sage Foundation, 1982.

Handlin, Oscar. *The American People in the Twentieth Century*. Boston: Beacon Press, 1954.

————. *Boston's Immigrants: A Study of Acculturation*. New York: Atheneum, 1968.

Haraven, Tamara K., and Randolph Langenbach. *Amoskeag: Life and Work in an American Factory City*. New York: Pantheon Books, 1978.

Harlon, Alvin F. *The Road of the Century*. New York: Creative Age Press, 1947.

Hartz, Louis. *The Liberal Tradition in America*. New York: Harcourt, Brace and World, 1955.

Hay, Douglas, et al. *Albion's Fatal Tree: Crime and Society in Eighteenth Century England*. New York: Random House, 1975.

Hennessey, James J. *American Catholics: A History of the Roman Catholic Community in the United States*. New York: Oxford University Press, 1981.

Higham, John. *Send These to Me: Jews and Other Immigrants in Urban America*. New York: Atheneum, 1975.

Hirsch, Susan. *Roots of the American Working Class: The Industrialization of Crafts in Newark, 1800–1860*. Philadelphia: University of Pennsylvania Press, 1978.

Holbrook, Stewart. *The Story of American Railroads*. New York: Bonanza Books, 1947.

Howard, Helen Addison. *Northwest Trail Blazers*. Caldwell, Idaho: Caxton Printers, 1963.

Howard, Robert P. *Illinois: A History of the Prairie State*. Grand Rapids, Mich.: William B. Eerdman Publishing Co., 1972.

Hulbert, Archer Butler. *The Great American Canals*. Cleveland: A.H. Clark Co., 1904.

Hungerford, Edward. *The Story of the Baltimore and Ohio Railroad, 1827–1927*. New York: G.P. Putnam's Sons, 1928.

Hutton, Paul Andrew. *Phil Sheridan and His Army*. Lincoln: University of Nebraska Press, 1985.

Joyce, William Leonard. *Editors and Ethnicity: A History of the Irish-American Press, 1848–1883*. New York: Arno Press, 1976.

Kee, Robert. *The Green Flag*. 3 vols. London: Quartet Books, 1979.

Kelley, Robert. *The Cultural Pattern in American Politics*. New York: Alfred A. Knopf, 1979.

Kelley, William F. *The Jesuit Order in Higher Education in the United States*. Milwaukee: Wisconsin Jesuit Province, 1966.

Kelly, Joseph John. *The Irish in Camden County*. Camden, N.J.: Camden County Historical Society, 1984.

Kemble, Frances Anne. *Journal of a Residence on a Georgia Plantation in 1838–1839*. New York: Harper and Row, 1961.

Kennedy, William. *O Albany: An Urban Tapestry*. New York: Viking Press, 1983.

King, Joseph A. *The Irish Lumberman-Farmer: Fitzgeralds, Harrigans and Others*. Lafayette, Calif.: Joseph A. King, 1982.

Kneiss, Gilbert. *Bonanza Railroads*. San Jose: Stanford University Press, 1941.

Kupperman, Karen Ordahl. *Settling with the Indians: The Meeting of English and Indians in the Cultures of America, 1580–1640*. Totowa, N.J.: Rowman and Littlefield, 1980.

Lane, Roger. *Violent Death in the City*. Cambridge: Harvard University Press, 1979.

Lavender, David. *Bent's Fort*. Garden City, N.Y.: Doubleday and Co., 1954.

———. *The Southwest*. New York: Harper and Row, 1980.

Le Massena, Robert A. *Rio Grande to the Pacific*. Denver: Sundance, Ltd., 1974.

Le Roy, Edwin D. *The Delaware and Hudson Canal*. Honesdale, Penn.: Wayne County Historical Society, 1950.

Levin, Murray B. *The Compleat Politician: Political Strategy in Massachusetts*. Indianapolis: Bobbs Merrill Co., 1962.

Levine, Susan. *Labor's True Woman: Carpet Weavers, Industrialization, and Labor Reform in the Gilded Age*. Philadelphia: Temple University Press, 1984.

Leyburn, James G. *The Scotch-Irish: A Social History*. Chapel Hill: University of North Carolina Press, 1962.

Licht, Walter. *Working for the Railroad: The Organization of Work in the Nineteenth Century*. Princeton, N.J.: Princeton University Press, 1983.

Lingeman, Richard. *Small Town America: A Narrative, 1620 to the Present*. Boston: Houghton Mifflin Co., 1980.

Lockhart, Audrey. *Some Aspects of Emigration from Ireland to the North American Colonies between 1660 and 1775*. New York: Arno Press, 1976.

Lockridge, Kenneth A. *A New England Town: The First Hundred Years*. New York: W.W. Norton, 1970.

McCaffrey, Lawrence. *The Irish Diaspora in America*. Bloomington: Indiana University Press, 1976.

McClellan, George B., Jr. *The Gentleman and the Tiger*, ed. Harold C. Syrett. Philadelphia and New York: J.B. Lippincott Co., 1956.

McCluskey, Neil G. *Catholic Education in America: A Documentary History*. New York: Columbia University Teachers College, 1964.

MacCurtain, Margaret. *Tudor and Stuart Ireland*. Dublin: Gill and Macmillan, 1972.

Magdol, Edward, and Jon L. Wakelyn, eds. *The Southern Common People: Studies in Nineteenth Century Social History*. Westport, Conn.: Greenwood Press, 1980.

Mahoney, Patrick. *It's Better in America*. Washington: Institute for the Study of Man, 1964.

Maloney, Margaret E. *Fág An Bealach: The Irish Contribution to America*. Pittsburgh: United Irish Societies of Pittsburgh, 1977.

Mandelbaum, Seymour. *Boss Tweed's New York*. New York: John Wiley and Sons, 1965.

Mann, Arthur. *Yankee Reformers in the Urban Age: Social Reform in Boston, 1880–1900*. New York: Harper and Row, 1954.

Mark, Frederick. *A History of the Westward Movement*. New York: Alfred A. Knopf, 1978.

Martin, Albo. *James J. Hill and the Opening of the West*. New York: Oxford University Press, 1976.

Mason, Charles. *The History of Dublin, New Hampshire*. Boston: John Wilson and Son, 1855.

Masterson, V.V. *The KATY Railroad and the Last Frontier*. Norman: University of Oklahoma Press, 1952.

Melville, Herman. *Moby Dick or, The Whale*. New York: Random House, 1950.

Menzies, Elizabeth G.C. *Passage between Rivers*. New Brunswick, N.J.: Rutgers University Press, 1976.

Mercey, Arch. *The Laborer's Story, 1903–1953*. Washington: Ransdell, Inc., 1954.

Miller, Kerby A. *Emigrants and Exiles: Ireland and the Irish Exodus to North America*. New York: Oxford University Press, 1985.

Miller, Randall M., and Jon L. Wakelyn, eds. *Catholics in the Old South*. Macon, Ga.: Mercer University Press, 1983.

Mitchell, John. *McSorley's Wonderful Saloon*. New York: Duell, Sloan and Pearce, 1943.

Mohl, Raymond A., and Neil Betten, eds. *Urban America in Historical Perspective*. New York: Weybright and Talley, 1970.

Morison, Samuel Eliot. *The Oxford History of the American People*. New York: Oxford University Press, 1965.

Niehaus, Richard. *The Irish in New Orleans, 1800–1860*. Baton Rouge: Louisiana State University Press, 1965.

Norwood, Christopher. *About Paterson: The Making and Unmaking of an American City*. New York: Harper and Row, 1974.

O'Brien, Michael J. *A Hidden Phase of American History: Ireland's Part in America's Struggle for Liberty*. New York: Dodd, Mead and Co., 1920.

O'Connor, Edwin. *The Last Hurrah*. Boston: Little, Brown and Co., 1956.

O'Flanagan, Rev. Michael. *Letters of John O'Donovan Containing Information Relative to the Antiquities of Londonderry*. Bray, Ireland: Michael O'Flanagan, 1927.

Oliphant, G. Talbot. *Annual Report to the Board of Managers of the Delaware and Hudson Canal Company for 1860*. New York: Nathan Lane, 1861.

Olmstead, Frederick Law. *The Cotton Kingdom*. 2 vols. New York: Mason Publishers, 1861.

O'Neil, Dennis A. *A Whale of a Territory: The Story of Bill O'Neil*. New York: McGraw-Hill Book Co., 1966.

Osofsky, Gilbert. *Harlem, The Making of a Ghetto: Negro New York, 1890–1930*. New York: Harper and Row, 1966.

Overton, Richard C. *A History of the Burlington Lines*. New York: Alfred A. Knopf, 1965.

Parks, Robert J. *Democracy's Railroads: Public Enterprise in Jacksonian Michigan*. Port Washington, N.Y.: Kennikat Press, 1972.

Parmet, Herbert S. *JFK: The Presidency of John F. Kennedy*. New York: The Dial Press, 1983.

Perrigo, Lynn I. *The American Southwest*. New York: Holt, Rinehart and Winston, 1971.

Philbrick, Francis S. *The Rise of the West, 1754–1830*. New York: Harper and Row, 1965.

Platt, Rutherford. *The Great American Forest*. Englewood Cliffs, N.J.: Prentice-Hall, 1965.

Porteous, J. Douglas. *Canal Ports: The Urban Achievement of the Canal Age*. New York: Academic Press, 1977.

Purdue, Howell and Elizabeth. *Patrick Cleburne: Confederate General*. Hillsboro, Tex.: Hill Junior College Press, 1973.

Reagan, John H. *Memoirs*. New York: The Pemberton Press, 1968.

Reed, John Shelton. *One South: An Ethnic Approach to Regional Culture*. Baton Rouge: Louisiana State University Press, 1982.

Reinhardt, Richard, ed. *Workin' on the Railroad: Reminiscences from the Age of Steam*. Palo Alto: American West Publishing Co., 1970.

Ridge, John T. *The Flatbush Irish*. Brooklyn: Division 35, Ancient Order of Hibernians, 1983.

Riis, Jacob. *How the Other Half Lives*. New York: Young People's Missionary Society, 1890.

Rischin, Moses. *The Promised City: New York's Jews, 1870–1914*. New York: Corinth Books, 1962.

Roberts, Edward R. *Ireland in America*. New York: G.P. Putnam's Sons, 1931.

Rogin, Michael Paul. *Fathers and Children: Andrew Jackson and the Subjugation of the American Indian*. New York: Random House, 1976.

Rohrbough, Malcolm J. *The Trans-Appalachian Frontier: People, Societies and Institutions, 1775–1850*. New York: Oxford University Press, 1978.

Roucek, Joseph, and Bernard Eisenberg, eds. *America's Ethnic Politics*. Westport, Conn.: Greenwood Press, 1982.

Ryan, Dennis P. *Beyond the Ballot Box: A Social History of the Boston Irish, 1845–1917*. Madison, N.J.: Fairleigh Dickinson University Press, 1983.

Ryan, Mary P. *Womanhood in America: Colonial Times to the Present*. New York: New Viewpoints, 1975.

Sally, A.S., ed. *Warrants for Lands in South Carolina, 1672–1711*. Columbia: University of South Carolina Press, 1973.

Scheer, George F., and Hugh F. Rankin. *Rebels and Redcoats*. New York: World Publishing Co., 1957.

Shaeffer, Louis. *O'Neill: Son and Playwright*. 2 vols. Boston: Little, Brown and Co., 1968.

Shannon, Fred A. *The Farmer's Last Frontier, 1860–1879*. New York: Harper and Row, 1945.

Shannon, William V. *The American Irish: A Political and Social Portrait*. New York: The Macmillan Co., 1963.

Shaughnessy, Gerald. *Has the Immigrant Kept the Faith?* New York: The Macmillan Co., 1925.

Shaw, Douglas V. *The Making of an Immigrant City: Ethnic and Cultural Conflict in Jersey City, New Jersey, 1850–1877*. New York: Arno Press, 1976.

Shea, John Gilmary. *History of the Catholic Church in the United States*. 4 vols. New York: The American Press, 1892.

Shoemaker, Floyd C. *Missouri's Struggle for Statehood: 1804–1821*. New York: Russell and Russell, 1916.

Shulim, Joseph I. *John Daly Burk: Irish Revolutionary and American Patriot*. Philadelphia: The American Philosophical Society, 1964.

Sigafoos, Robert A. *Cotton Row to Beale Street: A Business History of Memphis*. Memphis: University of Tennessee Press, 1979.

Sinclair, Bruce. *Philadelphia's Philosopher Mechanics: A History of the Franklin Institute, 1824–1865*. Baltimore: The Johns Hopkins University Press, 1974.

Siracusa, Carl. *A Mechanical People: Perceptions of the Industrial Order in Massachusetts, 1815–1880*. Middletown, Conn.: Wesleyan University Press, 1979.

Skorda, Gust. *The Early Settlers of Maryland*. Baltimore: Geneological Publishing Co., 1968.

Slocum, Charles E. *History of the Maumee River Basin*. Defiance, Ohio: Published by the author, 1905.

Smith, Abbott Emerson. *Colonists in Bondage: White Servitude and Convict Labor in America: 1607–1776*. New York: W.W. Norton Co., 1971.

Solomon, Barbara Miller. *Ancestors and Immigrants: A Changing New England Tradition*. New York: John Wiley and Sons, 1956.

Spalding, M.J. *Sketches of Early Catholic Missions in Kentucky*. Louisville: D.J. Webb and Brother, 1844.

Spencer, Wilbur. *Pioneers on Maine Rivers*. Baltimore: Geneological Publishing Company, 1973.

Stack, John F., Jr. *International Conflict in an American City: Boston's Irish, Italians, and Jews, 1935–1944*. Westport, Conn.: Greenwood Press, 1979.

Still, Bayrd. *Mirror for Gotham: New York as Seen by Contemporaries from Dutch Days to the Present*. New York: New York University Press, 1956.

Susman, Warren I. *Culture as History: The Transformation of American Society in the Twentieth Century*. New York: Pantheon Books, 1984.

Sydnor, Charles. *The Development of Southern Sectionalism: From Nationalism to Sectionalism, 1819–1848*. Baton Rouge: Louisiana State University Press, 1969.

Taylor, George Rogers. *The Transportation Revolution, 1815–1860*. New York: Harper and Row, 1951.

Thernstrom, Stephan. *The Other Bostonians: Poverty and Progress in an American Metropolis, 1880–1970*. Cambridge: Harvard University Press, 1973.

————. *Poverty and Progress: Social Mobility in a Nineteenth Century City*. New York: Atheneum, 1969.

Thompson, E.P. *Whigs and Hunters: The Origin of the Black Act*. New York: Random House, 1975.

Time-Life Books. *The Railroaders*. New York: Time-Life Books, 1973.

Trout, Charles H. *Boston: The Great Depression and the New Deal*. New York: Oxford University Press, 1977.

Tyndall, George Brown. *The Emergence of the New South*. Baton Rouge: Louisiana State University Press, 1967.

Unruh, John D. *The Plains Across: The Overland Emigrants and the Trans-Mississippi West, 1840–1860.* Urbana: University of Illinois Press, 1979.

Verhoeff, Mary. *The Kentucky River Navigation.* Louisville: John P. Morton, 1917.

Ver Steeg, Clarence L. *Origins of a Southern Mosaic.* Athens: University of Georgia Press, 1975.

Walsh, James P., ed. *The Irish: America's Political Class.* New York: Arno Press, 1976.

Ward, David. *Immigrants and Cities: A Geography of Change in Nineteenth Century America.* New York: Oxford University Press, 1971.

West, Elliott. *The Saloon on the Rocky Mountain Mining Frontier.* Lincoln: University of Nebraska Press, 1979.

Whitford, Noble E. *History of the Canal System of the State of New York.* New York, 1905.

Wilcox, Frank. *The Ohio Canals.* Kent, Ohio: Kent State University Press, 1969.

Willison, George F. *Saints and Strangers.* New York: Time-Life Books, 1945.

Wills, Gary. *The Kennedy Imprisonment: A Meditation on Power.* Boston: Little, Brown and Co., 1981.

Wilson, O.M. *The Denver and Rio Grande Project, 1870–1901.* Salt Lake City: Howe Brothers, 1982.

Wittke, Carl. *The Irish in America.* Baton Rouge: Louisiana State University Press, 1956.

Wolf, Peter. *Land in America: Its Value, Use and Control.* New York: Pantheon Books, 1981.

Wolfe, Thomas. *Of Time and the River: A Legend of a Man's Hunger in His Youth.* New York: C. Scribner's, 1935.

Wood, Robert L. *Men, Mules and Mountains: Lieutenant O'Neil's Olympic Expedition.* Seattle: The Mountaineers, 1976.

Wooster, Ralph. *Politicians, Planters and Plain Folks: Courthouse and Statehouse in the Upper South, 1850–1860.* Knoxville: University of Tennessee Press, 1975.

Wuttall, Thomas. *A Journal of Travels into Arkansas Territory, 1819.* Norman: University of Oklahoma Press, 1980.

Yellowitz, Irwin. *Industrialization and the American Labor Movement, 1850–1900.* Port Washington, N.Y.: Kennikat Press, 1977.

Yoder, C.P. *Delaware Canal Journal.* Bethlehem, Penn.: Canal Press, 1977.

Zinn, Howard. *A People's History of the United States.* New York: Harper and Row, 1980.

INDEX

About the Author

DENNIS CLARK is Executive Director of the Samuel S. Fels Fund, a private foundation. Among his books are *Cities in Crisis, Work and the Human Spirit*, and *The Irish Relations: Trials of an Immigrant Tradition*. He has published numerous articles on urban problems, urban history, ethnic history, and Irish issues.